D0858709

Adolescent Literature as a Complement to the Classics

Addressing Critical Issues in Today's Classrooms

Adolescent Literature as a Complement to the Classics

Addressing Critical Issues in Today's Classrooms

Joan F. Kaywell

Credits

Every effort has been made to contact copyright holders for permission to reproduce borrowed material where necessary. We apologize for any oversights and would be happy to rectify them in future printings.

Copyright © 2010 by Christopher-Gordon Publishers, Inc.

All rights reserved. Except for review purposes, no part of this material protected by this copyright notice may be reproduced or utilized in any form or by any means, electronic or mechanical, including photocopying, recording, or in any information and retrieval system, without the express written permission of the publisher or copyright holder.

Christopher-Gordon Publishers, Inc.
Bridging Theory and Practice

1420 Providence Highway, Suite 120, Norwood, MA 02062
800-934-8322 (in U.S.) 781-762-5577
www.Christopher-Gordon.com

Printed in Canada

10 9 8 7 6 5 4 3 2 1   14 13 12 11 10 09

ISBN: 978-1-933760-30-8

Library of Congress Catalogue Number
2009939901

To the next two generations
Stephen M. Kaywell and Katelyn Jean Baggerly,
Christopher S. Maida and Kylie Rain Maida

Make the world a better place because you have lived in it!

Contents

Preface

My co-authors and I were inspired to write *Adolescent Literature as a Complement to the Classics: Addressing Critical Issues in Today's Classrooms* because teachers have responded so enthusiastically to using *Adolescent Literature as a Complement to the Classics,* Volumes 1 (1993), 2 (1995), 3 (1997), and 4 (2000) in their classrooms. We have updated our lists of recommended books, adding many new titles, and have incorporated the use of new media and technology into our strategies. Consistent with the series, this text makes two assumptions: (a) The classics constitute the canon of literature most frequently taught in our schools, and (b) most teachers, though familiar with young adult (YA) literature, are unsure how best to use it in their classrooms. This book gives teachers the information they need to confidently use YA novels to complement their teaching of the classics.

When we were selecting classics appropriate for middle-level students and organizing them chronologically—*The Adventures of Huckleberry Finn, The Miracle Worker, To Kill a Mockingbird, Anne Frank: The Diary of a Young Girl,* and *A Raisin in the Sun*—the theme of continuing prejudice became glaringly apparent. Because we live in a post-9/11 society and the United States is currently at war, I decided to end the book with the chapter "Using Young Adult Literature to Develop a Comprehensive World Literature Course with several classics" to build understanding.

Every summer for the past 11 years, I've had the good fortune to teach a world literature course at the University of South Florida. Since 2001, my students tell me that 9/11 forever changed the way they view the world. By reading and studying world literature, however, my students learn to appreciate diversity and realize how fortunate they are to live in a free and wealthy country. They also learn that Americans are a minority of the world's population but use a majority of the world's resources. With a growing population, limited resources, and the Internet making the world an increasingly smaller place, we must help our students to understand and promote peace among all residents of our global village. Using strategies in this book, teachers can help students to identify and address prejudice based on race, religion, age, class or status, lifestyle, disabilities, and ethnicity. By exploring these issues at a time when they are developing their ability to think in abstraction, secondary school students can learn, through the class's study of world literature, that hatred leads to pain and destruction and be inspired to choose peace instead.

Each chapter is designed so that every student, from least to most talented, can learn at his or her optimum level. Each chapter can stand alone, and an experienced teacher can easily adapt any chapter's strategies to fit his or her needs. For example, a teacher who is not required to teach *The Adventures of Huckleberry Finn* may choose to adapt that chapter's multitext strategy to the study of another required classic. A teacher who *is* required to teach Twain's novel might prefer to use strategies from chapter 5, which explores the themes of race and family by using the YA novel *Crossing Jordan* as a bridge to understanding the classic play *A Raisin in the Sun*. In other words, a teacher can choose from any chapter's strategies, replacing that chapter's suggested novels with novels of his or her choice. The many suggestions and resources listed at the end of the book will assist teachers and their students in their search for YA novels that complement the classics.

We initially targeted this revised edition toward English teachers of middle school students, but teachers of high school students can certainly benefit as well. University professors who teach preservice teachers and graduate students may also find this text valuable.

Acknowledgments

My first thanks must go to my colleagues who agreed to assist in the writing and revising of these chapters, who met their deadlines, and who extended their friendship: Michelle Dixon, Bonnie Ericson, Joan Fowinkle, Jo Higgins, Patricia P. Kelly, Kara Larson, Jennifer Loadman, Tara Foote Lorentsen, April Templeton, and Leandra Sambrine Vera.

A very special thanks is extended to Sue Canavan, the executive vice president of Christopher-Gordon Publishers, whose confidence made this book happen, and to Jennifer Bengtson for her extraordinary patience and encouragement. I am also grateful to the reviewers who made excellent suggestions and to the many, many teachers who have successfully used the previous four volumes of *Adolescent Literature as a Complement to the Classics*. Every teacher who wrote to share her or his success story using young adult literature to complement the classics made a positive difference, motivating me to update this work.

It probably goes without saying, but I'd like to thank my family, friends, and various faculty and staff at the University of South Florida for supporting me and giving me the time and encouragement necessary to complete this task.

Finally, I'd like to thank the authors who write for young adults, for without them, these units would not be possible. Books give us hope. Books give us understanding. Books can help us to create peace.

Chapter 1

The Adventures of Huckleberry Finn, Prejudice, and Young Adult Literature

Jo Higgins, Joan Fowinkle, & Joan F. Kaywell

> People fail to get along
>   because they fear each other.
> They fear each other
>   because they don't know each other.
> They don't know each other
>   because they have not properly
>   communicated with each other.
> —Martin Luther King, Jr.

Introduction

When assigned the classic novel *The Adventures of Huckleberry Finn* (Twain, 1885/2002), students often say, "Why do we have to read this? Slavery was a long time ago" or "I don't see what this has to do with me." They raise a good point. Young adult (YA) literature can help students understand why reading about Huck Finn still matters. By creating a bridge to the reading of this classic, YA novels help make relevant this seemingly outdated aspect of racial prejudice by allowing students to examine several contemporary forms of prejudice. We chose the YA novels listed in this chapter for several reasons: They reflect many kinds of prejudice, promote thoughtful exploration of the human dilemma, and are relevant to the lives of our students. Although *The Adventures of Huckleberry Finn* is often studied as the original foster child, dysfunctional family, abusive father, ward-of–the-state story, we have designed this chapter (revised from *Adolescent Literature as a Complement to the Classics,* Volume 1) to help students vicariously experience situations in which prejudice occurs in this and in other novels. Vicariously experiencing and responding to prejudice through literature can help students develop their sense of empathy and enable them to clarify their attitudes and values regarding those they consider different.

This chapter provides students with the opportunity to work coopera-tively as well as individually. We have planned these activities to accommo-date students' various learning styles. Our goal is to offer students a variety of activities while still providing a structural base.

Preparation

The activities described in this chapter are designed to take place approx-imately 1 week before the actual teaching of *The Adventures of Huckleberry Finn*; however, some additional preparation is necessary before beginning these activities.

Three to Four Weeks Before Teaching *The Adventures of Huckleberry Finn*

Several weeks before teaching *The Adventures of Huckleberry Finn*, select a day when the class can brainstorm their ideas about prejudice, divide into groups, and be assigned novels to read outside class. We suggest that you and your students brainstorm all possible types of prejudice, list them on the board, and break the list down into categories. Usually, students will name prejudices that fall into one of five major categories: racial, age, class or status, religious or lifestyle, and disabilities (Figure 1.1). You may use any category for which corresponding YA novels can be found.

Next, divide the class into five groups, each of which will read YA novels grouped by theme: One group will read novels about racial prejudice, an-other about age prejudice, and so on. Although you may assign the groups, you'll generate more interest in the activity if each student is allowed to pick the type of prejudice he or she finds most compelling.

After the groups are formed, introduce students to YA novels about preju-dice. You can do this in a variety of ways. You can give book talks (brief oral book summaries) to the students, students can peruse the books themselves, or each group can do a book pass.

Book Talks

For each book, you can present a *book talk*, a 1- to 3-minute dynamic pre-sentation designed to motivate students to read that book. Book talking, an acquired skill that develops with practice, is a fine line between storytelling and book reviewing. By preparing your material, knowing your audience, and deciding just what and how much to tell about a book, you can quickly generate a lot of reading interest. You should never book-talk a book you don't like or haven't read. Do not, under any circumstances, tell the ending. To learn more about book talking, visit Joni Richards Bodart's Web site at http://www.thebooktalker.com.

Figure 1.1. Novel Distribution

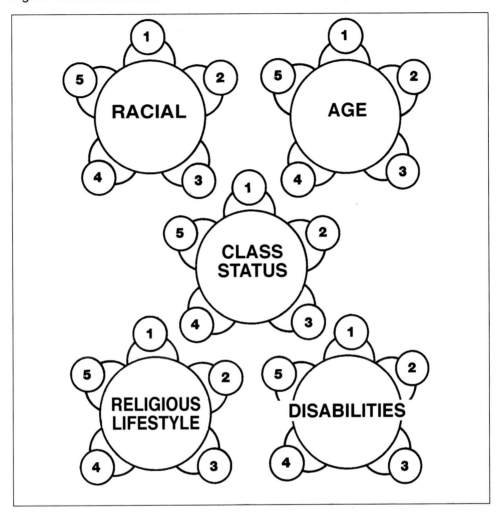

Conducting a Book Pass

The purpose of a *book pass* is to expose each student to as many books as possible in a limited amount of time. You should provide at least one YA novel per student. Have students write down the book's title and author on a sheet of paper and instruct them to find out as much about the book as they can before time is called. Direct them to look at the front cover, to read the back cover and inside flaps, and then to begin reading the book. After a few minutes, or when you sense that students are getting antsy, call time. Have the students rate the book on a scale from 1 to 5, with a 1 meaning "No way! I'd rather clean the oven" and a 5 meaning "Get out of the way! I must read this book." Students should also include a one-line description of the book. At this point, each student should pass his or her book to the next person. This continues until each student has had a chance to peruse and rank about 15 books. Allow students in each group to negotiate their book assignments; for example, those students who ranked only one book a 5 can choose their novel first, and so on. By the end of the class period, each student should have selected a YA novel within his or her designated area of prejudice to read outside of class. The length of time given to read the novel will depend on the class size, concurrent activities, and the ability level of the students.

We have compiled a suggested reading list of YA novels that address the various forms of prejudice mentioned above. This is by no means an exhaustive list but rather a place to start. (See Figure 1.2) Complete bibliographic information can be found at the end of the book.

Figure 1.2. Suggested Reading List of Young Adult Novels

Racial

1. *The Absolutely True Diary of a Part-Time Indian* by Sherman Alexie (240 pp. (MS)
2. *Warriors Don't Cry* by Melba Pattillo Beals (336 pp.) (HS)
3. *The Opposite of Love* by Helen Benedict (290 pp.) (HS)
4. *Naughts and Crosses* by Malori Blackman (386 pp.) (HS)
5. *Abeng* by Michelle Cliff (176 pp.) (MS-HS)
6. *Getting Away With Murder* by Chris Crowe (231 pp.) (MS)
7. *Mississippi Trial, 1955* by Chris Crowe (231 pp.) (MS)
8. *Whale Talk* by Chris Crutcher (224 pp.) (MS-HS)
9. *Elijah of Buxton* by Christopher Paul Curtis (352 pp.) (MS)
10. *The Watsons Go to Birmingham* by Christopher Paul Curtis (224 pp.) (MS)
11. *Fire From the Rock* by Sharon Draper (240 pp.) (MS-HS)
12. *Crossing Jordan* by Adrian Fogelin (160 pp.) (MS)
13. *Brendan Buckley's Universe and Everything in It* by Sundee T. Frazier (208 pp.) (MS)
14. *White Bread Competition* by Jo Ann Yolanda Hernández (208 pp.) (MS-HS)
15. *Saying Goodbye* by Marie G. Lee (240 pp.) (HS)
16. *A Friendship for Today* by Patricia C. McKissack (176 pp.) (MS)
17. The *War Between the Classes* by Gloria D. Miklowitz (158 pp.). (MS)
18. The *Legend of Buddy Bush* by Shelia P. Moses (224 pp.) (MS)
19. *Rosa Parks: My Story* by Rosa Parks with Jim Haskins (208 pp.) (MS-HS)
20. *Yankee Girl* by Mary Ann Rodman (216 pp.) (ES–MS)
21. *Words by Heart* by Ouida Sebestyen (176 pp.) (MS)
22. *Roll of Thunder, Hear My Cry* by Mildred Taylor (288 pp.) (MS)
23. *The Other Side* by Jacqueline Woodson (32 pp.) (ES)

Age

1. Postcards From No Man's Land by Aidan Chambers (312 pp.) (HS)
2. The Mind's Eye by Paul Fleischman (112 pp.) (MS)
3. The Slave Dancer by Paula Fox (144 pp.) (MS)
4. Summer Secrets by Patricia Hermes (144 pp.) (MS)
5. Bearstone by Will Hobbs (160 pp.) (MS)
6. Schooled by Gordon Korman (224 pp.) (MS)
7. Pool Boy by Michael Simmons (176 pp.) (MS–HS)
8. Loser by Jerry Spinelli (224 pp.) (MS)
9. The Pigman by Paul Zindel (176 pp.) (MS)
10. The Pigman's Legacy by Paul Zindel (176 pp.) (MS)

Class or Status

1. *Alt Ed* by Catherine Atkins (208 pp.) (MS)
2. *Waiting for Normal* by Leslie Connor (304 pp.) (MS)
3. *Money Hungry* by Sharon Flake (192 pp.) (MS)
4. *The Skin I'm In* by Sharon Flake (176 pp.) (MS)
5. *The Clique* by Lisi Harrison (220 pp.) MS
6. *The Misfits* by James Howe (288 pp.) (MS)
7. *Alice, I Think* by Susan Juby (304 pp.) (MS–HS)
8. *Deliver Us From Normal* by Kate Klise (240 pp.) MS
9. *Spite Fences* by Trudy Krisher (283 pp.) (MS–HS)
10. *Twists and Turns* by Janet McDonald (135 pp.) (MS)
11. *Blind Sighted* by Peter Moore (272 pp.) (HS)
12. *Bad Boy: A Memoir* by Walter Dean Myers (206 pp.) (MS–HS)
13. *Rhymes With Witches* by Lauren Myracle (224 pp.) (HS)
14. *Esperanza Rising* by Pam Muñoz Ryan (288 pp.) (MS)
15. *Stargirl* by Jerry Spinelli (208 pp.) (MS)

Religious or Lifestyle

1. *Playing the Field* by Phil Bildner (181 pp.) (MS)
2. *The Geography Club* by Brent Hartinger (226 pp.) (MS–HS)
3. *Split Screen* by Brent Hartinger (304 pp.) (HS)
4. *Nailed* by Patrick Jones (216 pp.) (HS)
5. *Talk* by Kathe Koja (133 pp.) (MS–HS)
6. *Drummers of Jericho* by Carolyn Meyer (308 pp.) (MS–HS)
7. *Keeping You a Secret* by Julie Anne Peters (256 pp.) (HS)
8. *Luna* by Julie Anne Peters (256 pp.) (HS)
9. *Love Rules* by Marilyn Reynolds (224 pp.) (HS)
10. *Never Mind the Goldbergs* by Matthue Roth (360 pp.) (HS)
11. *The God Box* by Alex Sanchez (272 pp.) (HS)

12. *Rainbow Boys* by Alex Sanchez (272 pp.) (HS)
13. *Parrotfish* by Ellen Wittlinger (304 pp.) (HS)
14. *True Believer* by Virginia Euwer Wolff (272 pp.) (MS–HS)
15. *From the Notebooks of Melanin Sun* by Jacqueline Woodson (141 pp.) (MS)

Disabilities

1. *Tangerine* by Edward Bloor (blind) (304 pp.) (MS-HS)
2. *The Crazy Horse Electric Game* by Chris Crutcher (head injury) (308 pp). (HS)
3. *Of Sound Mind* by Jean Ferris (deaf) (224 pp.) (MS)
4. *Bronx Masquerade* by Nikki Grimes (dyslexia, weight, etc.) (176 pp.) (MS)
5. *My Louisiana Sky* by Kimberly Willis Holt (mentally deficient parents) (208 pp.) (MS)
6. *Slot Machine* by Chris Lynch (overweight) (256 pp.) (MS-HS)
7. *Petey* by Ben Mikaelsen (cerebral palsy) (256 pp.) (MS)
8. *Peeling the Onion* by Wendy Orr (disfigurement) (166 pp.) (MS)
9. *The Last Book in the Universe* by Rodman Philbrick (epilepsy) (224 pp.) (MS)
10. *What Happened to Lani Garver* by Carol Plum-Ucci (leukemia) (328 pp.) (MS-HS)

Application

The next part of the chapter is divided into three primary sections (Figure 1.3). The first section, Introductory Activities, includes an overview of prejudice and organizes the students' collaborative group activities. The second section, Concurrent Activities, involves teaching the novel while allowing students time to work in their groups on various projects. The third section, Concluding Activities, synthesizes the themes of *The Adventures of Huckleberry Finn* with the theme of prejudice in general.

Introductory Activities

You'll need 2-4 days to complete the following introductory activities. For the sake of clarity, we refer to each section as a day, but this can mean one or more actual teaching days. You can expand or reduce any of these activities to meet your and your class's needs, interests, and schedule.

Day 1

The first day should begin with something that hooks your students' interest in the topic. In our case, we use a slide presentation on racism that Jo created, which involves a series of black-and-white slides set to the music of Paul McCartney's "Ebony and Ivory." Read or show something that has a strong visual or auditory impact—perhaps a clip from the evening news, a feature article from the local paper, a video of the Civil Rights Movement during the 1960s, or a poignant scene from a YA novel.

Figure 1.3. The Structure of Application

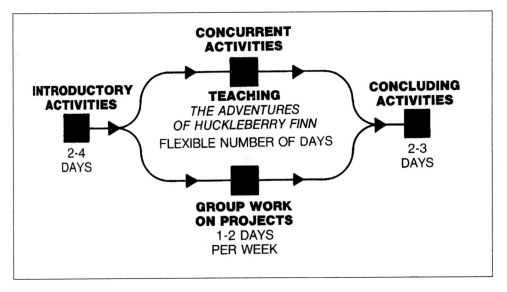

After your introduction, students can free-write a response to your presentation for a few minutes. Ask for volunteers to share their free-writes and discuss them. At this point, you can segue into a discussion of key terms, defining and making distinctions among them. We suggest the following terms:

- *Discrimination*—acting differently toward people on the basis of their membership in a particular group
- *Prejudice*—prejudgment of people on the basis of their membership in a particular group
- *Racism*—holding negative attitudes toward and discriminating against people on the basis of a belief that one race is inherently superior to another

Now it is time to distribute the list of the prejudice types and categories previously brainstormed by the class to each student and give an overview of the coming week's activities.

Day 2

Begin with an opening activity called *picture categorizing*. Display around the room a group of approximately 10 pictures, clearly numbered.

Include pictures of all kinds of people: Black, White, young, old, men, women, and so forth. Three or four of the pictures should be of people who *are*—but might not *look*—successful. Ask each student to categorize the people shown in the pictures by rating each between a 1 and a 10 (1 being the least likely, 10 the most likely) in response to the following questions:

1. Who is the most intelligent?
2. Who is the nicest?
3. Who is the most successful?

After the students have rated the pictures, reveal the identities of the people in the photographs. Follow this activity by having students discuss why they rated some people higher than others. You may also want to discuss the multiple meanings of the word *discriminate* and when it might be appropriate to discriminate. Students should then assemble into their groups and list the ways in which prejudice manifests itself and causes conflicts in their YA novels. Students can list how these prejudice-based conflicts were or could be resolved. Students can write both lists on large pieces of paper and share them with the other groups, thus exposing the whole class to a wide range of prejudices and possible solutions.

Day 3

You may or may not be comfortable with group work. We have found that our groups work most efficiently when we provide some basic structure. We operate groups on the premise that each person is an integral part of the group and that in order for the group to function, each person must be responsible for specific tasks. A group folder containing organizational material is essential to the success of the group. To help build group unity, you may allow students a few minutes to come up with a group name, which can then be used to decorate the group folder. At this point, we distribute the Group Projects Responsibility Sheet (Figure 1.4).

We then discuss each responsibility in detail with the entire class. After we have answered any questions, each student chooses a responsibility and the group fills out the sheet. Next, each group decides how its project will reflect the type of prejudice identified in their members' YA novels. Once the decision has been made and recorded, the sheet can be glued to the inside of the group's folder.

Groups can approach the projects in one of three ways (Figure 1.5). The group's first option is to concentrate on the one novel it feels best represents the type of prejudice it is addressing. In this case, the group member who read that book will need to share the plot details and may even want to provide a written outline or plot summary. The group's second option is to incorporate into its project some of the ideas or events from all of the group's YA novels. In the third option, group members can do individual projects but present them cohesively as a group. This option allows the most independence but requires the most creativity for presenting the projects. (Figure 1.5)

Figure 1.4. Group Projects Responsibility Sheet

Group Name _____ **Period** _____

Ambassador _____

The ambassador monitors and assesses the group's functioning, is responsible for designating tasks and running the group, and talks to the teacher if the group has any questions or problems.

Extra or Encourager _____

The extra or encourager fills in for anyone who is absent, is willing to perform all roles within the group, helps in any capacity that is needed in order to complete the project, and encourages everyone to participate.

Record Keeper _____

The record keeper is responsible for the writing and record keeping for the group, updates and maintains this sheet, and writes and submits a detailed daily progress report that contains an account of all the activities the group completed that day.

Supplies and Equipment Manager _____

The supplies and equipment manager is responsible for gathering the supplies needed to complete the project, and submits a written list to the record keeper to attach to the daily progress report so the teacher will be aware of the group's needs and can offer assistance.

Time and Task Coordinator _____

The time and task coordinator is responsible for developing a schedule to ensure that the group is able to complete the project on time. The schedule should be written and submitted to the teacher at the beginning of the second class period. This person is also responsible for keeping the group focused and on task in relation to this schedule.

Group Project Decision: _____

_____

Figure 1.5. Three Options

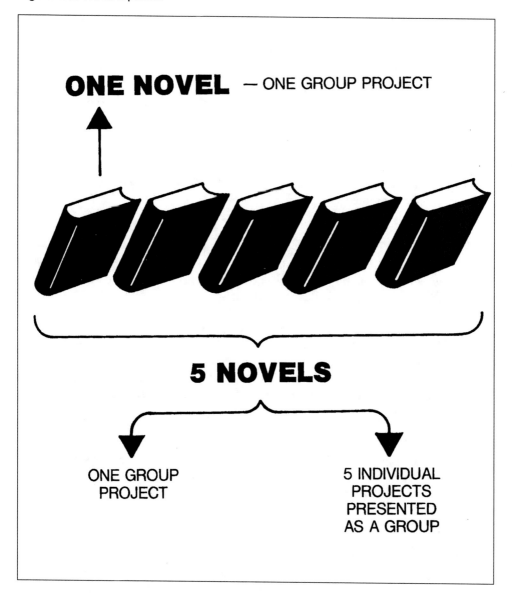

When explaining these three options to the class, the teacher may distribute the Group Projects handout (Figure 1.6).

Figure 1.6. Group Projects

Your group can choose to do either a group project or five individual projects that can be presented cohesively. Your group project can concentrate on one particular book or can bring together a theme or an idea presented in several books. If your group chooses to do individual projects, one person can act as a spokesperson to describe your theme and to introduce your individual projects.

If you have another idea, you can present it to your teacher. If your idea is accepted, it will be permanently added to the idea file for future group projects. Your group should decide on a project or projects fairly quickly.

After your group chooses a project (or projects) to work on, look up the project details in the idea file box at the back of the room. The ideas for projects are filed alphabetically. Once a project is selected, your group should begin working on a plan of action. Be sure each of you does your part.

Your group's presentation to the class should be 5–10 minutes long. Presentations will be graded according to appropriate content, creativity, evidence of time spent, thoroughness, neatness, and cohesiveness or flow.

Group Projects—One Novel

Chronological Scenes
Group Debate
Group Role-Play
Mock Trial
Newspaper
Panel Discussion
Rewrite as a Play
Time Period Presentation

Group Projects—Several Novels

Create a Book
Group Debate
Group Role-Play
Newspaper
Panel Discussion
Rewrite as a Play
Slide, Photo PowerPoint Presentation

Individual Projects—To Be Presented as a Group

Alternative Ending
Background Music
Book Jacket
Bulletin Board Character Sketch
Bulletin Board Display
Cartoon Strips
Character Sketches
Create a Book
Create a Collage
Create a Diary
Design a Game
Design a Symbol
Diorama or Model
Dramatic or Mood Lighting
Multimedia Presentation
Newspaper Articles
Oral Presentation
Personality Folder
Story Sales Pitch
Take on the Author
TV Commercial
Vocabulary

This list of projects is by no means exclusive. Projects can be added or deleted. You can distribute detailed project descriptions as handouts to each group, or you can place the project descriptions on index cards and keep them in a file box somewhere in the room, as mentioned in Figure 1.6. The projects listed in the Group Projects handout are detailed in Figure 1.7 and formatted so that copies can be cut and pasted onto index cards for students' use.

Figure 1.7

Group Projects (One Novel)

Chronological Scenes

If your topic includes events that have unfolded over time, your group can write and act out a series of short scenes that depict your topic's stages of development. For example, if your topic is the Civil Rights Movement, you might act out a scene from before the Civil War, just before the turn of the century, the Depression, the 1960s, and the present. Each scene need not include every group member, but be sure all group members are included in at least one scene. As alternatives to having all group members act, one or two members can be script writers or narrators for the dramatized scenes. A written script must accompany the presentation.

Group Debate

Knowing that a debate is the intelligent, constructive exchange of ideas and opinions, have each person in your group choose a character in the story he or she wants to represent and set up a debate between these characters. The debate may center around one particular conflict or an entire theme. If there are not enough characters in the story for each person to have a part, one person can act as the moderator. The debate should be written up and submitted at the time of the presentation.

Group Role-Play

Role-playing is the taking on of another's point of view to gain greater insight into that person's psyche. Have each person in your group choose a character in a novel and play out a scene (or several scenes). Each person should assume that character's perspective as much as possible. A written script must accompany the presentation.

Mock Trial

Set up a mock trial to determine the guilt or innocence of a character in your novel. You can have one person be the judge, one the accused, one the prosecutor, one the defense attorney, and the rest as jurors. Be sure the attorneys ask questions that effectively reveal the crime so that the jury will know what happened. An alternative is to put the author of the book on trial. This is particularly effective if you think the author was unjust or biased in his or her writing. A written script must be submitted at the time of the presentation.

Newspaper

Design a newspaper (a minimum of two pages) that includes articles reporting different conflicts from the story. Be sure to include catchy headlines, a few pictures, and one or two advertisements. You can divide your group according to specific tasks:

one person can be the editor, one or two the reporters, one a layout person, and so forth, or all members can work together on each aspect of the paper.

Panel Discussion

Each person is responsible for presenting the views of one person in the novel. If there are not enough main characters, one person can be the moderator and ask key questions. Questions should be made up ahead of time and should reveal the details of the book's main conflicts so the rest of the class can follow. Some questions can be given to members of the class ahead of time, and, if time permits, classmates can ask questions that are not preselected. An alternative to this activity is to create a panel of experts (e.g., doctor, lawyer, clergy) to answer questions about the events of the novel from their perspectives.

Period Presentation

Authors are often strongly influenced by the times in which they lived. Present a skit that depicts the period in which your story took place or the period in which your author wrote or grew up. Be sure to study and include appropriate costumes, lingo, and mannerisms. A written script must accompany the presentation.

Rewrite as a Play

Rewrite the novel as a short play. Be sure to include as many of the main events as possible. Your group can work on the script together, or you can divide the story and have each person write a scene. If you divide it up, however, you will need to make your writing styles match. If you are having difficulty writing a scene, have some of your group mates act out the conflict to give you a better idea of how it actually happened.

Slide, Photo, or PowerPoint Presentation

Create a photo, slide, or PowerPoint presentation that depicts scenes from the novel or that represents the novel's theme. Scenes can be staged using a few props and some costumes. Write a script or find some dramatic music to accompany your presentation. You can tape-record the music or narration to play along with the pictures or slides, making sure that the timing is accurate.

Group Projects (Several Novels)

Create a Book

Create a book that reflects the main theme or idea of the novels your group has read. Your book can include sections of poetry, illustrations, interviews, comic strips, and so on. Each person can contribute one page for each section, or one person can be in charge of creating an entire section. Your presentation to the class will consist of reading the book aloud and explaining how the illustrations relate to the theme.

Group Debate

Pick one person to be the moderator and divide the rest of your group into two. Knowing that a debate is the intelligent, constructive exchange of ideas and opinions, have each group take a side concerning your topic and debate that position's pros and cons. Preparing and writing down questions and arguments before presenting your debate is helpful. You can also involve your classmates by letting them ask questions.

Group Role-Play

Role-playing is the taking on of another's point of view to gain greater insight into that person's psyche. Each group member should write a short skit depicting a conflict from her or his novel. Assign the roles and act out the scenes. Make sure your topic is clearly represented in each skit.

Newspaper

Design a newspaper (two or three pages is sufficient) that includes articles reporting different conflicts from the novels your group members have read. Be sure to include catchy headlines, a few pictures, and one or two advertisements. You can divide your group according to specific tasks (an editor, one or two reporters, one layout person, etc.) or all members can work together on each aspect of the paper.

Panel Discussion

Each group member should generate a list of questions that would help reveal the major events in his or her novel (group members can help by asking questions about other member's books). Pick several of your classmates and give each of them one question to ask your panel. If time permits, classmates can ask questions of their own.

Rewrite as a Play

Write a play that incorporates conflicts from all the novels your group members have read. Choose roles and perform them. Your group can work on the entire script together or divide it up according to scenes. If you divide it up, however, you will need to make your writing styles match. If you are having difficulty writing a scene, have some of your group members act out the conflict to give you a better idea of how it actually happened.

Slide, Photo, or PowerPoint Presentation

Use photos, slides, or a PowerPoint presentation to depict prejudice-based conflicts from your novels. Scenes can be staged using a few props and some costumes. Either write a script or find some dramatic music to accompany your presentation. You can tape-record the music or narration to play along with the pictures or slides, making sure that the timing is accurate.

Individual Projects to Be Presented as a Group

Alternative Ending

This is a good project to do if you are not pleased with the way your novel ended. Pretend that you are the author and write an alternative ending to the story. Be sure to include information that tells the reader where your ending begins. Try to imitate the author's style as much as possible. When you present your ending to the class, you will also need to give a brief explanation of the story and how the author ended it.

Background Music

Provide appropriate music or sound effects, live or recorded, to accompany your group's presentation. CDs of sound effects may be a helpful resource. Provide a narrative explaining your selection.

Book Jacket

Create a book jacket for your novel. Include the title and the author's name, and create an illustration depicting an important incident, character, or object from the story using any medium you prefer (chalk, crayons, paints, magazine cutouts). On the inside flaps, write a brief book summary, which should include an allusion to the significance of the cover illustration. If possible, include a paragraph about the author.

Bulletin Board Character Sketch

Create cutout sketches of your novel's main characters, and mount the sketches on a bulletin board. Write a short script to dramatize the characters' development throughout the novel. Read the script aloud to the class and move the sketches on the bulletin board accordingly. You can dramatize the entire novel or several important scenes.

Bulletin Board Display

Fill a bulletin board with pictures, quotes, and original art. Number each item. Make a tape or write a script that identifies each item and tells why it is significant to your novel and to your group's topic. Play the recording or read the script to the class.

Cartoon Strips

Create a series of cartoon strips (at least five) that reflect the main theme of your novel. Be sure to include some of the major conflicts presented in the book or portray your cartoon characters experiencing modern-day conflicts similar to those in the novel.

Character Sketches

Create a character sketchbook. Have each page display an image or images that represent one character. You can cut out pictures from magazines, use clip art, or create your own drawings. At the bottom of each page, write a caption (perhaps a quotation from the book) or briefly explain why the images are appropriate for that character.

Create a Book

Create a book that reflects the main theme or idea of your novel. Your book can include poetry, illustrations, comic strips, interviews, and so forth. Your presentation to the class will consist of reading the book aloud and explaining how the illustrations relate to the theme. A variation of this project is to target your book toward—and present it to—elementary-age students.

Create a Collage

Draw or find pictures that illustrate the main theme of your novel, and create a collage by gluing the pictures to a large piece of poster paper. Add some appropriate quotations and write a detailed explanation of the significance of each picture.

Create a Diary

Create a diary that might have been kept by the most or least likable character in your novel. Writing as that character, include entries that reflect the story's main events or what you think will happen to the character in the future. Your entries should be consistent with that character's actions, personality, and lingo.

Current Events

Gather a large collection of printed items that reflect current events (newspaper clippings, advertisements, magazine articles, cartoons) that closely parallel events in your novel. You can place your items in a scrapbook, make a collage, or create another way to display them. Include a few sentences that tell how each item relates to your book.

Design a Game

Create a game (crossword puzzle, word find, word scramble) that uses character names, place names, and key words from the novels your group has read. Present your game to the class and explain the words or names used. The game can later be distributed to the class and used as a review.

Design a Symbol

Design a symbol (a coat of arms, a flag, or other motif) for your novel or for a character in your novel. You can then draw, sew, or sculpt your design. Write about the symbol, detailing what each part of your design represents.

Diorama or Model

Create a diorama or a model of a climactic scene in your novel. A diorama is a three-dimensional miniature scene you can create by placing painted models, wax figures, or stuffed animals against a background. You can also re-create a scene using cloth transparencies; shine various lights through the cloths to produce changes in effect when viewed through a small opening. For more information, you can talk to the art teacher or consult an art book.

Dramatic or Mood Lighting

Design lighting to create a dramatic mood or atmosphere for your group's presentation. Use different colored spotlights to add emphasis to a dramatic conflict, or project slides of appropriate scenes on a wall (or a sheet) to provide a background. Write about what inspired your design choices and explain the thought process behind your ideas.

Multimedia Presentation

Develop a multimedia presentation of your book's plot, but don't give away the ending. Be sure to present the scenes that highlight prejudice. The goal of your presentation is to inspire classmates to want to read your book immediately.

Newspaper Articles

Write two newspaper articles, each about a major event from your novel. If your novel is set in a particular period, you can write in the style of that time. Create a front-page layout for your articles, including catchy headlines, pictures, and captions.

Oral Presentation

Memorize a poignant scene from your novel and perform it for the class. You can use costumes, props, and so forth to make your audience empathize with the character or characters presented. Be sure to pick a scene that reflects the type of prejudice your group is studying.

Personality Folder

Choose a colorful character (one with a lot of personality) from your novel. Open a file folder and, on one side, create a picture montage that represents that character's personality: likes, dislikes, interests, occupation. On the other side, write a detailed explanation of the significance of each picture.

Story Sales Pitch

Create a sales pitch designed to persuade your classmates to read the book you've read. Use some advertising lingo, and be as persuasive as possible. Make posters or collages to accompany your pitch, or persuade a group member to be part of your presentation by dressing up as a character or as the author.

Take on the Author

Write a letter to the author detailing how you feel about the book. Don't be afraid to challenge the author concerning something in the book you found questionable. Pretend you are a character in the novel and write a letter to the author about your treatment in the story. Write dialogue for a staged interview between you and the author. You can ask another member of the group to play the part of the author and perform the interview for the class.

TV Commercial

Write a TV commercial that promotes your novel. Be sure to include some quotations from the book when you write your "copy." You can create dialogue and include staging directions for actors, scenery, lighting, props, and music. You can submit your commercial in its written form or perform it for the class.

Vocabulary

If the novel's author or one of the characters uses unusual vocabulary, make a creative presentation of those words for the class. For example, you can design a book by putting each word on a separate page and illustrating it with magazine images or original drawings. Write on the bottom of each page a sentence from the novel using that word.

Day 4

If students need more time to look over their project options, or if you think the groups need more time to get organized, take another day to address this. We have found that groups work best when given enough time in the beginning to firmly establish their ideas. Allowing extra time also gives all students a chance to finish reading their YA novels.

Concurrent Activities

During instruction of *The Adventures of Huckleberry Finn*, provide regular times for the groups to work on their projects—usually 1 or 2 days a week. Since most teachers are familiar with the novel, we do not include a specific approach to its instruction but offer a few suggestions and ideas that might be helpful.

Because many school districts have banned *The Adventures of Huckleberry Finn* due to its language, we believe it is wise to address this issue head-on. Dr. Elliot Engel's tape, *The Genius of Mark Twain*, provides a sensitive discussion of this issue that can help students prepare to read Twain's book. Dr. Engel's tape also provides insight by quoting some of Mark Twain's statements concerning his character, Jim, and about people of color in general.

Displaying a map of the Mississippi River can help you overcome one of the greatest challenges of teaching and reading this classic: keeping track of its many characters and events. You can laminate the map and use dry-erase markers to color-code the characters' routes, highlight important locations, and mark sites of significant events.

You can make an interesting comparison between *The Adventures of Huckleberry Finn* and Hans Christian Andersen's popular fairy tale "The Emperor's New Clothes." (A free audio version is available at http://lightupyourbrain. com/emperors-new-clothes-audio=story.html.) In each story, society tries to uphold a falsehood as a truth—in one case, that all people of color are subhuman, and in the other, that the emperor's "clothes" are wonderful—and places a considerable amount of pressure on its members not to challenge those falsehoods. However, if someone who has not succumbed to the dictates of that society challenges those dictates, the truth is revealed. In both stories, a boy ignores what society has told him and follows his own sense of truth. Huck decides that no matter what everyone has told him about Black people, Jim is a pretty swell guy. The boy who views the royal procession and hears the crowd praise the emperor's new clothes simply says, "He doesn't have any clothes on!"

Toward the end of instruction, you might provide an activity that connects the novel to the group work. Ask students to compare the relevance of their YA novels to that of *The Adventures of Huckleberry Finn*. They can also discuss how they think Huckleberry Finn would have dealt with the prejudice confronted by the characters in their group's novels.

Concluding Activities

When you have finished teaching the novel, it is time for the groups to present their projects. This generally takes 1 or 2 days, depending on the class size and the length of the presentations. There are many ways to evaluate projects of this type. You can evaluate the project itself; the project and its presentation; or the project, its presentation, and how well the group worked together. For example, in addition to assigning a grade to the project and its presentation, you may wish to give a grade that reflects the overall functioning of the group, including its cooperation, punctuality, attitudes, and use of time. Many strategies can be used. Figure 1.8 shows a form we use to evaluate group projects.

Figure 1.8. Group Project Evaluation

Group Name _____

Group Members' Names & Responsibilities

_____ - _____

_____ - _____

_____ - _____

_____ - _____

_____ - _____

Presentation   _____

Creativity   _____

Appropriateness   _____

Timeliness   _____

Cooperation   _____

Comments _____

_____

_____

_____

_____

_____

_____

Total Grade _____

You may also wish to consider using some sort of peer evaluation to help you assess the group projects.

We believe that in addition to receiving the teacher's evaluation of their group work, students need an opportunity to analyze their own group experience. This forces students to assess how their individual roles contributed to the success or failure of the group and will aid them when participating in group projects in the future. You can also use their valuable insights to better structure group activities. We use the form shown in Figure 1.9 to solicit student response.

Figure 1.9. Group-Process Evaluation

Cooperative learning is a skill that many educators believe is the key to our future. More and more researchers are studying group dynamics to find out how we can work together most effectively. Because of this, I'd like to know your opinions and observations about your group. Please help me conduct my own research by taking a few minutes to fill out this form. I will keep all your answers confidential.

Team Name: _____

Your Name: _____

Your Group Responsibility: _____

How many times were you absent during the time your group was working on its projects? What was the reason for your absence(s)?

Was each group member responsible? Did he or she do the job as listed on the group task sheet? Why or why not?

How did your group make decisions? Was it a democracy, a dictatorship, or something else? Explain.

Did the group as a whole have a positive or a negative attitude? Did attitudes change? Explain.

Overall, did your group work well together? Why or why not? Explain.

Are you satisfied with how your group project turned out? Why or why not?

What did you learn from this experience?

Did you have fun?

A unit on *The Adventures of Huckleberry Finn* could end at this point; however, we have found it helpful to devote an additional day to ensuring closure regarding ideas, activities, and the topic of prejudice in general.

Day 5

We begin the last day by reading selected pieces of poetry. We prefer to use students' original or favorite poems about prejudice, but you can use any poem that discusses prejudice from a personal point of view.

After reading and discussing the poetry, we define four additional terms:

- *Acceptance*—regarding with favor or approval

- *Tolerance*—allowing or respecting the beliefs or behavior of others when these differ from one's own

- *Individuality*—the quality of existing as a distinct entity; single; separate

- *Diversity*—variety in form; multiformity

We discuss these terms with our students to provide a balance for the three terms (i.e., *prejudice, discrimination, racism*) discussed at the beginning of the unit. We believe students should also identify the positive aspects of our diversity and individuality. We then ask students to answer some key questions, which they can discuss in their groups or as a whole class:

1. What is the difference between tolerance and acceptance?

2. Is it enough for us to be tolerant of people who are different, or do we also need to accept them? Explain.

3. The word *discriminate* also means "to make a distinction or to use good judgment." Can you name a situation in which it might be necessary to discriminate (e.g., in the presence of a hitchhiker or a stranger on the street)? Justify your answer.

4. Would the world be a better place if everyone were the same? Explain.

5. What is the value of diversity?

Finally, we challenge our students to, like Huck, make a difference in the world. In an informal discussion, we invite our students to brainstorm practical ways to create positive change in our own community.

After the discussion, students engage in an activity called "Have a Better Day." Each student makes a list of 10 people and writes down one nice thing he or she could do to make each person on the list have a better day. Give students a couple of days to complete the tasks on their lists, then have them turn in a summary about what they learned from this experience. Discuss the results, and have individuals share their experiences with the class. In the words of Toni Morrison (1998), author of the Pulitzer Prize-winning novel *Beloved*, "Racism is a scholarly pursuit. . . . Human beings can change things."

Additional Resources for Teachers

Web Sites

Discovery Education (http://school.discoveryeducation.com) provides lesson plans that include objectives, materials, procedures, adaptations, discussion questions, evaluation, extensions, suggested readings, links, vocabulary, and academic standards. A lesson plan that helps students understand that thinking about a key quote or symbol in Twain's novel can help them extract a greater meaning is available at http://www.teachervision.fen.com/reading/lesson-plan/6296.html.

EDSITEment was created in fulfillment of a National Endowment of the Humanities Grant and helps students to critically analyze *The Adventures of Huckleberry Finn*. For specific plans, go to http://edsitement.neh.gov/view_lesson_plan.asp?id=447.

TeacherVision has a variety of resources and activities, including printables, slide shows, links, and much more. Your students might enjoy seeing the pictures of the summer house Twain lived in with his family during the 1870s and 1880s and playing the memory-building game about the author. Go to http://www.teachervision.fen.com to see what's available.

The Web English Teacher contains a thorough list of outside links to student study guides, teacher guides, activities, handouts, vocabulary words, historical research sites, illustrations, an online scrapbook project, and more. For specific information about Twain and this classic, go to http://www.webenglishteacher.com/huckfinn.html.

Joy F. Moss's article "Breaking Barriers, Building Bridges: Critical Discussion of Social Issues" is available at http://www.readwritethink.org/lessons/lessonviewprinterfriendly.asp?id=86. This Web page provides teachers with five detailed lesson plans that allow students to explore the issues of race, class, and gender. Drawing from the work of Jerome Harste, who uses picture books to engage students in critical discussion, Moss suggests activities that range from looking at historical context and literary terms—viewpoint, setting, and metaphor—to comparing and contrasting the experiences of a White child and an African American child.

The Annenberg Foundation's Annenberg Media has http://www.learner.org a wonderful resource and a recommended site regardless of the topic being studied. Specifically, the "American Passages: A Literary Survey" site http://www.learner.org/resources/series164.html offers 16 half-hour videos, one of which is on regional realism and "compares Twain's depiction of Southern vernacular culture to that of Charles Chestnutt and Kate Chopin and, in doing so, introduces the hallmarks of American Realism."

Journal Articles

"Exploring Prejudice in Young Adult Literature through Drama and Role
   Play" by Barbara T. Bontempo (3 pp.).
   This article reviews how to connect students dramatically to the issue of
prejudice using Mildred Taylor's *Roll of Thunder, Hear My Cry*. Through role
play and improvisation, students will respond to the feelings and events that
are portrayed.

"Shoot the Author, Not the Reader" by Mark Franek and Nyaka NiiLampti
   (3 pp.).
   Read this piece to understand why some African American students may
still be uncomfortable reading this classic work no matter how well you prepare them for the N-word.

"Creating a Space for YAL with LGBT Content in Our Personal Reading" by
   Katherine Mason (7 pp.).
   Most teachers do not know how to incorporate YA literature with LGBT
(lesbian, gay, bisexual, transgender) content into their curriculum, and Mason offers suggestions on how and why it is necessary: "Think about what
we are teaching students when we downplay or ignore acts of hate and prejudice."

"'Sturdy Black Bridges': Discussing Race, Class and Gender" by KaaVonia
   Hinton (4 pp.).
   Once you have read the piece by Franek and NiiLampti, you should read
this piece on applying Black Feminist Theory to the discussion of these issues.

"PowerPoint Presentations: A Creative Addition to the Research Process" by
   Alan E. Perry (6 pp.).
   This article provides a rationale and instructions for having students cre-
ate an online scrapbook. An example of an online scrapbook about Mark
Twain can be found at http://www.readwritethink.org/lesson_images/
lesson787/MTScrapbook.ppt#285.

Video, Film, and Audio

Several movie versions of *The Adventures of Huckleberry Finn* are available; the most recent (1993) stars Elijah Wood and Courtney B. Vance. For
fun, have your students notice the following mistake: At the beginning of the
film, when Huck's father is carrying Huck out of the house over his shoulder,
observant students will notice a sprinkler head on the ceiling.
   Hairspray (2007), starring John Travolta and Michelle Pfeiffer, tells the

story of an overweight White teenager named Tracy Tumblad (played by Nikki Blonsky), whose dream it is to become a regular dancer on the Corny Collins Dance Show. At school, she befriends kids of color who help her in more ways than one. This film presents more than one kind of prejudice in a comedic fashion.

Christian Z. Goering has developed LitTunes, a great resource for helping teachers use popular music to complement the study of classic literature. Available at http://www.corndancer.com/tunes/tunes_main.html. LitTunes is a collaborative online community designed to serve three purposes: (a) to provide educators with a centralized source of materials and support for using popular music in the classroom, (b) to provide a forum for educators to share their successful experiences and research involving the use of popular music, and (c) to inspire educators to reach the disenfranchised using their own language—music. The site lists the following songs to complement *The Adventures of Huckleberry Finn*:

- "Barefoot Children" from *Barometer Soup* by Jimmy Buffett (MCA Nashville, 1995).
- "Mmm Mmm Mmm Mmm" from *God Shuffled His Feet* by Crash Test Dummies (Arista, 1993)
- "Song for America" from *Song for America* by Kansas (Sony, 1974)
- "Fly Away" from *The Longest Yard Soundtrack* by Nelly (Universal, 2005)
- "Southern Accents" from *Southern Accents* by Tom Petty (MCA, 1985)
- "Youth of the Nation" from *Satellite* by P.O.D. (Atlantic, 2001)
- "Born to Run" from *Born to Run* by Bruce Springsteen (Sony, 1975)

Chapter 2

The Miracle Worker and Young Adult Literature About Disabilities

Patricia P. Kelly, Joan F. Kaywell, Michelle Dixon, Kara Larson, Jennifer Loadman, & Tara Foote Lorentsen

Introduction

Each of us is, in some way, disabled. We might read, see, or hear less well than we should. We might suffer from a physical or an emotional problem. We adjust to our limitations because this is the way we are, this is the way we know ourselves to be. In 1990, the Individuals with Disabilities Education Act (IDEA) made it possible for more and more physically and emotionally disabled students to become part of the regular classroom setting. In 2004, Congress revised IDEA to help improve the quality of education for disabled students and to align IDEA with the 2001 No Child Left Behind Act. Today, we must develop ways to help disabled students and their peers relate to and appreciate one other.

Of course, when students interact and work together on a daily basis, they usually learn to understand their classmates' feelings. Nevertheless, students may need some direct guidance to help them manage physical interactions. For example, people often do not know how to relate to someone who is in a wheelchair or who is blind or deaf. If we do not know how to react to or help another person with a disability, we may unintentionally make that person feel uncomfortable. How better to raise students' awareness than by pairing their reading of young adult (YA) novels about young people with disabilities with their study of the classic play about Helen Keller, one of the most profoundly disabled—and highly successful—people in modern times.

Prereading for *The Miracle Worker*

Read Aloud Two Essays

As an introduction to *The Miracle Worker* (Gibson, 1956-2002), you or your students can read aloud excerpts from or, if time and grade level permit, the entire text of two essays by Nancy Mairs. Mairs (1997) is a writer, poet, and former English teacher and university professor who was crippled by multiple sclerosis when she was in her 30s. Two essays from *Waist-High in the World: A Life Among the Nondisabled* provide excellent insight into life as a disabled person and are appropriate for most middle and secondary students. "Young and Disabled" includes several short passages from women who responded to a *Glamour Magazine* request to write about their lives as disabled persons. "The Wider World," the final essay in the collection, briefly explores Mairs's adventures as an international traveler. Mairs humorously compares the American and British responses to disabled people.

Mairs's essays provide an excellent starting point for the class to discuss what it means to be disabled and how nondisabled Americans view the disabled. You may want to encourage students to respond to the essay(s) in journal entries or through poetry or art.

Prereading Team-Building Activity

As an extension of the class discussion on disabilities, the following team-building activity lets students briefly experience what it is like to have a physical limitation. In this activity, students work together in groups of four to complete a puzzle. Students should be able to complete the puzzle activity in about 20 minutes and devote another 20 minutes to small-group discussions.

Materials Required for Each Participating Group
- A puzzle with few pieces, such as a 25-piece puzzle
- Blindfold
- Earplugs
- Twine

Instructions
Divide the students into groups of four. In each group, one student is blindfolded, one is given earplugs, one's arms are tied with twine behind his or her back, and one is not allowed to speak. To put the puzzle together, this team of "disabled" students must now rely on each other's abilities.

After students complete the puzzle, they should record their feelings as a think-write in their journals. This can lead to small- or large-group discussions. Small groups can list their three main observations, and each member can describe one "aha" moment or insight he or she experienced during the puzzle activity.

Sensitivity Training

You can invite sensitivity training professionals to visit your classroom. Many states have a department (e.g., the health department) that deals with disability issues and offers free services or suggests other sources for this type of training. Several agencies for disabilities have informative Web sites, such as the Technical Assistance Alliance for Parent Centers at http://www. taaliance.org/index.htm or the federal government's http://www.disability info.gov. Teachers might also find guidance in this matter from their district office. For example, the District School Board of Pasco County, Florida, through the Exceptional Student Education (ESE) Department, offers disability awareness programs that include a visit to the classroom to help make students more aware of what disabilities are and how to handle them.

Reading *The Miracle Worker*

We recommend that students read the play aloud in small groups, which allows more students to actively participate; however, the reading is also effective when done in readers' theater style in the front of the class. You may prefer to use the film version of the play as "the text," which helps students learn to "read" performances. The 1962 black-and-white film, directed by Arthur Penn and starring Anne Bancroft as Annie Sullivan and Patty Duke as Helen Keller, is available on video (running time 105 minutes) and on DVD (released 2001). We also use the film to show students those scenes from the play that are lengthy or that contain intense action but no dialogue and which are, therefore, difficult for students to visualize. You can coordinate the showing of these movie clips with the students' reading of the play.

We do not recommend that students read the play and then see the film version because we do not want students to believe that seeing a movie is a reward for or easier than reading a text. The two "readings" are different; one is not better or easier than the other. On the other hand, plays are meant to be performed, whether by students or by professionals, and we always include a performance of the play in our lesson. Whether students are reading and performing the play or seeing the film, the class activities can be the same.

As students read or view *The Miracle Worker*, they should reflect on what it felt like to have a "disability" during the prereading puzzle-making activity. Have students discuss how their experiences during the activity might compare to those of Helen, who had three of the four disabilities. This can also make a good class discussion at the end of the unit.

First Impression and Last Impression

Our feelings toward a character can change either because the character undergoes a transformation or because we get to know that character better, and our attitude toward him or her changes. To chart these changes, students can list these major characters' names in their journals—Arthur Keller (Helen's father), Kate Keller (her mother), James (her half-brother), Annie Sullivan (her teacher), and Helen—leaving enough room to write about their first and their last impressions of each character.

Students can make their first entries at the end of act one (about one-third of the way through the film). Ask them to then choose two adjectives or nouns that describe each character at that point in the play. On a large sheet of butcher paper on a bulletin board, create a "skeleton web" for each character: Circle each character's name and draw several lines emanating from each circle. On these lines, students should write, in red, some of the words they chose to describe the characters at first impression. When they have finished reading or viewing the play, students can record in their journals their last impressions of each character. Students can then choose two words that now best describe the characters and add those words—this time in blue—to the skeleton web.

Students are usually amazed at how much their feelings toward the characters have changed. For example, students may have initially viewed Arthur Keller as cold and uncaring, but, in the end, he poignantly communicates his love for Helen; and James, whom students may have labeled as weak and lazy, eventually stands up to his father in a way that is decisive for Helen's development. The "evidence" on the webs can generate excellent class discussions.

Dramatic Freeze Frames

Whether students have read the play or have seen the film, they can use dramatic freeze frames as one of their culminating activities. Divide the class into groups of four or five, using students' regular cooperative learning groups or teams. Ask students to select four key scenes from the play. All group members must appear at least once in a scene, but each student decides how she or he will contribute to the action. Allow 15 minutes for the groups to select their scenes, to decide on the order of scene presentation, to discuss how to portray the action, and to rehearse. After a 1-minute "curtain time" call, students assemble their desks in theater style for the show.

Students can decide on the order in which the groups will present, or groups can draw numbers. The students in the audience should close their eyes for the few seconds it takes the first performing group to arrange its first scene. When you signal the students to open their eyes, they should look at the scene for about 10 seconds, then close their eyes again while the performing group arranges its second scene. Continue this process until the group performs all four scenes. Completing every group's freeze frames in a single class period is important to the success of this activity; otherwise, students lose their "edge" and the class's excitement fades.

All is not quiet during the performances: Students clap and laugh, show their appreciation and approval of particular interpretations, and even point out the most effective aspects of the dramatizations. At the end of the class, we discuss how each group's interpretations varied. Usually, at least one key scene is performed by all groups, which provides a good basis for comparison. Seeing different presentations of the same scene allows students to begin trusting in and enjoying a wide range of artistic interpretations, including their own.

Pairing *The Miracle Worker* With Contemporary Young Adult Novels

Many YA novels feature disabled teens. When choosing one of these novels for the classroom, keep in mind the following adapted criteria (Landrum, 2001):

- Choose novels that portray a disabled character as an active participant in the plot.
- Although the focus of the plot should be on what the disabled character can do, the character should not be portrayed as a "superhero."
- Curing the disability should not be the solution to the character's problems.
- Information related to the disability should be accurate.
- The disabled character should be multidimensional, expressing the same range of emotions, desires, and conflicts as his or her nondisabled peers.

Accidents of Nature by Harriet McBryde Johnson

Seventeen-year-old Jean has cerebral palsy and is confined to a wheelchair, but she has always felt like a "normal" girl. This changes in the summer of 1970 when she attends Camp Courage and meets, for the first time in her life, other kids with disabilities. Jean makes friends with strong-willed Sara and easygoing Willie. Sara, who affectionately refers to Camp Courage as Camp Crip, quickly nicknames Jean "Spazzo," and over the course of a mere 10 days, Jean's conception of what is normal and what is right changes forever. (240 pp., HS)

Literature-Composition Activity

Literature-composition (Lit-Comp) activities use book excerpts to stimulate ideas, critical thinking, and written responses from students without their having to read an entire text. By reading a brief passage and answering a series of related composition questions, students are able to participate in meaningful in-class writing and class discussions about themes and issues fundamental to the work. We design the questions that follow the passage (typically two or three) so that students can choose to write an in-depth response to only one of the questions or to write briefer responses to the series of questions, each of which builds upon the previous question. Figure 2.1, a passage from Johnson's *Accidents of Nature* (2006), serves as an example.

Figure 2.1. Lit-Comp Activity for *Accidents of Nature*

...It seems that everyone had a good time. Maybe they didn't notice that the games were rigged, or didn't care. They all feel like winners.

When the games are rigged, does it make everyone a winner—or no one? All I know is that I don't feel much like a winner. But I don't feel like a loser either. That's something. It is better that I didn't get with the program this time. I believe in competition. The program seems to say that handicapped people aren't up to it; we can only pretend to be winners. I don't want to pretend. I want to achieve, really achieve. Or I will take my disappointments just like anyone else. (p. 137)

Time to Write

Directions: Answer the following questions as sincerely as possible.

1. Think about a situation in which you or someone you know won an individual award. Write a paragraph that describes how you (or your friend) felt achieving this distinction.

2. Now think about a situation in which you or someone you know "won" an award like "Cleanest Desk" or "Best Smile" during an occasion in which all members of a group received some sort of award. Write a paragraph that describes how you (or your friend) felt receiving this award.

3. Before Annie Sullivan's arrival, Helen's family tolerated her misbehavior because they pitied her disabled status. Their coddling actually prevented Helen from learning appropriate social norms that would allow her to interact with people outside her family. In a sense, Helen was "rewarded" simply for existing. How does winning an award for something that you did or achieved "better" than anyone else compare to winning an award for showing up and participating in a group activity? In the latter situation, would you feel that you had achieved something? Would you value this award as much as you might have valued an individual award? In competitions, if everyone wins an award, is everyone a winner? Explain your answers.

Stuck in Neutral by Terry Trueman

This controversial but humorous story (2000) is told from the point of view of Shawn, a 14-year-old boy with cerebral palsy who is "stuck" in a wheelchair. He loves life and believes he might even be a genius. But Shawn is unable to voice his contentment to his loving parents. In fact, his dad believes that Shawn is in pain every day and is growing increasingly concerned about Shawn's condition. Shawn believes that his dad is going to kill him in the name of love. (114 pp., MS)

Small- and Large-Group Discussion Topics

Compare the brother in *Stuck in Neutral* with the brother in *The Miracle Worker*. In both works, the brother seems bothered by the situation and irritated by the difficulties his disabled sibling has placed on the family. Yet each brother appears to be fiercely protective of his sibling. When the future of the disabled child becomes threatened, the older brother takes charge and stands up to anyone who may hamper the success of the younger child.

Students may want to discuss the pros and cons of assisted suicide. Possible class projects include a debate or mock trial about assisted suicide or an individual or group persuasive essay either for or against assisted suicide. Have students consider the following points:

- The effect of Annie's refusal to give up on Helen
- The Keller family's struggle during the weeks Helen spent alone with Annie
- Shawn's belief that his father is going to kill him
- Shawn's inability to express his feelings to his father

Students may also want to discuss the pros and cons of institutionalizing the disabled. Have students consider the following questions:

- What might have happened if Helen or Shawn had been put in an institution instead of kept at home under the care of loved ones?
- Is it better for the disabled individual to be placed in an institution under a doctor's care or left in the familiar environment of his or her home? Explain.
- How important is it to consider the feelings, obligations, and preferences of the family members who are responsible for caring for the disabled individual? Explain.

Gathering Blue and *The Messenger* by Lois Lowry

Kira is a young orphan with a special gift; unfortunately, most of the people in her village consider her useless because she has a crippled leg. Can Kira prove them wrong when the Council of Guardians asks her to perform an important task?

The story of Kira continues in *The Messenger* as the worlds of Forest and Village collide. Can Kira's friend Matty help her escape from Forest before Village closes its borders to immigrants? Who will survive the meeting of these two communities? (240 pp., 184 pp., MS)

Double Literature-Composition Activity

A double lit/comp activity presents students with two brief passages, each from one of two related texts. These passages are followed by a series of composition questions that address issues common to both books. Again, students should be able to participate in in-class writing and class discussions related to the texts without having read either book. We have developed the following example based on passages from Lowry's *Gathering Blue* (2006) and *Messenger* (2004) (Figure 2.2).

Figure 2.2. Lit-Comp Activity for *Gathering Blue* and *The Messenger*

Directions: Read silently through the following passages and then answer both of the questions below in your writing journal.

> It was a long journey for Kira, dragging her twisted leg. Her stick caught at roots knotted under the earth of the path, and she stumbled from time to time. But she was accustomed to the awkwardness and the ache. They had always been there for her. (*Gathering Blue*, p. 79)

> He could see, too, that she was accustomed to her stick and twisted leg. A lifetime of walking in that way had made it, as she had pointed out, part of her. It was who she was. To become a fast-striding Kira with two straight legs would have been to become a different person. (*The Messenger*, p. 129)

The first quotation from *Gathering Blue,* and the second quotation from *The Messenger,* both talk about how Kira's disability is part of who she is. When we say that we "accept" someone, it means that we are not trying to change them but are trying to understand them just as they are—even if they have a disability, are in a wheelchair, or use canes and seeing-eye dogs.

Time to Write

1. Think about something that you consider to be an important "part of who you are." How would you respond if someone asked you to change it? Write an imagined dialogue with a specific person, or just create a general response, but be sure to include an explanation of why you value that aspect of yourself that others might consider to be an imperfection.

2. If that part of you could speak, what would it say? What would the rest of you say back to it?

Truesight by David Stahler, Jr.

In Jacob's community, everyone is blind. The community is set up so that blind people can easily do what seeing people take for granted: cook, compose music, work as harvesters, and play hide-and-seek. Everyone there is so content with their lives that they have no desire to see. As Jacob nears his 13th birthday, he begins to question his community and the philosophies on which it was founded. (256 pp., MS)

Interview on a Talk Show

Hosting a talk show can be an insightful and fun activity. Students can interview other students who are acting as characters from *Truesight* (2004) and *The Miracle Worker*. For example, the host can ask Jacob what it was like to experience first sight and then ask Helen Keller to comment or to give him advice. Students often want to ask Jacob about the decision he makes at the book's end. Both guests might be asked if blind people can live truly happy lives in spite of their disability and how blindness might actually be a gift.

Tying All the Books and the Play Together

The Values Profile Activity (Figure 2.3) can help your students bring together the perspectives of many different characters. Model for students how to create a Values Profile for Helen Keller and Annie Sullivan, citing examples from the play to support your choices. Each student can then choose to independently analyze any other person from the play. When you are satisfied that they fully understand the assignment, students can work in their learning teams to create Values Profiles for characters from their YA novels.

When students have finished and shared their results with the class, they can do a critical analysis of the authors' belief systems. We recommend that you display an adaptation of Landrum's (2001) criteria to help students formulate their judgments (Figure 2.4).

Extension Activities

Individual or Group Projects

At the conclusion of the unit, we offer a variety of extension activities that students may do as a group or individually. Many prefer reading or investigating something on their own. Students are also encouraged to develop their own project ideas.

1. Read the first four chapters of Helen Keller's autobiography, *The Story of My Life* (1904-1990), and compare Helen's and the play's account of events. How are they different? Why do you think the differences occur? Are the differences significant? Explain.

2. Read *The Helen Keller Story*, a biography by Catherine Owens Peare (1959-1990), which covers not only the period in which the play is set but also the time during which Helen learns to read, write, and talk— all particularly difficult tasks for someone who is deaf and blind. The book continues to follow Helen's life as she goes to college, writes books, makes speeches, and works for the deaf-blind.

Figure 2.3. Values Profile Activity

(Title of Book and Author)

Directions: Use the values listed below to analyze two or three characters. What does each character value most? List his or her top three values, and include an example from the book to support each choice.

Values

1. Achievement	2. Approval of others	3. Beauty	4. Creativity
5. Family	6. Freedom or independence	7. Friendship	8. Honesty
9. Justice	10. Knowledge	11. Love	12. Loyalty
13. Physical beauty	14. Pleasure	15. Power	16. Religion
17. Self-respect	18. Skills	19. Tradition	20. Wealth

21. Other: _____

Values Most

Character One: _____

Values 1. _____ 2. _____ 3. _____

Example for 1: _____

_____ (page(s):   )

Example for 2: _____

_____ (page(s):   )

Example for 3: _____

_____ (page(s):   )

Character Two: _____

Values 1. _____ 2. _____ 3. _____

Example for 1: _____

_____ (page(s):   )

Example for 2: _____

_____ (page(s):   )

Example for 3: _____

_____ (page(s):   )

Character Three: _____

Values 1. _____ 2. _____ 3. _____

Example for 1: _____

_____ (page(s):   )

Example for 2: _____

_____ (page(s):   )

Example for 3: _____

_____ (page(s):   )

Directions. Now use the values listed above to identify what each character values least. List his or her bottom three values, and include an example from the book that supports each choice.

Character One: _____

Values 1. _____ 2. _____ 3. _____

Example for 1: _____

_____ (page(s):   )

Example for 2: _____

_____ (page(s):   )

Example for 3: _____

_____ (page(s):   )

Character Two: _____

Values 1. _____ 2. _____ 3. _____

Example for 1: _____

_____ (page(s):   )

Example for 2: _____

_____ (page(s):   )

Example for 3: _____

_____ (page(s):   )

Character Three: _____

Values 1. _____ 2. _____ 3. _____

Example for 1: _____

_____ (page(s):   )

Example for 2: _____

_____ (page(s):   )

Example for 3: _____

_____ (page(s):   )

Figure 2.4. Analysis of Authors' Belief Systems

_____

(Title of Book and Author)

Directions. Based on your values profile for characters, what do you think the novel's author values most? Values least? List your choices, and include an example from the book that supports each choice. Then answer the five questions that follow.

Values

1. Achievement	2. Approval of others	3. Beauty	4. Creativity
5. Family	6. Freedom or independence	7. Friendship	8. Honesty
9. Justice	10. Knowledge	11. Love	12. Loyalty
13. Physical beauty	14. Pleasure	15. Power	16. Religion
17. Self-respect	18. Skills	19. Tradition	20. Wealth

21. Other: _____

Values Most

_____

Example_____

_____ (page(s):   )

Values Least

_____

Example_____

_____ (page(s):   )

1. Did [name of author] portray a disabled character as an active participant in the plot? Use evidence from the book to justify your answer.

2. Did [name of author] portray any character as a "superhero"? Use evidence from the book to justify your answer.

3. Did name of author] suggest that curing the disability would be the solution to the character's problems? Use evidence from the book to justify your answer.

4. Did [name of author] present accurate information related to the disability? Use evidence from the book to justify your answer.

5. Did [name of author] present the disabled character as a multidimensional person, expressing the same range of human emotions, desires, and conflicts faced by his or her nondisabled peers? Use evidence from the book to justify your answer.

---

3. Read *Gentle Hand to Victory: The Life of Annie Sullivan (Helen Keller's Teacher)* by Jean Welt Taylor (2004). Annie's early difficulties and visual problems were alluded to in the play, but this biography brings Annie's story to life. Called "Teacher" by Helen, she became Helen's

eyes and ears for the remainder of her life. How does the additional information about Annie's early years illuminate the scenes in *The Miracle Worker* in which she is remembering her brother and her own blindness?

4. Research how people in the fields of medicine and engineering have collaborated to address the needs of those with disabilities—for example, creating voice computers for the blind that can take voice directions and read written material aloud, new technologies for aiding the deaf, and breakthroughs that help people walk after spinal injuries. Share your findings with your classmates.

5. Learn sign language, and prepare a project in which you demonstrate your knowledge.

6. Learn about the Braille alphabet, and prepare a project to share that knowledge with your classmates.

7. Research the various ways that print media and art forms are presented for the blind today. Bring examples to class, if possible.

8. Volunteer at a nursing home to read to or write for a sight-impaired person, go for a walk with someone in a wheelchair, or find another way to be helpful to a disabled person. Then write a letter to that person explaining what you learned from the experience.

9. Read a play written by a teenager about a teenager with disabilities, such as Risa Yanagisawa's *The Invisible Room* (1993), in which a girl struggles to understand the dyslexia that is affecting her life, or Max Moore's *In the Dark* (1993), which centers on a blind student in a multicultural high school. These and other plays are published each year by the Young Playwrights Program, which encourages students to think about disabilities in modern society and write stage scripts expressing those ideas. After reading one of these plays, you or your group may want to write your own short play about a teen who has a disability.

Young Adult Books About Disabilities

As a final activity, ask students to read and respond to an individual YA novel of their choice in their reader response journals. To help students decide which book to read, we recommend that you give brief book talks on several YA novels about disabilities. Although our list below is limited to YA books about deaf or blind characters, we often make available for our students novels about characters who have other disabling conditions, such as diabetes, epilepsy, mental illness, and learning disabilities. A good short story collection that addresses several different types of disabilities is Don Gallo's *Owning It: Stories About Teens With Disabilities* (2008).

Some students prefer nonfiction accounts. Three excellent sources for identifying resources on disabilities, as well as other subjects, are *Using Literature to Help Troubled Teenagers Cope With Health Issues* edited by Cynthia Ann Bowman (2000); *Adolescents at Risk: A Guide to Fiction and Nonfiction for Young Adults, Parents, and Professionals* by Joan F. Kaywell (1993b); and *Voices From the Margins: An Annotated Bibliography of Fiction on Disabilities and Differences for Young People* by Marilyn Ward (2002).

Young Adult Novels With Deaf Characters

1. *Dangerous Games* by Joan Aiken (256 pp.) (E–MS)
2. *Girl in the Shadows* by V. C. Andrews (416 pp.) (HS)
3. *Nick's Secret* by Claire H. Blatchford (175 pp.) (E–MS)
4. *A Sudden Silence* by Eve Bunting (144 pp.) (E–MS)
5. *Of Sound Mind* by Jean Ferris (224 pp.) (MS)
6. *My Most Excellent Year: A Novel of Love, Mary Poppins, and Fenway Park* by Steve Kluger (416 pp.) (HS)
7. *Love Rules* by Dandi Daley Mackall (256 pp.) (HS)
8. *Deaf Child Crossing* by Marlee Matlin (208 pp.) (E–MS)
9. *Miss Spitfire: Reaching Helen Keller* by Sarah Miller (240 pp.) (MS–HS)
10. *Wait for Me* by An Na (240 pp.) (MS–HS)
11. *Friends Everywhere* by Donna Jo Napoli (96 pp.) (E–MS)
12. *Gaps in Stone* by John Neufeld (186 pp.) (MS)
13. *Silent Time* by Paul Rowe (200 pp.) (MS–HS)
14. *Finding Abby* by Virginia M. Scott (177 pp.) (MS–HS)
15. *Feathers* by Jacqueline Woodson (208 pp.) (E–MS)

Young Adult Novels With Vision-Impaired Characters

1. *On My Own: The Journey Continues* by Sally Hobart Alexander (165 pp.) (MS–HS)
2. *She Touched the World: Laura Bridgman, Deaf-Blind Pioneer* by Sally Hobart Alexander and Robert Alexander (96 pp.) (MS)
3. *Tangerine* by Edward Bloor (304 pp.) (MS–HS)
4. *Brian's Bird* by Patricia Anne Davis (32 pp.) (E)
5. *Sees Behind Trees* by Michael Dorris (128 pp.) (MS)
6. *Louis Braille: The Blind Boy Who Wanted to Read* by Dennis Fradin (32 pp.) (E)

7. *The Window* by Jeanette Ingold (208 pp.) (MS–HS)

8. *Can You Feel the Thunder?* by Lynn E. McElfresh (144 pp.) (MS)

9. *Sarah's Sleepover* by Bobbie Rodriguez (32 pp.) (E)

10. *The Schwa Was Here* by Neal Shusterman (228 pp.) (MS–HS)

11. *Into the Dark* by R. L. Stine (176 pp.) (MS)

12. *The Cay* by Theodor Taylor (144 pp.) (MS)

Conclusion

There's an old saying that reflects how difficult it is to truly understand another's life: "How do I know how you feel unless I've walked in your shoes?" One way to "walk in another's shoes" is through reading, which allows us to gain empathy by vicariously experiencing a character's feelings, difficulties, and courage. Not only do we enter a character's mind, we can also use his or her story as a mirror with which to view more clearly our own lives and attitudes. YA novels provide just that mirror for their teenage readers.

Additional Resources for Teachers

Web Sites

The Council for Exceptional Children (CEC), www.cec.sped.org, is the largest international professional organization dedicated to improving educational outcomes for individuals with exceptionalities, students with disabilities, and the gifted. The Teaching and Learning Center on the Web site provides teachers with numerous resources, including research articles, professional standards, and instructional strategies. The latest news related to special education is updated daily. The National Dissemination Center for Children with Disabilities, www.nichcy.org, has a Web site devoted to educating people about disabilities in children. Research-based information about IDEA (the law that authorizes special education) and the No Child Left Behind Act is also available.

Education World, http://www.education-world.com, a handy Web site for all teachers, contains the article, "Understanding Kids Who Are Different: Activities for Teaching About Disabilities," available at http://www.education-world.com/a_lesson/lesson115.shtml. Teachers may download a lesson plan for teaching nondisabled students about disabilities in a mainstreamed classroom. The site links to other Web sites appropriate for student's independent study.

The Deafblind Children's Fund, www.deafblindchildren.org, is a nonprofit organization dedicated to finding teachers to work with children who are both deaf and blind. The organization calls these teachers *interveners*. *Interveners* work with deaf-blind children just as Annie Sullivan did with Helen Keller. The Web site also has information about Helen Keller's story and the impact Annie Sullivan had on Helen Keller's life.

The Special Olympics created "SO Get Into It: A Curriculum That Breaks Barriers," available at www.specialolympics.org/getintoit. This site provides a free, downloadable curriculum on celebrating the diversity of persons with disabilities, ranging from elementary through secondary grade levels. This Web site and curriculum also teaches students about the Special Olympics and how students can get involved with the Special Olympics in their own communities.

Journal Articles

"Selecting Intermediate Novels that Feature Characters with Disabilities" by Judith Landrum (2001)

Landrum outlines criteria for selecting intermediate literature that portrays characters with disabilities and provides an annotated bibliography of such novels published between 1990 and 1999.

"Perceptions of Deaf Characters in Adolescent Literature" by Sharon Pajka-West (2007)

In this study, the author examines the authenticity of six YA novels, three written by deaf authors and three by hearing authors. The bottom line is that the positive portrayal of deaf characters benefits deaf and hearing students alike.

"Using Technology to Teach About Individual Differences Related to Disabilities" by Spencer J. Salend (2005).

This article provides resources for teachers who want to include disability-awareness lessons in their classrooms, including a brief summary of how one teaching team used technology to help nondisabled students view the world from a different perspective and activities for expanding students' understanding of what it means to be disabled.

Video, Film, and Audio

Movies

Hunchback of Notre Dame (1996, G). Directors Gary Trousdale and Kirk Wise. Starring Jason Alexander, Demi Moore, and Kevin Kline. Walt Disney Pictures.

Loosely based on the original 19th-century novel by Victor Hugo, Walt Disney's animated version features Quasimodo, a young man with physical deformities who is forced to live secretively with the cruel overseer, Claude Frollo. Quasimodo finds friends in the most unlikely place—the Festival of Fools. He bands together with his new friends, Esmeralda and Phoebus, to battle Frollo, who is attempting to destroy the home of the Gypsies.

Little People, Big World (2006). TV series. TLC. Gay Rosenthal Productions.

This reality TV series follows the lives of the Roloff family. Parents Matt and Amy are both dwarfs; their 15-year-old son Zack, also a dwarf, is 2 feet shorter than his twin brother Jeremy; Molly and Jacob are the couple's two other children. Watching this family go through life's daily challenges will open the eyes of the viewer to a new perspective.

Murderball (2005, R). Directed by Henry Alex Rubin and Dana Adam Shapiro. A&E Indie Films.

Winner of the 2005 Audience Award at the Sundance Film Festival and nominated for an Oscar, *Murderball* follows the U.S. Quad Rugby Team as it competes in the 2002 World Championships and the 2004 Paralympic Games in Athens, Greece. Although the film is rated R for language and sexual content, *Murderball* provides a compelling look at the lives of these quadriplegic athletes, both on and off the court. A similarly themed and inspirational children's book is Patricia McMahon's *Dancing Wheels* (48 pp., E-MS), based on Mary Verdi-Fletcher's dream of being a dancer in spite of having spinal bifida. More information about Verdi-Fletcher's Dancing Wheels dance company can be found at http://www.gggreg.com/DW/pages/dancingwheels.htm.

Powder (1995, PG-13). Directed by Victor Salva. Starring Mary Steenburgen, Sean Patrick Flanery, and Jeff Goldblum. Caravan Pictures.

An albino boy with strange psychic powers makes enemies in a small country town but ends up touching the lives of the community members and making lifelong friends.

Radio (2003, PG). Director Michael Tollin. Starring Cuba Gooding, Jr., and Ed Harris. Revolution Studios.

A high school football coach befriends a developmentally challenged young man named Radio who is harassed by the team. Radio teaches the coach and team that life is more than what happens on the football field.

The Secret Garden (1993, Not rated). Directed by Agnieszka Holland. Starring Maggie Smith, Kate Maberly, Heydon Prowse, Andrew Knott, and Laura Crossley. Warner Brothers.

A young orphaned girl is sent to live with her reclusive uncle in the English countryside. She finds a secret garden while exploring the estate and is befriended by a maid, Martha, and Martha's younger brother, Dickon. She soon finds another hidden secret—her bedridden cousin, Colin. The children decide to take on the challenge of restoring the garden to its former grandeur.

Through Your Eyes (2007, Not rated). Directed by Donny Hall, Cory Hudson, and James Paul. Narrated by Michael Madsen and David Carradine. Hands Free Entertainment.

Produced by Hands Free Entertainment, a nonprofit organization devoted to the deaf-blind, this documentary is about the only known set of triplets who are all deaf-blind. The film also highlights how the children's single mother deals with their handicaps. Unlike Helen Keller, who lost her sight and hearing as an infant, the triplets did not lose their hearing until they were 2 years old. For more information about this film, go to http://www.handsfreeentertainment.com.

Wild Hearts Can't Be Broken (1991, G). Directed by Steve Miner. Starring Gabrielle Anwar, Michael Schoeffling, and Cliff Robertson. Walt Disney Pictures.

This movie follows the life of Sonora, a teenager who joins a carnival and becomes the main stage fair attraction, riding a horse as it dives from a high tower into deep water. When she suffers a fall that leaves her permanently blind, no one thinks she will ever ride and dive again, but Sonora is determined to prove them wrong.

Note: We encourage teachers of students with special needs to read Joseph Coencas (2007), "How Movies Work for Secondary Students with Special Needs," in which he presents an effective case for the power of film to help kids overcome disabilities.

Songs

Harwin. (2007). "Behind Those Eyes." *Through Your Eyes*. Hands Free Entertainment.

The song explores the loneliness experienced by children who are both deaf and blind.

Rascal Flatts. (2006). "Stand." *Me & My Gang*. Lyric Street.

Applauding those who have survived life's struggles, this song encourages individuals who have fallen to stand again and keep pursuing their dreams.

The Who (Pete Townsend). (1969). "Pinball Wizard." *Tommy*. Polydor.

A "deaf, dumb, and blind" boy is a master pinball wizard despite his handicaps. Because today's youth are reembracing classic rock, students may have heard this song before but may not have listened closely to the lyrics.

Chapter 3

Introducing *To Kill a Mockingbird* With Collaborative Group Reading of Related Young Adult Novels

Bonnie O. Ericson, Joan F. Kaywell,
& Leandra Sambrine Vera

Introduction

The Pulitzer Prize–winning *To Kill a Mockingbird* (1960-2006) is a perennial classroom favorite. Unlike other standard required works, this modern classic is accessible to most middle and high school students. Its young characters—Scout, Jem, and Dill—are appealing, and its themes—growing up and losing innocence, finding the courage to do what is right, accepting others who are different, discovering the power of family love and community, and recognizing the dehumanizing effects of prejudice and hypocrisy—are compelling.

Why, then, do we use companion young adult (YA) novels to teach *To Kill a Mockingbird*? In spite of its appeal, Harper Lee's novel does present some obstacles, especially for readers of average ability. These include a sometimes bewildering array of characters, an unfamiliar setting, interwoven plots and subplots, and complex themes. To help students overcome such obstacles, we use collaborative group reading of carefully selected YA novels. By reading these companion YA novels, students become familiar with settings and themes similar to those in *To Kill a Mockingbird*: small-town Southern life, the influence of family and relationships, coming-of-age issues, prejudice, and injustice. Students' enjoyable and relatively easy experience reading a YA novel can lead them to a better understanding of and richer responses to the core novel. By comparing different authors' treatments of similar issues, students are inspired to more deeply examine their own beliefs and ideas—certainly an outcome we want to encourage.

To organize students' collaborative reading of the companion YA novels, we use reading circles, which we prefer to either a guided whole-group reading or to unguided independent readings. Each reading circle (a small group of 4 to 6 students who all read the same YA novel) reads and discusses 1 YA novel, which it has chosen from several offerings, then reports on that novel to the rest of the class. Because each circle assumes full responsibility for choosing, reading, discussing, and presenting its book, student-centered responses to the novels become not only possible but central. Furthermore, when students read collaboratively, they clarify, reexamine, verify, and extend their initial responses more than they would if reading independently. Using this approach, we hope that students establish the habit of using group discussions to extend and explore their initial individual responses to literature. We intend for this approach to continue not only as the class moves from its collaborative reading of YA novels to the whole-class reading of *To Kill a Mockingbird*, but to become a habit when approaching literature in any unit.

We follow the small-group readings of YA novels with a whole-class reading of *To Kill a Mockingbird*. Below, we describe in detail how best to organize this two-part approach. Although the time you'll need to complete this unit depends on your particular class, plan to spend about 3 weeks on the collaborative reading portion and about 4 weeks on the core reading portion.

Using Young Adult Literature in Reading Circles

The main facets of reading circles are (a) student selection of novels based on teacher presented previews, (b) individual reading, (c) writing of literature log entries, (d) group discussions of the novel, and (e) group presentations to the class.

Student Selection of Young Adult Novels

On the first day, preview each YA novel available for group reading by showing your students the cover and giving a book talk, a brief summary of the main characters, events, and conflicts. Your book talk should create excitement about reading the book in the same way that a movie preview creates excitement about seeing a movie. Read aloud the novel's beginning pages or choose one of its most exciting or emotional passages. Your book talk should also give students an idea of the book's style and level of difficulty.

To introduce *To Kill a Mockingbird*, we recommend the following YA novels. The choices described below are all compelling reads that have themes similar to those explored in *To Kill a Mockingbird*.

***The Trial* by Jen Bryant** (2004). Set during the Depression, this book, written in blank verse poetry, is based on the real-life trial of Bruno Richard Hauptmann, the man accused of kidnapping the baby son of Anne and Charles Lindbergh. Although its themes are not racial, the story is told from the perspective of 12-year-old Katie, who, like Scout, attends the courtroom trial and relays the events in her own words. (176 pp., MS) (Note: Photos and information relating to the actual trial can be accessed at http://www.law.umkc.edu/faculty/projects/ftrials/Hauptmann/Hauptmann.htm.

Mississippi Trial, 1955 **by Chris Crowe** (2002). It's been 7 years since 16-year-old Hiram has been to Greenwood, Mississippi, to visit his Grampa Hillburn. He is expecting this summer to be just like old times, but Hiram soon finds out that things are not as he remembers. He is beginning to understand why his father, a believer in civil rights, does not get along with Grampa. That summer, a Black teenager named Emmett Till is murdered, and Hiram believes he has information about who one of the killers might be. Will Hiram find the courage to come forward and testify in court? This coming-of-age story is based on a real murder and trial that took place in Mississippi in 1955. There is also a movie version of this novel. (231 pp., MS–HS)

Francie **by Karen English** (1999). Sixteen-year-old Francie works hard at everything she does: She's a top student, cooks for her family, and helps her mother clean and cook at "White people" homes. She's also tutoring 16-year-old Jessie, helping him learn to read. When Jessie is framed for attacking a White man, Francie decides to help him, in spite of the possible danger. At the same time, she wonders when and if she and her family will ever join her father in Chicago, leaving their segregated Alabama lives behind. (208 pp., MS)

Witness **by Karen Hesse** (2001). Set in 1924, *Witness* is based on the true story of a small Vermont town infiltrated by the Ku Klux Klan. This means trouble for Lenora, a 12-year-old African American girl, and Esther, a 6-year-old Jewish girl. When Lenora and her father are shot at through a front door, the town must respond. Written using free verse and dialect, *Witness* presents five "acts," in which characters tell the story in their own words. (161 pp., MS)

The Legend of Buddy Bush **by Shelia M. Moses** (2003). Set in North Carolina in 1947, this fictionalized account of actual events is told through the eyes of Pattie Mae, a 12-year-old African American girl. Her uncle, Buddy Bush, is jailed after being falsely accused of attempting to rape a white woman. When members of the Ku Klux Klan unlock his cell so that they can lynch him, Buddy escapes into the swamps and heads north, becoming legendary. Interested readers may want to read the sequel, *The Return of Buddy Bush* (2005, 160 pp. MS) in which Pattie Mae travels to Harlem, finds her uncle, and convinces him to return with her to North Carolina, where he must face trial. (224 pp., MS)

Monster **by Walter Dean Myers** (1999). Maybe he was just in the wrong place at the wrong time, but 16-year-old Steve Harmon finds himself on trial for felony murder when a Harlem store owner is shot and killed during a robbery. The only person who believes in him is his mother—even his attorney doubts his innocence. The fast-paced story is told through the journal entries and movie screenplay that Steve, an aspiring filmmaker, writes from his prison cell. Will he survive his incarceration? Is he the monster the prosecutor says he is? Steve must find a way to hold on to hope and maintain his humanity. (209 pp., MS–HS)

***Lizzie Bright and the Buckminster Boy* by Gary D. Schmidt** (2004). People in Phippsburg don't like newcomer Turner Buckminster. He's just not behaving like a son of a minister should. Turner's life in his new town is completely miserable until the day he meets Lizzie Bright. Lizzie lives on Malaga, a nearby island first colonized by former slaves. As their friendship grows, so does the disapproval of Turner's father and many town residents. What will happen when the town elders decide Malaga should be a tourist destination, not a home to its African American residents? Will Turner stand up for what is right? This Newbery Honor and Printz Honor book, set in a historically accurate 1912 Maine, uses lyrical language to explore prejudice, intolerance, courage, and character. (224 pp., MS–HS)

You will want to read and evaluate these works with your students in mind, making modifications in the choices, as needed. With larger numbers of struggling readers in a class, for example, you may opt to select shorter books or those that are easy or relatively easy to read. Shelia P. Moses' *The Baptism* (2007) is another title to consider for such a class. Helpful sources for other possible titles are *The ALAN Review* and the National Council of Teachers of English's *Books for You, High-Interest Easy Reading,* and *Your Reading.*

For a class of 30 students, 5 copies of 6 different titles will be needed. For a class of 40 students, you could either arrange for 5 copies of 8 different novels, or you may wish to have 6 copies of 7 titles (so that 2 different groups could be reading the same work). Many English departments are willing to purchase paperback novels, but in some cases, students can purchase the books or borrow them from a public or a school library.

Once the books have been previewed, display them at different desks in the room and let students browse through them. Students can then form reading circles, with a maximum of five students per group. As an alternative, students could list their first-, second-, and third-choice books, and teachers could establish groups based on their preferences.

After groups have been established, each reading circle should meet to develop a work schedule for the next 3 weeks. The group decides how many pages or chapters to complete by midweek and by the end of the week. Students should finish reading the book by the end of the second week. A fair amount of class time should be allotted for students to read their novels and to write their reading response log entries. At least twice during each of the 2 weeks, groups should schedule discussion days. Groups should spend some time at the beginning of the third week developing the presentations they will be giving during the latter part of the week.

Reader Response Logs

Students write daily entries in their reader response logs—spiral or three-ring notebooks—which they share with you and with their peers in the group. The log entries may be open; that is, a student can write down thoughts and feelings about the book only or react in writing to any of the topics or questions that you provide. See Figure 3.1 for some suggestions.

Figure 3.1. Suggestions for Daily Reader Response Logs

Describe a problem or choice facing one character. What advice do you have for that character?

Explain why you think a character is acting as he or she is.

Copy a provocative, interesting, important, or enjoyable passage and comment on it.

From what you have read so far, predict what might happen next, explaining the reasons for your predictions.

Explain why you would or would not like to have a particular character as a friend.

Explain why you would or would not like to have lived in the time and place of this novel.

Write questions about a part you had difficulty understanding. Choose one question and explore possible answers.

Examine the values of a character you like or dislike.

What real-life people or events are you reminded of by characters or events in the story? Explain.

Reread your entries to date and discuss what your main reactions to this book have been so far. Have you had any change of heart during the reading? Explain.

We skim students' reader response log entries once or twice a week and write comments intended to encourage their thoughtful reading and responding. We may agree with the content of one student's entry or write a question that probes another's vague or more superficial response. If a student has a question, we may respond to it or, more likely, ask the student to bring it up in the group discussion. This is not the time to grade students' mechanical or grammatical errors, but we do encourage giving a completion grade.

Group Discussions to Clarify, Verify, and Extend Responses

Each group meets at least 4 times during the 2-week period to discuss its chosen novel. The conversation usually begins with a quick review of characters and events and moves to addressing any questions group members have. Individuals also select a reader response entry or entries to share so that others may react. During this discussion, students inevitably better articulate their judgments about the book and begin to make connections between the book and their own experiences.

We like to sit in on the discussions for brief periods, mostly because we are curious about the students' responses. Occasionally, we participate by encouraging students to expand their own responses in light of what others have to say. With gentle questioning, a student will explain the reasons for his or her comments and will begin to make connections between the book and personal experience. Modeling this sort of questioning also helps other students in the group adopt this sort of questioning themselves. Also, joining small-group discussions assists you in your assignation of participation grades.

Group Activities for Sharing and Comparing Responses to Novels

During the third week, groups meet to plan a 10- to 15-minute presentation about their novel to the rest of the class. Students may work together or do individual written projects to show their personal understanding of the novel. See Figure 3.2 for suggestions for group and individual presentations.

The presentations serve a number of purposes. Perhaps the most obvious is that students can learn about the books read by other groups. A strong presentation may even encourage students to independently read the novels presented by other groups. Most important, this requirement lets students reread and reexperience the novel. As a highlight of the entire unit, you can videotape the students' presentations and share them with parents, administrators, and visiting credentialing teams.

Figure 3.2. Suggestions for Classroom Sharing

Group Presentations

- Give a readers' theater presentation of a key scene.
- Script and present an interview of characters or the author, perhaps in the style of Oprah Winfrey or Montel Williams.
- Focus on a central character's development, and have different group members read passages from various points in the novel that depict the character's growth.
- Create an original book display that represents the book your group read. Displays might include collages or drawings illustrating the book's themes or scenes, pictures of well-known actors and actresses who could play the characters in a film version of the book (along with an explanation of those choices), excerpts from reader response logs, and so forth. Each member can also present a booktalk. (Bushman & Haas, 2006, p. 159)
- Create a PowerPoint presentation about the book, including a summary of the book's plot, a presentation of its main characters and their traits, and facts about the time and place in which the novel is set. Include music when possible.

Individual Presentations and Projects

- Write a letter to a friend explaining why she or he would enjoy reading this novel.
- Write a letter of advice to one of the characters in the novel.
- Write a letter from one of the novel's characters to another, and then write the second character's response.
- Write an original short story featuring one of the most interesting characters from the novel (not the novel's main character).
- Create a newspaper for the novel's town. In addition to writing front-page stories, you can include an advice column, letters to the editor, obituaries, classified ads, and so on.

Note: You are encouraged to explore the many media formats possible for students' presentations, including audio theater, video projects, storyboards, hyperlinked essays, and Web design by checking out Bushman and Haas (2006, pp. 205–251). The text includes handy Web site addresses, useful examples, and rubrics that you can easily adapt for this unit.

Preview Questions for *To Kill a Mockingbird*

Following the presentations and in preparation for reading *To Kill a Mockingbird*, have students form new groups composed of one representative from each of the collaborative reading groups. In other words, each student in the new group will have read a different YA novel. These new groups will function throughout the reading of *To Kill a Mockingbird*. Have groups discuss the questions found in Figure 3.3.

Figure 3.3. Whole-Group Discussion Questions

---

1. Do any of the characters in these novels grow up over the course of the book? What changes do they make? What kinds of challenges do they face? What do you think the authors are saying about the process of growing up or becoming mature? Do you agree or disagree? Explain.

2. How are families and communities depicted in these novels? What influences do they have on the characters? What are these authors saying about family and community? Do your own experiences lead you to similar or different conclusions? Explain.

3. What forms of prejudice appear in these novels? How does prejudice affect those who display it and those who are the object of it? Do the authors or characters offer any solutions to the problem of prejudice? Are they right or wrong? Explain.

4. Do any of the characters display courage? Describe that courage and your responses to it. What are the authors saying about courage? Do your own experiences lead you to different or similar conclusions about courage? Explain.

5. Is tolerance or acceptance displayed toward any of the characters? Give examples of that tolerance and describe your responses to it. What are these authors saying about accepting others who are different? Could their ideas apply to your world? Explain.

Groups share their conclusions about these issues in a whole-class discussion.

Viewings Clips

For many students, viewing and discussing clips of movies that have themes similar to the novel's can be a valuable closing activity. These viewings can also be a great introductory activity. We recommend that, before students read *To Kill a Mockingbird*, you show them portions from some of the following movies: *American History X* (1998, R), *Crash* (2005, R), *Coach Carter* (2005, PG-13), *The Color Purple* (1985, PG-13), *Do the Right Thing* (1989, R), *Driving Miss Daisy* (1989, PG), *Guess Who's Coming to Dinner* (1967, NR), *The Hurricane* (1999, R), *Monster's Ball* (2001, R), *Pleasantville* (1998, PG-13), *Remember the Titans* (2000, PG), *The Shawshank Redemption* (1994, R), *A Time to Kill* (1996, R), and *X-Men* (2000, PG-13). You should preview the clips, selecting those scenes that best relate to *To Kill a Mockingbird*. Students can also use the clips to make further connections to the themes explored in their YA novels and might suggest other relevant movies or television shows.

Whole-Class Reading of *To Kill a Mockingbird*

Students are now well prepared to begin their study of this classic core novel. This portion of the unit includes individual and class reading, individual reading response log entries, and small-group and whole-class discussions and activities. We will also describe several unit closure activities. To accomplish this progression, we have divided the novel into 10 chapter groupings: chapters 1, 2–3, 4–6, 7–8, 9–11, 12–15, 16–18, 19–22, 23–27, and 28–31. The pace at which you proceed depends on the time available and the abilities of the students in your class.

During-Reading Activities

Listening

You might want to read the novel's first chapter aloud to the students or, better yet, play an audio version of the chapter so that students can hear the dialect and inflections of the reader. Students occasionally volunteer to read aloud in their small groups. Assign independent reading for homework so that students make timely progress.

Viewing and Performing

Use a readers' theater format to bring to life the trial described in chapters 16–22. Students will need practice time and should perform their production for the class.

Creating a Character Chart

Students can keep track of characters on paper by creating a character chart, updating it as new characters are introduced. Keep the chart on a bulletin board and make sure the students include names, brief descriptions, character traits, and important incidents involving each character. Though not a central activity, the chart allows students to organize and display information about many characters and helps them to distinguish major from minor characters.

Map of Maycomb

Students make a map of Maycomb. Be sure they site the school, the town square, and the homes of the Finches, Mrs. Dubose, Miss Rachel, Mr. Avery, Miss Maudie, Miss Stephanie Crawford, and the Radleys. The map helps students more vividly picture a number of scenes, including Bob Ewell's attack on the children.

Reader Response Logs and Group Discussions

Students should write reader response log entries for each of the 10 chapter groupings. Students may write free responses or get ideas from the topics and questions used for the YA novels. Assign one reader response log entry, to be written in class, by having students respond to the following: "After Atticus's closing argument at the trial, comment on Tom Robinson's guilt or innocence, predict the jury's decision, and explain the reasons for their predictions." Although prepared for the jury's verdict, like Dill, some students will believe that justice will prevail. Read and comment on the reader response log entries, and encourage each student to connect *To Kill a Mockingbird*, the YA novel read earlier, and her or his own experiences. Use the entries to be certain that students are keeping up with the reading and as an inspiration for small-group and whole-class discussion topics. Although key issues for discussion arise in the log entries, you might want to pose questions that prod students to think about and discuss other important points in small-group and whole-class conversations.

After reading chapter 8, the class's attention will shift from the Radleys to the trial of Tom Robinson. At this juncture, have small groups discuss the five issues (Figure 3.4), which connect *To Kill a Mockingbird* to the previously read YA novels and to the students' personal experiences.

Figure 3.4. Whole-Group During-Reading Discussion Questions

---

1. Why do you think Harper Lee chose Scout to narrate this story? What effect does this choice have? Did any of your novels have first-person narrators? Compare these narrators to Scout.

2. What are the attitudes of Scout and Atticus toward school and education? How do these attitudes compare with those of characters from the young adult novels? How do these attitudes compare to those held by you and your parents?

3. How would you describe the relationship between Atticus Finch and his children? How does this compare to parent-child relationships in the young adult novels? Which relationships do you think are positive? Negative? Why?

4. Contrast the different ways that Jem, Scout, Dill, Atticus, and Miss Maudie view the Radleys. How do characters from the young adult novels view those who are different? What are your ideas about this issue?

5. Why should you never kill a mockingbird? What characters from *To Kill a Mockingbird* and the young adult novels might be thought of as mockingbirds? Who are the mockingbirds in society today? Explain.

After-Reading Activities

After they have finished reading the novel, writing their individual responses, and discussing the ending, students can enhance their understanding, enjoyment, and appreciation of *To Kill a Mockingbird* by doing any or all of the following activities:

- Students bring in current newspaper stories about justice and injustice, hypocrisy, prejudice, courage, and so forth, and post them on a bulletin board for all to read. This makes the point that the issues central to *To Kill a Mockingbird* aren't limited to the South during the Depression years but are still issues relevant today.

- Students view the 1962 movie version of *To Kill a Mockingbird* (NR), starring Gregory Peck and Mary Badham. They compare and contrast the film with the novel and discuss the effectiveness of both. Students can also discuss why the film does not include some of the novel's scenes and why the director might have chosen to exclude them.

- Students reread the beginning of chapter 1 and attempt to answer Scout's question about when "it" all began. Students also discuss what "it" is and speculate about what kind of adult Jean Louise will become.

- Throughout the novel, there are many allusions that students may not fully comprehend. Give a minilesson on allusions, and have the students find at least two allusions from the text, guess what the allusion refers to, and share their ideas with their respective groups. Once their hypotheses have been formulated, they can research the allusion through the Internet, *The Oxford Dictionary of Allusions*, or any other available source. Students might find it helpful to log on to Ask Oxford's Web site at http://www.askoxford.com and search for "allusions."

- Students work in groups to update *To Kill a Mockingbird* for a film about a trial set in the present. Who would portray the characters? What would they wear? How would they act? Where would the movie take place? Who would be on trial and for what? What kinds of issues would the film explore? Students should create a realistic plot line and resolution, a believable setting, and at least 5 fully developed main characters.

- Literature has long been a source of inspiration for writing assignments, and *To Kill a Mockingbird* is no exception. Encourage the class to generate ideas for writing, keeping in mind their reading response log entries and discussions. As an alternative, students can select from the topics found in Figure 3.5.

Unit Closure

We use several ways to provide closure for the unit. The first is to ask each student to complete a Response Guide (Figure 3.6). Such guides are usually used to introduce units, but they can effectively challenge students to address and connect the complex issues of *To Kill a Mockingbird* with their YA novels. An animated discussion invariably ensues when individuals share the reasons for their answers.

Our second suggested unit-ending activity is the biopoem (Figure 3.7), a structured, biographical poem that allows students to show their understanding of a favorite character. After choosing a character from one of the

YA novels, students can use the form to provide the framework for their biopoem. Have students write a final draft of their biopoem on paper and make a creative background or frame using images that relate to the novel. (Bushman & Haas, 2006, p. 99)

Figure 3.5. Writing Ideas for *To Kill a Mockingbird*

---

1. Reflect on the meaning of courage, prejudice, justice, hypocrisy, or another central concept from *To Kill a Mockingbird*. Use examples from the other novels and from your own experiences to come to some conclusions about your topic. (Reflective essay)

2. Compare and contrast related characters from *To Kill a Mockingbird* and the young adult novel you read. (Analysis)

3. Scout vividly describes many of her school experiences. Describe a significant school experience of yours and explain the direct and indirect consequences of this experience. (Autobiographical incident)

4. The prejudice obvious at the trial of Tom Robinson strongly impacts Dill and Jem. Describe a situation in which you witnessed prejudice or discrimination. Explain what happened and what impact this incident had on you. (Eyewitness account)

5. Tom Robinson's skin color was vital to the novel's plot. Do you believe that skin color still plays an important role in the way a person is perceived? Why or why not? Document with factual evidence and explain thoroughly. (Evaluation)

6. Aunt Alexandra is often critical of Atticus's parenting decisions, yet most readers consider Atticus a very able parent. Define and explain what you think makes a good parent. According to your criteria, is Atticus a good parent? Think about a parent from the young adult novel you read. Does his or her parenting meet your criteria? Why or why not? (Evaluation)

7. Imagine that the Ewells are a Black family. How would this have changed the events of the book? Would the townspeople care? Explain. (Evaluation)

Figure 3.6. Response Guide

Directions: In column 1, indicate your personal reaction to each of the statements; in column 2, respond to the statement as if you were Harper Lee; in column 3, respond to the statement as if you were the author of the young adult novel you read.

A = I agree; D = I disagree.

Be prepared to share and give reasons for your answers.

1   2   3

___ ___ ___   1. Discrimination is inevitable because everyone has prejudices.

___ ___ ___   2. Values and attitudes are learned from parents and developed during childhood.

___ ___ ___	3.	All people are created equal and should be treated equally.
___ ___ ___	4.	In America, the legal system ensures that justice will be served.
___ ___ ___	5.	An important part of growing up is learning to accept life's unfairnesses.
___ ___ ___	6.	The time and place you live in have minimal influence on your attitudes and values.
___ ___ ___	7.	Real courage is rarely displayed.
___ ___ ___	8.	All people who are emotionally or mentally disabled should be treated with tolerance.
___ ___ ___	9.	Fear is the main reason for the existence of prejudice.
___ ___ ___	10.	A good education is necessary for doing well in life.

Figure 3.7. Biopoem

Line 1:	(Write character's first name) _____
Line 2:	(List four adjectives that describe the character) _____, _____, _____, _____
Line 3:	(Brother, sister, friend, etc.) of _____ (names of family members or friends)
Line 4:	Who loves _____, _____, _____ (name three things or people)
Line 5:	Who feels _____, _____, _____ (name three feelings)
Line 6:	Who believes _____, _____, _____ (name three beliefs)
Line 7:	Who wants _____, _____, _____ (name three desires)
Line 8:	Who fears _____, _____, _____ (name three fears)
Line 9:	Who _____, _____, _____ (name three accomplishments)
Line 10:	Who wants to see _____, _____, _____ (name three dreams)
Line 11:	Resident of _____(name neighborhood or town, etc.)
Line 12:	(Write character's last name) _____

Students can also create a poetry booklet by assembling a collection of poems (original or published) that address prejudice, discrimination, or stereotypes. Poems chosen should relate to one or both of the novels that students have read during this unit. Have students include in their booklets a short critical or explanatory essay about the poems and why they belong together.

Our third suggested activity is a mock trial. Reassembled into their original collaborative reading groups, students prepare to act out a trial scene from one of this unit's novels. Many of the books already contain trial scenes, and others can easily be adapted to the courtroom. Students can even create a mock trial that combines characters from their YA novel and *To Kill a Mockingbird*. For example, Atticus can be Steve Harmon's attorney in *Monster*. Students may choose any character to put on trial, then write a script and perform it for the class.

For our last closure activity, we ask students to write a final entry in their reading response logs. To do this, they should reread their reading response logs and then write one more entry to describe their thoughts about the entire unit. In particular, ask them to comment on the collaborative reading of the YA novels, how well it prepared them to read *To Kill a Mockingbird,* and how their responses to the whole-class novel developed as they read further. Be sure to ask them which activities were most enjoyable or helpful. We've learned a great deal from the final log entries, and so have the students, who only occasionally are asked to reflect on their own learning. Requesting student evaluations is an extension of an approach that recognizes the importance of student responses, both for the literary and the classroom experience.

Conclusion

Introducing *To Kill a Mockingbird* with the collaborative reading of a variety of YA novels is our attempt to provide students with a satisfying literary and classroom experience. Our hope is that such positive and rewarding experiences will translate to students' lifelong love of reading literature. By experiencing a reader-response approach, participating in reading circles, and completing authentic projects, students begin to understand why literature matters. In this unit, students have explored prejudice through the experiences of characters in novels and have used that exploration to better identify and understand prejudice in the world around them.

Additional Resources for Teachers

Web Sites

The Understanding Prejudice Web site, http://www.understandingprejudice.org, is actually the home page for the McGraw-Hill anthology *Understanding Prejudice and Discrimination*. This academic site, which is open to all, provides surveys, demonstrations, and links to help teachers address various forms of discrimination—such as racism, sexism, and heterosexism—and the various ways in which society judges the "other."

The Public Broadcasting Service (PBS) has "The Rise and Fall of Jim Crow," based on a popular television series of the same name, available at http://www.pbs.org/wnet/jimcrow/index.html. The site gives a history of segregation and provides teacher resources, including lesson plans.

The Film Foundation partnered with Turner Classic Movies and IBM to create "The Story of Movies," available at http://storyofmovies.org. *To Kill a Mockingbird* is one of three films featured in this project, which provides "an interdisciplinary curriculum introducing students to classic cinema and the cultural, historical, and artistic significance of film." Teachers must register to use the site, which provides free DVDs and lessons plans to any middle or high school teacher of English language arts.

Journal Articles

"Living on the Edge: Confronting Social Injustices" by Marshall A. George (2002).
    This article explores the usefulness of using novels and expository texts to teach thematic units based on social themes like tolerance and injustice. For example, one eighth-grade teacher complemented the teaching of *To Kill a Mockingbird* with his class's reading of expository texts relating to civil rights and Jim Crow laws.

"Promoting Social Justice through Historical Young Adult Literature: An Action Research Project" by Marshall A. George (2006).
    George takes the study of *To Kill a Mockingbird* one step further. His students not only read injustice-themed YA novels—they take a real-life stand against social injustice.

"Multicultural Literature and Young Adolescents: A Kaleidoscope of Opportunity" by Susan M. Landt (2006).
    This article exposes the need for using multicultural literature in the English classroom. It includes an extensive list of multicultural books, many of which would be appropriate for the study of racism and prejudice.

"Myth Education: Rationale and Strategies for Teaching Against Linguistic Prejudice" by Leah A. Zuidema (2005).
    Zuidema exposes how prejudice lurks within our literature and lesson plans and examines the discrimination that results. For example, we often draw negative conclusions about people based on their dialects or use of language, often based on misconceptions about language and its correct usage. This article enlightens teachers and helps them develop an acceptance of and understanding about linguistic differences.

"Interracial Myths Still Nag Couples" by Mark Mathabane (2001).

More than 40 years have passed since one brave interracial couple challenged—and the Supreme Court struck down—Virginia's antimiscegenation laws. But as author Mathabane writes in this personal op-ed piece, many misconceptions about interracial relationships persist to this day. Mathabane, a Black man who escaped apartheid South Africa and now lives in Oregon with his wife, Gail, offers many insights, facts, and personal anecdotes to dispel these stereotypes. This short, contemporary piece is available at http://www.usatoday.com/news/opinion/2001-08-22-ncguest2.htm.

Songs

LitTunes is a Web site designed to help students make connections between popular music and classic literature; http://www.corndancer.com/tunes/tunes_main.html. Dr. Christian Z. Goering created this collaborative online community to serve three purposes: (a) to provide educators with a centralized source of materials and support for using popular music in the classroom, (b) to provide a forum for educators to share their successful experiences and research involving the use of popular music, and (c) to inspire educators to reach the disenfranchised with their own language—music. The site lists the following songs to complement the study of *To Kill a Mockingbird*:

- "Man in Black" from *A Man in Black* by Johnny Cash (Columbia, 1971)
- "Folsom Prison Blues" from *Johnny Cash With His Hot and Blue Guitar* by Johnny Cash (Varese, 1957)
- "Mrs. Dubose" from *Pizza Deliverance* by Drive By Truckers (Ghostmeat, 1999)
- *"What's to Become of the Mockingbird" from *SIBL (Songs Inspired by Literature) Contest Winners* by Angie Heimann (unreleased)
- "Strange Fruit" from *The Commodore Master Takes* by Billie Holiday (GRP, 1939)
- "Imagine" from *Imagine* by John Lennon (Capitol, 1971)
- "Losing My Religion" from *Out of Time* by R.E.M. (Warner Brothers, 1991)
- "The Peace Train" from *Teaser and the Firecat* by Cat Stevens (A&M, 1971)

*This song was inspired by the artist's reading of the classic work, confirmed through album liner notes and published interviews that specifically mention the artist's sources of inspiration.

Chapter 4

Anne Frank: The Diary of a Young Girl: World War II and Young Adult Literature

Joan F. Kaywell

Introduction

When I first taught *Anne Frank: The Diary of a Young Girl* (Frank, 1942-1993), now required reading for eighth-grade students, I presented it in a very traditional fashion. We read the book, discussed certain sections, and saw the movie. No doubt, I did most of the work, leading the discussions while several students simply dismissed the topic as being irrelevant to modern times. Now that young adult (YA) literature is readily available, my classes have a depth and breadth to them that I always wanted but didn't know how to achieve as a beginning teacher. Through YA literature, students are exposed to a myriad of perspectives concerning World War II. In this unit, students will acquire enough background knowledge about the Holocaust to participate in meaningful class discussions and to produce several unique group projects. This is not the teacher telling students what to think; instead, each student is responsible for reading and sharing something about World War II. In essence, the students are responsible for their own learning, and the teacher learns, too. Through YA literature, all students—even the least motivated—become engaged with the material.

There are many ways to set up a classroom to achieve the same goals. Ideally, you will present the following annotated bibliography of YA novels and let each student select a different book; choice is key in this unit. For less skilled readers, you can suggest some shorter or less difficult novels, such as Chana Byers Abells' (1986) *The Children We Remember* (a picture essay) or Hana Volavkova's (1994) *I Never Saw Another Butterfly* (a collection of drawings and poems produced by children in concentration camps). Art Spiegelman's graphic novels, *Maus I* (1986) and *Maus II* (1992), are so engrossing that even nonreaders feel the intensity of this work, which won Spiegelman a Pulitzer Prize. These 4 books allow the least skilled readers in your classes to make powerful contributions to class projects. Because the material in this unit is extremely inspirational, many students will be motivated to read beyond their current reading level.

Already I am anticipating many of you saying, "Yeah, right! I have a hard enough time getting my students to read the required book, let alone read another one!" To be successful, the group projects require participation from each group member; therefore, I've chosen projects that are meaningful, relevant, and fun. This unit also has built-in peer pressure. After hearing one classmate's presentation about 9-year-old Piri in Aranka Siegal's *Upon the Head of a Goat* (2003b), students will want to make sure that whoever chooses to read the sequel, *Grace in the Wilderness* (2003a), which tells about Piri as a teenager, finishes its reading and gives a good presentation. The same is true for students who choose Graham Salisbury's *Under the Blood Red Sun* (1995) and its sequel, *House of the Red Fish* (1994).

After the students select the book they want to read outside class, group them according to topic, with no more than 5 students in one group. For the sake of convenience, I have included an annotated bibliography of the books that I would use in clusters organized by topic. I have provided group project suggestions following my list of book recommendations, but you should encourage students to develop their own group project ideas if they are interested in a specific subject.

For more book suggestions, you can consult resources readily available from the National Council of Teachers of English (NCTE), such as *The ALAN Review, English Journal*, and several NCTE publications, such as *Books for You: A Booklist for Senior High Students* and *Your Reading: A Booklist for Junior High and Middle School Students*. The International Reading Association (IRA) also has information pertaining to YA literature, which you can find in *SIGNAL* and the *Journal of Adult and Adolescent Literacy*. One of the finest collections of resources is *Learning About the Holocaust: Literature and Other Resources for Young People* (1995), compiled by Elaine Stephens, Jean Brown, and Janet Rubin. This text provides an amazing list of organizations, books, and teaching strategies relevant for all grade levels. Finally, you are encouraged to refer to the end of this chapter for a list of recommended articles, Web sites, and movies that can enhance this unit of study.

Group 1: Other Jewish Children's Experiences During the Holocaust

Anne Frank and Me by Cherie Bennett and Jeff Gottesfeld

The authors have adapted their 1998 play of the same title into this easy-to-read novel (2001). When tenth grader Nicole Burns questions why she must read *Anne Frank: The Diary of a Young Girl*, she is mysteriously transported in time, becoming Nicole Bernhardt, a 15-year-old Jewish girl living in occupied France. There Nicole meets Anne Frank, who helps her understand that studying the Holocaust is still important today. (287 pp., MS)

London Calling by Edward Bloor

Martin Conway hates his snobby school. When his grandmother dies and leaves him an old 1940s radio, he mysteriously time-travels to London during the Blitz. There he meets Jimmy, who desperately needs his help. As he alternates between the past and present, Martin helps expose serious wrongs committed during both times. (304 pp., MS–HS)

We Are Witnesses by Jacob Boas

Boas, who was born in the Westerbork concentration camp, tells the story of the Holocaust through the wartime diary entries of five real-life teenagers: David Rubinowicz, Yitzhak Rudashevski, Moshe Flinker, Eva Heyman, and Anne Frank. As Boas points out, "Alongside the other four diaries, Anne's looks different than when you read it by itself as the sole voice of the Holocaust." (208 pp., MS)

I Am David by Anne Holm

Twelve-year-old David has known life only in a Bulgarian labor camp. When the opportunity to escape presents itself, David seizes it and begins his dangerous journey on foot to Denmark and freedom. Walden Media, which made a movie of this book, markets the film to educators and provides teaching materials and resources at http:// iamdavidmovie.com. (256 pp., MS)

Memories of My Life in a Polish Village: 1930–1949 by Toby Knobel Fluek

Toby Fluek is a happy child living in Poland when World War II begins. By the war's end, she and her mother are the only family members who have survived. Through her art and words, Fluek recounts her childhood, her family's move to a Jewish ghetto, her life in hiding, and her escape. Fluek is now an artist living in New York City. (110 pp., MS)

Room in the Heart by Sonia Levitin

After learning that the Germans have plans to capture all of the Jewish people in Denmark, Julie and her family escape to Sweden. Her friend, Niels, joins the resistance when he discovers the Nazi plot. Niels's friend, Emil, is captivated by and admires the power of the Germans. Based on true events and told through the alternating narration of Julie and Niels, this story (2003) reveals how the Danes fought the Nazi occupation and saved almost all of Denmark's Jews. (285 pp., MS–HS)

Tug of War by Joan Lingard

Hugo and Astra, 14-year-old twins, are separated amid the chaos of a busy train station as their family and throngs of others flee the 1944 Russian invasion of Latvia. Hugo ends up on a train to Hamburg, where a German family takes care of him until the end of the war. Meanwhile, his family waits out the war in a refugee camp. When Hugo and Astra are, by chance, finally reunited, Hugo is faced with a difficult choice. (208 pp., MS–HS)

No Pretty Pictures: A Child of War by Anita Lobel

A winner of the Caldecott Award for Illustrators, Anita Lobel wrote this memoir (1998) about growing up in Krakow, Poland, during the Holocaust. Only 5 when the Nazis invaded, Anita, along with her younger brother, is sent to live with their Catholic nanny in the countryside. When the children are finally discovered after years of flight, they are deported to a concentration camp, where they live until the liberation. When she comes to America as a teenager, Anita finds that art and books are her saving grace. (193 pp., HS)

In My Enemy's House by Carol Matas

Blonde-haired, blue-eyed Marisa loses her family when the Germans invade Poland. Assuming the identity of a Christian Polish girl, she goes to work as a servant for a Nazi family. As she gets to know and care about the family, Marisa must question her basic beliefs about humanity. (167 pp., MS–HS)

Four Perfect Pebbles by Lila Perl

Five-year-old Marion Blumenthal and her family want to escape the Nazis. They have tickets to travel by ship from Holland to America, but their voyage is delayed, and the Germans invade. The Blumenthals became a bargaining chip for the Nazis, who have agreed to send German Jews to Palestine in exchange for the release of German POWs. But instead of going to Palestine, they are sent to the concentration camp Bergen-Belsen. There Marion collects four perfect pebbles as a symbol of her hope that one day all four members of her family will be free. This riveting memoir (1996) is a story of determination and survival under the most dire circumstances. (130 pp., MS–HS)

We Were Not Like Other People by Ephraim Sevela

A Russian Jewish teenager is separated from his parents at the onset of World War II. Exhausted and practically starved, he is found and nursed to health by a peasant woman and her daughters. His life is a test of survival as he wanders in search of his parents for 6 years. This novel (1989) is based on the author's own experiences. (216 pp., MS–HS)

Milkweed **by Jerry Spinelli**

Misha Pilsudski is a young orphan boy living on the streets of Nazi-occupied Warsaw. He's got several names, including Stopthief, Stupid, Jew, and Gypsy. Uri, an older homeless boy, mentors Misha, helping him become more aware of what's happening around him. Misha learns from Uri that he needs to outsmart the "Jackboots," or Nazis, not emulate them. (208 pp., MS)

Behind the Secret Window: A Memoir of a Hidden Childhood During World War Two **by Nelly S. Toll**

When the Nazis invade Poland, 6-year-old Nelly Toll and her mother must go into hiding, first moving to a ghetto, then to a secret room in the home of a gentile couple. During the 2 years she is in hiding, Nelly writes in her diary and paints pictures of what she would be doing if she were free. The book is illustrated with 29 of her watercolors, which now hang in Yad Vashem, the Holocaust memorial museum in Israel. (161 pp., MS)

The Book Thief **by Markus Zusak**

Death narrates this story (2006) about Liesel Meminger, who lives near Munich, Germany, when the Nazis begin rounding up Jews and forcing young people to participate in the Hitler Youth. The first book young Liesel steals—even before she can read—is a gravedigger's handbook, which she takes during her brother's burial. Because most of her family is missing or dead, Liesel must live with a foster family who, she discovers, are hiding a Jew from the Nazis. Liesel continues to steal books because reading is what helps her survive. (560 pp., HS)

Group 2: The Concentration Camps

The Children We Remember **by Chana Abells**

This nonfiction photo essay (1986) focuses on the children in the concentration camps during World War II. (48 pp., E–MS)

Alicia: My Story **by Alicia Appleman-Jurman**

Alicia was only 13 years old when she began saving Jewish lives in war-ravaged Poland. In this nonfiction account (1990) of the Holocaust, Alicia recalls how she stood on her brother's grave and vowed she would tell his story. (433 pp., MS-HS)

The Seamstress by Sara Tuvel Bernstein

This posthumously published memoir (1999) tells of young Sara's resistance to anti-Semitism in Romania. Blonde-haired and blue-eyed, she is able to hide her Jewish identity to escape the Nazis for a while, becoming a sought-after dressmaker in Bucharest. She is eventually caught and sent to Ravensbruck, a German concentration camp for female prisoners in which 19 out of 20 prisoners did not survive. (384 pp., HS)

I Have Lived A Thousand Years by Livia Bitton-Jackson

Livia Bitton-Jackson (a.k.a. Elli Friedmann) was only 13 years old when the Nazis invaded Hungary. She recounts how she and her mother struggle to survive, first in the ghetto, then in the Plaszow concentration camp (shown in Stephen Spielberg's movie *Schindler's List*), and then while working in a factory in Augsburg. (224 pp., MS–HS)

Torn Thread by Anne Isaacs

After hiding the family from the Nazis for weeks in Poland, the father of 12-year-old Eva sends her to a labor camp in Czechoslovakia, where she will join her sister, Rachel, and avoid deportation to Auschwitz, where she would face certain death. Suffering from starvation and disease and struggling to survive from one hour to the next, the sisters are forced to make clothing for the German soldiers . The girls rely on each another and on their friendships with other prisoners as they wait for the camp to be liberated. This tension-filled story (2000) of human triumph is based on the real-life experiences of the author's mother-in-law. (188 pp., MS)

Fatelessness by Imre Kertesz

Kertesz's own experience as a youth who spent 1 year in Auschwitz inspired him to write this novel (2004) about Gyorgy, a 14-year-old Hungarian boy who has the ability to see beauty, even in a horrific concentration camp. *Publisher's Weekly* called its prequel, *Fateless* (1996), one of the best 50 books of 1992. In 2002, Kertesz won the Nobel Prize for Literature for this work. (272 pp., MS–HS)

All But My Life by Gerda Weissmann Klein

Little did Gerda know that her father's insistence that she wear her hiking boots one hot summer day would be her salvation from death. Gerda was able to see good even in the darkest moments of her life as she struggled to survive in several concentration and slave labor camps. From January through April 1945, those boots saved her from the cold during a brutal, 300-

mile death march from a labor camp in western Germany to Czechoslovakia, where she was the only one of 120 women to survive. (261 pp., HS)

Fragments of Isabella by Isabella Leitner and Irving A. Leitner

This American Library Association Best Book for Young Adults is the true, heart-wrenching, and unforgettable story of the author's experiences at Auschwitz during the Holocaust. The reader will be shocked by the atrocities and the horror that she faced but will be moved by her courage and determination to survive. (128 pp., HS)

I Am Rosemarie by Marietta D. Moskin

Drawn from the author's own experiences, this is the moving story (1999) of a young Jewish girl, Rosemarie Brenner, and her experiences in a concentration camp during World War II. (256 pp., HS)

Always Remember Me: How One Family Survived World War II by Marisabina Russo

Rachel always begs to hear Oma's (her grandmother's) stories. She especially wants to know the stories behind the photos in Oma's "sad" photo album, which tell of lives destroyed by the Nazis. As they look through Oma's two photo albums, one of her sad "first life" and the other of her happy "second life," Rachel learns about her family's history before, during, and after World War II. Oma and two of her three daughters spent time in concentration camps, but all survived and were reunited in the United States. The illustrations add to readers' understanding of this horrible time in history. (48 pp., ES–MS)

The Cage by Ruth Minsky Sender

In this memoir (1990), Holocaust survivor Riva Minska writes about her experiences as a teenager in the Lodz ghetto and at Auschwitz. Riva, who was only 12 when Germany invaded Poland, vividly shares how the Nazis destroyed her family, her community, and her way of life and tells how she survived the death camps of World War II. (224 pp., HS)

Upon the Head of the Goat: A Childhood in Hungary 1939–1944 by Aranka Siegal

Piri is 9 years old at the onset of World War II, and her life becomes a nightmare when the Nazis invade Hungary. Her Jewish family is placed into a ghetto to await the trains that will take them to the concentration camps.

Aware that the Nazis barely regard them as people, Piri's mother nonetheless courageously attempts to instill into her children the values of human dignity and respect for self and others. This sensitive fictionalized autobiography (2003b) depicts the contrast between those who know the value of life and others' total disregard for humanity. In the end, Piri survives the horrors of Auschwitz. (192 pp., MS)

Maus I: A Survivor's Tale and *Maus II* by Art Spiegelman

In these graphic novels, Spiegelman (1986, 1992) writes of his father's struggle as a Jew in Poland during World War II. In comic book form, the Jews are depicted as mice, the Nazis as cats, and those who side with the Nazis as pigs. *Maus II,* in which Spiegelman continues the story of his father's and Anja's struggles in Auschwitz and Birkenau, portrays Americans as dogs and the French as frogs. Spiegelman won a Pulitzer Prize in 1992 for this work. (166 pp., 144 pp., MS–HS)

I Never Saw Another Butterfly by Hana Volavkova

This is a collection of drawings and poems by children who lived in the Terezin concentration camp in Czechoslovakia between 1942 and 1944. This book (1994) vividly captures the wartime terror, the pleas for rescue, and the children's reflections about their beliefs and values. (80 pp., E–MS)

Night by Elie Wiesel

This short autobiographical novel (1972-2006) is Wiesel's rendering of his terrifying experiences as a teenager at the Nazi death camps Auschwitz and Buchenwald. A winner of the Nobel Peace Prize, Wiesel graphically describes witnessing the death of his father, his innocence, and his God. (112 pp., MS–HS)

The Devil's Arithmetic by Jane Yolen (176 pp.)

For students who resist studying the Holocaust, this is a must-read (2004). The protagonist, 12-year-old Hannah, has heard enough of her grandfather's stories about the Nazis and wishes he'd just stop bringing it up. When asked to open the door for the prophet Elijah during her family's Passover seder, Hannah is transported back to 1942 Poland and assumes the life of a young girl named Chaya. As Chaya, Hannah learns firsthand about the dehumanizing life in a concentration camp and why we must never forget. For a similarly themed book, consider *Briar Rose* (1993, 224 pp., MS–HS) in which Yolen links the story of Briar Rose, also known as Sleeping Beauty, to the Holocaust and to the Chelmno extermination camp. (176 pp., MS)

NOTE FOR TEACHERS: Because it is a good idea for you to read something new while your students are reading something new, I highly recommend *Etty Hillesum: An Interrupted Life—the Diaries, 1941–1943,* and *Letters from Westerbork* (Hillesum, 1996). Regarded as the adult counterpart of the diary of Anne Frank, Etty Hillesum's diary and letters capture 2 years of her life before she died in Auschwitz at age twenty-nine.

Group 3: Those Who Risked Their Lives

Rescuers Defying the Nazis: Non-Jewish Teens Who Rescued Jews (Teen Witnesses to the Holocaust) by Toby Axelrod

Rescuers Defying the Nazis (2002) actually includes three short texts: "In the Ghettos," "Rescuers," and "Hidden Children," replete with photo documentation. Axelrod tells the stories of Jewish teenagers who were assisted by non-Jews in Poland, Denmark, and Germany, and provides harrowing accounts written by the courageous survivors of the Lodz and Warsaw ghettos and the Theresienstadt concentration camp. (64 pp., E–MS)

Postcards From No Man's Land by Aidan Chambers

Jacob Todd, a British soldier wounded in World War II, falls in love with Geertrui, a Dutch teenager who hides him from his pursuers in 1944. Now his 17-year-old grandson, also named Jacob Todd, has traveled to Holland to visit the grave of the grandfather he never met. Upon arriving in Amsterdam, Jacob is not prepared for the perplexing experiences of the city, for seeing Anne Frank's house in Amsterdam, or for the shocking story that reveals family secrets. Two stories, young Jacob Todd's and Geertrui's, from two different times are intertwined throughout the book (2002) and raise some very thought-provoking questions. (312 pp., HS)

Number the Stars by Lois Lowry

One day in 1943, Annemarie and Ellen are playing in German-occupied Copenhagen, and the next day Ellen and her family face the possibility of relocation because they are Jewish. Annemarie decides that she must help her best friend escape from Denmark and go to Sweden, where they will be safe. Before she knows it, 10-year-old Annemarie finds herself involved in a dangerous mission. (144 pp., MS)

The Good Liar by Gregory Maguire

Three girls trying to complete a school assignment on World War II contact Marcel Delarue, an artist who grew up in France during the German occupation. In this primarily epistolary tale (1999), Marcel writes the girls a letter—in which he describes how he and his two brothers took pride in their ability to make a game out of successfully telling outrageous lies. Marcel even uses his lie-telling skills to hide his friendship with a Nazi soldier. Marcel didn't know, however, that the best liar in the family was his mother, who hid a Jewish family in their rural home for more than a year without the boys knowing. This sometimes humorous, sometimes sad story shows how ordinary people can become extraordinary heroes. (129 pp., MS)

The Hiding Place by Corrie ten Boom (with Elizabeth Sherrill and John Sherrill)

This nonfiction work describes how Corrie ten Boom, a heroine of the anti-Nazi underground in Holland, and her family hid persecuted Jews in their home. When the family members are betrayed, they, too, spend time in concentration camps. (272 pp., MS)

A Coming Evil by Vivian Van de Velde

As a measure of safety, 13-year-old Lisette Beaucaire is sent away from her home in Nazi-occupied Paris to live with an aunt in rural France. She's unhappy because she won't be with her friends to start a new school year and must now spend all her time with her annoying cousin, Cecile. She quickly realizes, however, that her time in the countryside will be anything but ordinary: Her aunt is hiding Jewish and Gypsy children from the Nazis, and she meets Gerard, the ghost of a 14th-century knight who plays a significant role in the outcome of this story. (213 pp., MS)

Group 4: The Japanese, Japanese American, and American Perspectives

Remembering Manzanar and *Fighting for Honor* by Michael Cooper

Ten thousand Japanese Americans were sent to the Manzanar relocation camp in eastern California between March 1942 and November 1945. In the first book (2002), Cooper shares what life was like for these imprisoned Americans. The second book (2000) examines the U.S. government's often shameful treatment of Japanese Americans before, during, and after World War II. Taking the reader from Pearl Harbor to the Japanese internment camps to the victories attained by an all-Asian battalion, these stories give readers insight into the Japanese American experience during this time in history. Photographs capture much of what words cannot adequately express. (96 pp., 128 pp. MS)

Lily's Crossing by **Patricia Reilly Giff**

Lily is looking forward to spending another summer with her grandmother at the family's beach house in Rockaway, New York, until her father announces that he must go to Europe with the U.S. Army Corps of Engineers during World War II. Angry at her widower father for leaving, Lily refuses to say goodbye to him and is certain that this summer will be lonely. Then she meets Albert, a Hungarian refugee who lost most of his family in the war and had to leave his sickly sister behind in Europe. The two friends help each other overcome their feelings of guilt in this story (1997) of how war affects the children at home. (180 pp., MS)

Looking Like the Enemy: My Story of Imprisonment in Japanese American Internment Camps by **Mary M. Gruenwald**

Mary Matsuda Greenwald's memoir (2005) begins when she is 16 years old. After Pearl Harbor is bombed by the Japanese in 1941, this teenager's typical life on a farm in Vashon Island, Washington, is completely changed. Because of their Japanese ancestry, Mary and her family are relocated to an internment camp. (240 pp., HS)

Shadows on the Sea by **Joan Hiatt Harlow**

Based on historical fact, this story (2003) is set on an island off the coast of Maine where Jill Winters has been sent to live with her grandmother. German submarines stalk the nearby waters, and Jill is feeling very nervous about the war, especially after she finds a carrier pigeon transporting a note written in German. After learning the contents of the note, Jill becomes suspicious. Determined to find the Nazi spy and solve the mystery, Jill finds herself in her own deep waters. (244 pp., MS)

Hiroshima by **John Hersey**

Pulitzer Prize-winner John Hersey (1946-1995) interviewed survivors of the atomic bombing of Hiroshima while the ashes were still warm. Hersey describes the lives of six people—a clerk, a widowed seamstress, a physician, a Methodist minister, a surgeon, and a German Catholic priest—shortly before and for about a year after the bombing. While describing the ordeals of these individuals, Hersey manages to convey the devastation and the suffering experienced by the people of Hiroshima on August 6, 1945. A final chapter was added in 1985 that catches up with the lives of these 6 people. (152 pp., MS)

Beyond Paradise by Jane Hertenstein

In 1941, 14-year-old Louise Keller and her family leave Ohio for the Philippines to join a missionary camp. Soon after their arrival, the Japanese invade. For a while, Louise hides in the jungle to avoid capture. This story (1999) tells what it was like for an American to be held in an internment camp established by the Japanese in the Philippines. (165 pp., HS)

Aleutian Sparrow by Karen Hesse

In June 1942, Japanese forces attack the Aleutian Islands of Alaska. In an effort to protect the native Aleuts, the U.S. military move them to relocation centers in southwestern Alaska. The conditions in these camps are deplorable; the Aleuts are often treated much worse than POWs, and many of them die. Hesse (2003a) combines poetry and prose to tell the Aleuts' story through the experiences of young Vera. (160 pp., MS)

Farewell to Manzanar by Jeanne Wakatsuki Houston and James D. Houston

This is the true story (2002) of one spirited Japanese American family's attempt to survive the indignities of forced detention, as seen through the eyes of Jeannie, the youngest daughter of the Wakatsuki family. The family was detained for 4 years at the Manzanar internment camp during World War II. (208 pp., MS–HS)

Weedflower by Cynthia Kadohata

After the bombing of Pearl Harbor, everything changes for Sumiko and her family. They are removed from their California flower farm and placed in an internment camp in the hot desert. Now, instead of flowers, there is only dust. The camp is on land that once belonged to the Mohave Indians, who resent the new inhabitants, and Sumiko and her family find themselves as unwelcome there as anywhere. When she and a Mohave boy become friends, they do their best to rebuild their lives and create a community. (272 pp., MS)

Dear Miss Breed: Stories of the Japanese American Incarceration During World War II and a Librarian Who Made a Difference by Joanne Oppenheim

This nonfiction book (2006) is a collection of letters written to Miss Breed, a librarian in San Diego. These actual letters, complete with spelling and grammar mistakes, show how one person can make a positive difference in the lives of many. (287 pp., MS–HS)

The Quilt by Gary Paulsen

During World War II, a 6-year-old boy is sent to live with his grandmother in Minnesota while his mother works in a munitions factory in Chicago. Because the men are away fighting in Europe, the women work the farm. The boy has many chores to do and plenty of animals to look after. When his cousin, Kristina, goes into labor, the women gather and work on a quilt as they await the birth. Through the tales he hears these women tell while they quilt, the boy learns about his family's stories of love and loss. (96 pp., ES–MS)

House of the Red Fish by Graham Salisbury

This sequel (2006) to *Under the Blood Red Sun* (1995, 246 pp., MS) continues the story of Tomi Nakajo. After his father and grandfather are arrested following the attack on Pearl Harbor, teenage Tomi is left in charge of the house. Prejudice abounds for Japanese Americans living in Hawaii in 1943, and Tomi meets it head-on when a former friend becomes his nemesis. (288 pp., MS)

Journey Home by Yoshiko Uchida

Readers first met young Yuki and her Japanese American family in *Journey to Topaz* (1988, 160 pp., MS), a story based on the author's experience of her own family being uprooted and sent to the relocation center in Topaz, Utah. This novel (1992) continues their story after they are released into a society full of prejudice and fear. (144 pp., MS)

Group 5: The Soldiers' Stories

Parallel Journeys by Eleanor H. Ayer (with Helen Waterford and Alfons Heck)

Ayer presents two alternating perspectives of the Holocaust: Helen Waterford, a young German Jew, struggles to survive; Alfons Heck, a member of the Hitler Youth, has ambitions to climb the ranks. After meeting in the Unites States long after the war, this pair becomes friends and, remarkably, joins forces to prevent this atrocity from ever happening again by educating young Americans about the Holocaust. (244 pp., MS)

Interested students may also want to find both of Alfons Heck's autobiographies, *Child of Hitler: Germany in the Days When God Wore a Swastika* (1985) and *The Burden of Hitler's Legacy* (1988).

Hitler Youth: Growing Up in Hitler's Shadow by Susan Campbell Bartoletti

This Newbery Honor book (2005) shows how Hitler manipulated young Germans to create the Hitler Youth, or *Hitlerjugend*, in 1926. Kathrin Kana narrates the stories of 12 young people who become patriotic supporters of the Third Reich. An epilogue tells what became of them when they realized the folly of their belief in Hitler, who was the very embodiment of the evil they thought they were eliminating. (176 pp., MS)

Under a War-Torn Sky by L. M. Elliott

At 19, Hank Forester has almost grown out of his teens, but he's still in the teens in terms of the number of bombings he's participated in as an American pilot during World War II. His luck runs out when he is shot down and parachutes into German-occupied territory. With the help of members of the French Resistance, he overcomes a number of perils and learns many lessons as he seeks safety in England. (288 pp., MS-HS)

Summer of My German Soldier by Bette Greene

In this American Library Association Notable Book (1973-1999), Patty Bergen is an abused girl who befriends an escaped German prisoner of war. In spite of what her parents and others say about the Germans, Patty gets to know Anton and falls in love with his gentle spirit. (208 pp., MS)

Children of the Swastika: The Hitler Youth by Eileen Heyes

This nonfiction book (1993) is carefully researched and includes photos and source notes to add to its credibility. It is fascinating to see how Hitler managed to brainwash children into doing things totally contrary to their parents' values. (96 pp., MS–HS)

Hansi, The Girl Who Loved the Swastika by Maria Anne Hirschmann

This is the true story (1982) of a young, orphaned Czechoslovakian girl who is raised in a Christian German home and serves in the Hitler Youth leadership. She eventually immigrates to the United States. Readers won't forget her story. (243 pp., HS)

The Last Mission by Harry Mazer

In this book (1999)—named American Library Association Best of the Best Books for Young Adults and *New York Times* Outstanding Book of the Year— Jack Raab uses an older brother's identity to join the service during World War II. This 16-year-old American Jewish boy vividly shares his experiences, including his harsh imprisonment in and release from a German camp. The horrors of a war in which Jack never should have fought make him an adult before his time. (188 pp., HS)

And No Birds Sang by Farley Mowat

Mowat (2004) retells his own experiences as a young soldier during World War II. At first idealistic, he romanticizes the war effort until his exposure to many atrocities forces him to see war as it is. (256 pp., HS)

Soldier X by Don L. Wulffson

Teacher Erik Brandt recalls his life as a member of the Hitler Youth. At only 16 years old, Erik is sent to fight for the Nazis on the Russian front because of his ability to speak Russian. Before long, he knows he wants out of this war, especially after witnessing the cruel treatment of the Jews. After a particularly brutal Russian attack, Erik puts on the uniform of a dead Russian soldier and feigns amnesia. As Soldier X, Erik escapes and lives to tell about his tormented past. (240 pp., MS–HS)

Group 6: Other Genocides

Forgotten Fire by Adam Bagdasarian

Once part of a wealthy, happy family, 12-year-old Vahan Kenderian now struggles to escape the horrors of the Armenian Genocide (1915–1918), during which Turks murdered 1.5 million Armenian men, women, and children. Based on the recollections of the author's great uncle, this historical novel (2000) is a vivid and chilling account of fate, perseverance, luck, and Vahan's determination to be like steel made stronger by this "forgotten fire." (272 pp., MS–HS)

When the Rainbow Goddess Wept by Cecilia Manguerra Brainard

Yvonne Macaraig's family flees its pleasant home in Ubec City to join a guerrilla movement in the jungle during the 1941 Japanese invasion of the Philippines. She grows to realize that even if her family survives and returns home, nothing will ever be the same. (272 pp., HS)

Zlata's Diary: A Child's Life in Wartime Sarajevo by Zlata Filipovic

First published as *Zlata's Diary* in 1994, this revised version (2006) includes additional photos. When Zlata Filipovic, "the Anne Frank of Sarajevo," began her diary entries on September 2, 1991, her life was like that of most 11-year-olds. By the time she ended her diary entries on October 13, 1991, the Serbian, Croatian, and Muslim warlords had changed her life forever. Her diary may prompt readers to seek additional information on Sarajevo, Bosnia, the Geneva Agreement, Anne Frank, and Icarus. (240 pp., MS)

The Other Victims: First-Person Stories of Non-Jews Persecuted by the Nazis by Ina R. Friedman

The Jews were not the only people persecuted on Hitler's orders. This nonfiction book (1995) is organized into these categories: "Those Unworthy of Life," "The War Against the Church," "Racial Purification: Breeding the Master Race," "Mind Control," and "Slaves for the Nazi Empire." (244 pp., MS–HS)

The Stone Goddess by Minfong Ho

Set during the Vietnam War, this book (2003) tells what happens to 12-year-old Nakri when the Khmer Rouge take over Cambodia. She and her sisters are forced to work in a child labor camp until they are liberated by the Vietnamese army and join two surviving family members at a refugee camp on Thailand's border. After they immigrate to the U.S, Nakri discovers that dancing can help her heal from her trauma. (208 pp., MS–HS)

The Aquariums of Pyongyang: Ten Years in the North Korean Gulag by Chol-hwan Kang and Pierre Rigoulot

Kang (2002) recounts growing up in Pyongyang after his Korean family returns to North Korea, leaving behind their affluent life in Japan. After Kang's grandfather is accused of high treason, Kang spends 10 years of his life in a remote labor camp, or *gulag*. Kang was only 9 years old when he was first imprisoned at the Yodok camp, in 1977. (238 pp., HS)

The Road From Home: A True Story of Courage, Survival and Hope by David Kherdian

Many people don't know about the Armenian Genocide, which occurred in 1915 and left more than a million innocent people dead. Kherdian (1995) captures the voice of his mother, Vernon Dumehjian Kherdian, who was born into a fine family just prior to the systematic killing of Armenians by the Turks. (242 pp., MS–HS)

Dawn and Dusk by Alice Mead

While growing up in a predominantly Kurdish town in Sardasht, Iran, 13-year-old Azad has known nothing but war. Iran's new religious leader, the Ayatollah Khomeini, wants to eliminate the Kurds, and Iraq's Saddam Hussein would like to occupy the Kurdish part of Iran. Readers get a glimpse into the heart of this young Kurdish refugee and will experience the losses and hopes of emigrees. (160 pp., MS–HS)

Under the Persimmon Tree by Suzanne Fisher Staples

Narration of this story (2005) alternates between that of Najmah and Nusrat—an Afghani girl and an American woman—whose very different lives are affected by religious extremism and eventually intersect in post-9/11 Pakistan. Najmah's father and older brother are kidnapped by the Taliban; her mother and little brother are killed during an unexpected American air raid. Disguised as a boy, Najmah begins a difficult journey on foot to Peshawar, Pakistan, hoping to find a refugee camp. Nusrat's story begins as she awaits the return of her husband, Faiz, who is in northern Afghanistan helping the wounded at a medical clinic while she is staying behind to help refugee children. Nusrat, whose American name is Elaine, converted to Islam and followed Faiz to Pakistan to help those hurt by religious fanaticism. (288 pp., HS)

Teenage Refugees from Rwanda Speak Out by Aimable Twagilimana

Eight teenagers who fled Ethiopia and Rwanda tell how they got to America and Canada, only to receive more prejudicial treatment. (64 pp., E–MS)

Group 7: After the War—The Effects on Families and What We've Learned or Not— Contemporary Prejudice

Silver Rights by Constance Curry

Mae and Matthew Carter want something more for their children than life on the cotton fields. When Title VI of the Civil Rights Act of 1964 is passed, the Carters decide to send 7 of their 13 children to an all-White school in Sunflower County, Mississippi, where they'll receive a better education. The Carter children, who were the only Blacks who chose to integrate and claim their civil rights at that time, bravely pioneered the difficult and lonely journey to desegregating the schools of Mississippi. (258 pp., HS)

Fire From the Rock by Sharon M. Draper

Imagine being asked to be one of the first Black students to integrate an all-White school in the 1950s. Sylvia Patterson must decide whether to be an agent of social change or to stay in the comfort of her inferior all-Black school. (231 pp., MS–HS)

Readers may want to refer to *Warriors Don't Cry* (1994), Melba Pattilo

Beals's memoir about being one of the nine teenagers who integrated Central High School in Little Rock, Arkansas, in 1957. (312 pp., MS-HS)

Child of Dandelions by Shenaaz Nanji

In 1972, Ugandan President Idi Amin dreams that he receives a message from God. Based on that dream, this dictator orders all noncitizen Indians and Pakistanis —the "Jews of Uganda"—to leave the country within 90 days. Fifteen-year-old Sabine thinks that she and her family will be spared because they are not like the other Indians--they are Ugandan citizens. Sabine soon learns that when an extremist like Amin controls a government, no one is safe. Even her Ugandan best friend comes to believe that Sabine and her family must be weeded from the land like dandelions. (214 pp., IIS)

Students will find similar themes explored in Gloria Miklowitz's (1999) *The War Between the Classes* and in Todd Strasser's (2005) *The Wave*.

Let Sleeping Dogs Lie by Mirjam Pressler and translated by Erik J. Macki

This story (2007) explores a situation that could erupt in any unsuspecting family of German descent. During a class trip to Israel, Johanna learns about the anti-Semitic laws that enabled her grandfather to "acquire" the family business from a Jewish family. What would you do if you discovered your grandfather was an enthusiastic Nazi supporter? (207 pp., MS–HS)

This novel is very similar to M. E. Kerr's *Gentlehands* (2001), in which Buddy finds out that his grandfather might have been the Nazi murderer "Gentlehands" in a concentration camp. (208 pp., MS–HS)

Never Mind the Goldbergs by Matthue Roth

Seventeen-year-old New Yorker Hava Aaronson is an Orthodox Jew who lives an unorthodox lifestyle in the world of punk. When she's "discovered" while acting in a play, she is offered a role in a sitcom about a modern American Orthodox Jewish family. Once in Hollywood, she discovers she is the only actual Jewish person on the show. Hava must now sort out who she is, what she believes in, and how she really feels about her religion. (368 pp., HS)

Grace in the Wilderness: After the Liberation, 1945–1948 by Aranka Siegal

Piri, 17, is living with a Swedish family while she searches for news of family and friends who also might have survived the Nazi concentration camps. Although the Swedish family accepts her as their own daughter, Piri strives to maintain her own identity and hold on to her dream of finding her blood relatives. The novel (2003a) is dedicated to the many people who assisted the Jews in their efforts to find their families after the war. (220 pp., MS)

Persepolis: The Story of a Childhood by Marjane Satrapi

In this autobiography, Satrapi (2004) recounts her life in Iran during the Islamic Revolution of 1979 and the Iran-Iraq War. She uses black-and-white illustrations to express her struggles as a rebellious girl living in a time of religious war and totalitarianism. In *Persepolis 2: The Story of a Return*, Satrapi tells about her life as a teenager when she leaves, then returns to, Iran (160 pp., 192 pp., MS–HS)

The Wave by Todd Strasser

Based on a true story, this book (1981-2005) will show contemporary students that the Holocaust could happen again—even today. (138 pp., MS-HS)

The Revealers by Doug Wilhelm

For those students who just don't understand how the desensitization of people toward other people begins, this book (2003) will show bullies in action and the complicit nature of others who allow it to happen. A reference to Anne Frank is made midway through the book.

For another book that examines the inner workings of the bully mentality, consider Jerry Spinelli's *Crash* (1997), (176 pp. MS), Nancy Garen's *Endgame* (2006, 304 pp., HS), or Suzane Phillips' *Burn* (2008, 279 pp., HS) (207 pp., MS)

Activities to Extend Learning

Students have several projects to choose from for their collaborative group assignments. Allow students to choose the ones that work best for their respective novels and topics. I have included examples when possible.

Single-Entry Literature-Composition Activities

Have students select a poignant passage from the book they have read. Students should copy the passage verbatim, including all bibliographic information. Then have students create 3 to 5 possible composition prompts that someone could respond to without having read the entire book. The example in Figure 4.1 was created by Jerri Norris.

During Lit-Comp activities, students learn how to cite material properly and are exposed to lots of new reading material, some of which might inspire them to read works beyond the class requirements. By having students spend 5 minutes doing free-writes, meaningful discussions can ensue.

Example 4.1. Single-Entry Lit-Comp

Richter, Hans Peter. (1987). *Friedrich*. Translated by Edite Kroll. New York: Viking Penguin/Puffin Books. 149 pp. (ISBN: 0-14-032205-1)

Jews are accused of being crafty and sly. How could they be anything else? Someone who must always live in fear of being tormented and hunted must be very strong in his soul to remain an upright human being. (p. 63)

Directions: Select one of the following writing assignments to complete. Be sure to provide examples whenever possible.

1. What minority groups could be substituted for "Jews" in the above paragraph? In what ways, to your knowledge, have these groups been tormented or hunted?

2. Define an "upright" human being. Do most people fit into this category? What happens to the ones who don't? What are the rewards, if any, for the ones who do?

3. Teacher Neudorf speaks of being strong in the soul. What does he mean, specifically? Give your opinion of what "strong in the soul" means. Include examples of people who best illustrate your definition and explain why.

Double-Entry Literature-Composition Activities

Have each student select a poignant passage from his or her book and team up with another class member. By juxtaposing the passages, students are able to generate some provocative writing prompts (Figure 4.2).

Figure 4.2. Lit-Comp, Double-Entry

In *Fire from the Rock*, Sylvia is treated as an inferior because she is Black:

I still feel like I've been hollowed out like a Thanksgiving turkey and stuffed with sharp knives instead of soft dressing. . . . I don't understand why people are so mean to each other, why one group of people can hate another group of people so much. It makes my head hurt to think about it, but I see it everywhere now. I can see it in the eyes of the bus driver who really doesn't want me on his bus, and the man at the Rexall drugstore, who thinks I'll probably steal something. I can feel it in the whispers of people who walk behind me on the street. (p. 130)

In *Summer of My German Soldier*, Anton, an escaped prisoner of war, gives Patty, an abused girl, a gift:

"The greater the value, the greater the pleasure in giving it. The ring is yours, P.B."

cont.

Then in the darkened silence, I heard him breathe in deeply. "Am I still your teacher?" Without pausing for an answer, he continued, "Then I want you to learn this, our last, lesson. Even if you forget everything else I want you to remember that you are a person of value, and you have a friend who loved you enough to give you his most valued possession." (pp. 134–135)

1. Hitler believed that the Germans were the Master Race, better than any other human beings; Sylvia faces an all-White school so she can get a better education; and Patty, who was verbally and physically abused by her parents, thinks she is a worthless human being. What makes people believe that they are better or worse than somebody else? Is there such a thing as a person who is better or worse than another? For someone who thinks that way, how do they treat others or how are they treated?

2. We have all been told to "love one another as ourselves." Why is that so hard to do? What makes people act so hateful toward and hurtful to other human beings?

Lines to Create a Feeling

Have each student choose five passages, each consisting of one to three lines. Working in groups of five, students should discard two lines apiece and rearrange what remains of the passages to evoke some kind of mood. Encourage them to add a visual or auditory touch to enhance the effect. The poem, "God or No God" was created by Amanda Burke, Shelley Perfect, Stacy Pelham, and Joan Kaywell (Figure 4.3).

Figure 4.3. Poem

Elliott's *Under a War-Torn Sky* (the French Resistance during World War II), Ryland's *But I'll Be Back Again: An Album* (losing a father, twice—not WWII), Staples' *Under the Persimmon Tree* (the war in Afghanistan), and Wiesel's *Night* (living in a concentration camp during World War II) were the books used.

This poem needs four readers who will take turns speaking the lines. Readers 1 and 2 should speak with dread in their voices and be looking at a dying plant. Readers 3 and 4 should stand behind them and listen. Readers 3 and 4 then interrupt 1 and 2, using forceful, determined voices to direct 1 and 2's attention to 3 and 4's drawing of a pretty tree.

God or No God

1. From the depths of the mirror, a corpse gazed back at me. (Wiesel, p. 9)

2. I sit in the dirt beside them quietly, not crying, not thinking, not even aware that I am breathing, and it occurs to me I might be dead, too. (Staples, p. 83)

cont.

3. He lies face down in the mud as the truck rolls forward, and he does not move. As the truck gathers speed, I think how short the distance is between life and death. (Staples, 158)

4. It is hard to lose someone, even harder to lose him twice, and beyond description to lose him without a goodbye either time. If I have any wish for my own life, it is a chance to say all my goodbyes. (Rylant, p. 8)

5. Never shall I forget those flames which consumed my faith forever. Never shall I forget the nocturnal silence which deprived me, for all eternity, of the desire to live. (Wiesel, p. 32)

6. . . . the only thing they live on is dreams of their farms, which no longer exist. (Staples, p. 186)

7. A sob tears itself from her deepest part, and she realizes . . . the world is ending. (Staples, p. 221)

8. Here, every man has to fight for himself and not think of anyone else. Here there are no fathers, no brothers, no friends. (Wiesel, p. 105)

9. Suck it up, boy. A whiner won't last long in this world. (Elliott, p. 4)

10. If you are a child who is never told the truth, you begin to make up your own. (Rylant, p.5)

11. The drain and pallet and the tubful of warm water look complicated and unimaginably extravagant to her. (Staples, p. 198)

12. She had an aura of knowing sadness that she counterbalanced somehow with a determined generosity and hope for happiness. (Elliott, p. 99)

13. I'm not about to die here after what I've been through and after all that people have sacrificed to save me because some lazy, spoiled Yankee good-for-nothin' hasn't got the guts to get up and walk. (Elliott, p. 192)

14. We shall see the day of liberation. Have faith in life. Above all else, have faith. (Wiesel, p. 38)

Dioramas

Have students create a visual representation of a memorable scene from their books using a shoebox as the stage. After reading *Alicia, My Story* (Appleman-Jurman, 1990), one of my students created a diorama of one of the bunkers (a small space dug underneath a room) in which Alicia hid during one of the Nazi actions. Because Nazis would shout and fire their guns so that babies would cry and reveal a hiding place, babies were hidden separately. In chapter 8, Alicia goes upstairs to give baby Shmuel more chamomile tea only to discover that he has been shot to death by a German soldier. Her family and friends in the rooms below are unaware of the tragedy they'll discover when they reemerge.

Memorabilia Bags

Students should gather a minimum of 15 objects that represent something of significance in their novels. I have students number their objects and provide a brief explanation for each. After reading *Summer of My German Soldier* (Greene, 1999), Laurie A. Van Zant created a memorabilia bag accompanied by the explanatory list in Figure 4.4.

Figure 4.4. Memorabilia Bag List

1. A female doll—represents Patty
2. A bag of sand—from Sharon's sandbox
3. A dictionary—Patty read it every day
4. Small red comb—the one Patty's mother made her use to comb her hair
5. A shoe—from the shoe department in Patty's parents' store
6. A belt—Patty's father beat her with one
7. Cotton balls—the prisoners were made to pick them
8. A train—the train brought the prisoners to town, and Anton escaped on the 10:15
9. A post card from Tennessee—represents Patty's trip to her grandmother's
10. Two hardcover books—Patty bought them using the money given to her by her grandmother
11. A monogrammed blue shirt with a blood stain on it—the one Patty gave to her father for Father's Day, which he never wore and which she subsequently gave to Anton to help him escape
12. $4.67—the amount of money Patty gave to Anton
13. A gold ring—Anton's prized possession, which he gave to Patty
14. A black Bible—the sheriff gave one to Patty
15. A yellow shoebox tied with a red ribbon—Ruth brought a box of chicken to Patty while she was in the reformatory

Collages

Students can create collages, using magazine pictures and print, that represent something significant from their novels. Each student is required to explain in an oral presentation how each image relates to the story. As an added bonus, while looking through magazines, students often read articles not required in your class.

Dictionary of Terms

Have each student select a minimum of 5 vocabulary words or terms from their individual YA books to be added to a class vocabulary book. Students who have identified the same word can work together to write a common definition. Definitions must be paraphrased (Figure 4.5). Using these words, students may write a composition at the end of the unit where they place themselves anywhere in the world during this period but look as they do at present.

Figure 4.5. Paraphrase Definitions

1. Allies: The nations fighting Germany during World War II: the Soviet Union, Britian, and the United States.

2. Anti-Semitism: Being hostile to or discriminatory against Jews.

3. Aryans: Hitler's imagined master race—tall, blond, and fair-skinned.

4. Auschwitz, Treblinka, Maidanek: death camps in Poland which had gas chambers.

5. Boche: an uncomplimentary nickname given to Germans, from the German word meaning "hard skull."

6. Dachau: an infamous concentration camp near Munich.

7. D-Day: On June 6, 1944, the combined Allied Forces crossed the English Channel to France to begin retaking occupied Europe.

8. Deport: to expel from a country.

9. Einsatzgruppen (special duty groups): When Germany invaded Russia in 1941, these groups rounded up the Jews, tortured them, made them dig their own graves, and shot them. Their estimated number of murders is 1.5 million.

10. Emigrate: to leave a county in order to reside elsewhere.

11. Fuhrer: Hitler's political title.

12. Ge(heime) Sta(ats)po(lizei): Germany's state police, better known as the Gestapo; led by Reinhard Heydrich.

13. Judenrat: Jewish councils in Germany ordered to carry out Nazi orders.

14. Kristallnacht: The Night of the Broken Glass, November 9–10, 1938, when SS members broke windows of Jewish shops and homes in response to the murder of the German ambassador to France by a young Jew whose Polish Jewish family had been expelled from Germany.

15. Liberation: release from oppression, such as the freeing of the Netherlands from German control.

Annotated List of Additional Nonfiction Articles

Each student should find one newspaper, journal, or magazine article that relates to the group's theme and write a "recommended reading" entry for it, including bibliographic information and an annotation of the article.

The following annotated entry, for example, could be part of a recommended reading list for the "Those Who Risked Their Lives" theme:

- Gies, Miep and Allison Gold. (1987, May 5). "The Woman Who Hid Anne Frank." *Family Circle,* 88–96. This excerpt from the book includes a detailed account of how Miep hid the Franks and how Anne's diary was preserved and returned to Mr. Frank.

The next example shows an annotated entry for a newspaper article that might be recommended by a student who read a book for the "After the War—The Effects on Families and What We've Learned" theme.

- Kim, Myung Oak. (2007, January 23). "Holocaust Survivors Hope Their Stories Outlive Them." *Rocky Mountain News.* Fred and Miriam Hoffman survived the Holocaust, but now most of the other survivors are either dead or nearing so. They speak about why it is important for them to continue to share their stories about the atrocity.

A Timeline

Tape some butcher paper on two walls or halfway around the classroom at eye level. Segment the paper by year, starting with 1938 and ending with 1945, but allow students to extend the timeline in either direction, if necessary. Draw a horizontal line about one-third of the way down the entire length of the paper. On the top third of the butcher paper, have students record in black ink the major historical dates and their corresponding events. On the bottom two-thirds, have students add corresponding vignettes and photos about the people who are the subjects of their books. (Students can prepare for the timeline project as they read by making notes about their book's important dates.) Color-code the vignettes by book. Students should initial their timeline entries so that other students who want to discuss a specific occurrence can consult "the expert." As material accumulates, the interest level is heightened and students gain a sense of chronology about the war (Figure 4.6).

A Map Display

Many of these books refer to a confusing number of specific locations. By charting a character's progress on a map, students gain a better sense of the story and acquire memorable geographical information. Maps should be displayed on one or more of the walls in the classroom.

A Classroom Museum

Each student brings in for display an artifact representative of World War II. For example, a student who brought in some Polish currency, zlotys, really helped make the period come alive for others.

Figure 4.6. Timeline

November 9, 1938—Kristallnacht

In May 1938, the Appleman family first experiences anti-Semitic violence when Alicia's oldest brother, Zachary, is attacked on his way to school by five Polish university students. They kicked him in the ribs, treated him like a punching bag, and smashed his violin, all because of his Jewishness.

In 1938, 18,000 Jews lived in the Polish city of Buczacz, about one-third of its total population.

December 7, 1941—the bombing of Pearl Harbor

America's entry of the war

In 1941, Alicia survives a jump from a moving train en route to a labor camp and learns that her brother, Bunio, has been murdered by the Nazis.

Each student should also bring in at least three pictures depicting the period. Have students form teams through the creation of logical groupings of the pictures, each team not exceeding 5 members. Have each team arrange the pictures for display on some room dividers. If room dividers are unavailable, makeshift displays can be made with two-by-fours, sheets of plywood, and wallpaper. Have students research, write, and then record information about their pictures on cassette recorders. Visitors and other students can use headphones to listen to the recorded information while they look at the photos.

A Documentary

Groups can prepare a documentary incorporating information from each of the books they read. Visuals such as timelines and maps should be used whenever possible. (Note: This can be incorporated into the timeline.)

Compare and Contrast: Then and Now

Not long ago, the 65th anniversary of the bombing of Pearl Harbor was commemorated by many television documentaries and newspapers. Students may find it interesting to read actual articles from newspapers dated December 7, 1941, and to view news footage from that time in order to compare and contrast that information with what we know today.

Another source of information for then-and-now comparisons is the United States Holocaust Memorial Museum, established in 1980. Elie Wiesel now serves as its chairman. Additional information about the organization can be obtained by writing to it at 2000 L Street, NW, Suite 588, Washington, DC, 20036, or by visiting it at www.ushmm.org.

Students can also interview World War II veterans about their impressions of the war. Students can then ask students in another grade level for their ideas about the value of fighting in World War II. The difference in attitudes is often frightening and lends itself to discussions about why Anne Frank's diary is required reading in most schools.

Examples of Prejudice Today

Each student is to find a newspaper or magazine article about current events involving prejudice or discrimination. When they read about incidents such as the genocide in Darfur, students become painfully aware of the relevance of World War II's lessons for us today. You may remind students that not so long ago, David Duke, a known racist, won a seat in the 1989 Louisiana state legislature and twice participated as a candidate in the presidential primary races. Students often find extreme examples of discrimination and prejudice in their own communities. California, for example, has more hate groups than any other state in the country, according to the Southern Poverty Law Center, available at http://www.splcenter.org/intel/map/hate.jsp. In Tampa, Florida, Neo-Nazi Skinheads have been known to beat up homosexuals. In Orlando, Florida, arsonists burned down Black churches. It is unfortunate that there is so much ill-treatment of people based on their differences, including race, religion, age, sex, sexual preference, disabilities, and diseases.

Their Own Ideas

By always having student ideas as an option, I have built up my repertoire of useful ideas through the suggestions made by my students. Students in my last class came up with these possibilities:

- Prepare a book talk.
- Create a dinner party and invite a key character from each book.
- Identify key scenes in each book and rewrite them in play form. Sequence the scenes and perform a readers' theater.
- Like Anne in *Anne Frank*, write a week's worth of diary entries for one of the characters in your young adult book.
- Contact one of the authors and invite him or her to speak to the class. (Note: One of my students contacted Alicia Appleman-Jurman and orchestrated a project to raise money to bring her to our school. By contacting an author's publisher, you may be able to arrange for him or her to speak for the price of a plane ticket and lodging.)

Conclusion

When studying *Anne Frank: The Diary of a Young Girl* by itself, I have been bombarded by students asking, "Why do we have to read this?" Since I began using YA literature to support the teaching of this classic, I have not once been asked that question. The 20th century was the most violent period in human history, and it's time to eradicate violence in this century. Most people know about the Holocaust, but few are familiar with the Armenian Genocide that followed World War I, the Ukrainian genocide of the 1930s, Pol Pot's killing fields, and, more recently, the 1994 Rwandan genocide and the ethnic cleansing in Yugoslavia. YA literature helps students to become aware of the hierarchies, manipulations, and prejudices involved in such events and to question how our own country's actions or inaction might have contributed. As part of this world of cultural diversity, we must teach our students to celebrate—not condemn or simply tolerate—our differences. We must learn from history, or we may repeat it. Next time, a genocide might be here.

Additional Resources for Teachers

Web Sites

Lesson Plans

The Southern Poverty Law Center's site, http://www.splcenter.org/index.jsp, and its companion site, Teaching Tolerance, http://www.tolerance.org/teach/, offer teachers an abundance of resources on how to combat hate and promote tolerance. Teachers may subscribe—for free—to their magazine, *Teaching Tolerance*, which offers teaching tips and important information about the different cultural groups in our schools. The Web site provides links that help teachers find activities sorted by grade levels, subject, and topic. The Southern Poverty Law Center has been an outspoken and major promoter of civil rights since its founding in 1971.

The Florida Center for Instructional Technology created "The Teachers Guide to the Holocaust," available at http://fcit.usf.edu/holocaust/resource/resource.html. This site uses photographs, documents, art, music, movies, and literature to provide teachers and students with a wealth of information about the people and events of the Holocaust. The California Center for the Book developed "Caught in the Crossfire: Young People and War," available at http://www.calbook.org/bcb/crossfire.html. This book discussion program is designed to help middle- and secondary-level students understand war's impact on children and teens. In addition to providing discussion questions, the site refers teachers to supplemental activities, books, author interviews, articles, and film and DVD titles. Laura Pringleton–from the Yale–New Haven Teachers Institute, has also put together an impressive list of resources and ideas for teaching the Holocaust, which can be found at http://www.yale.edu/ynhti/curriculum/units/1997/2/97.02.03.x.html.

To motivate your students to take action, go to http://www.emnsetmanus.net/paperclip-children-holocaust-memorial/ to see what middle school students in the small town of Whitwell, Tennessee, accomplished with their now famous Paper Clip Project. Shocked that such an incomprehensible number of Jewish people were exterminated by the Nazis, these eighth graders decided to see what 6 million actually looks like. Inspired by Europeans who wore paper clips on their lapels as a statement of protest of the Nazis, these students decided to collect 6 million paper clips. In the end, the students collected more than 20 million paper clips and received letters of support from many people, including Holocaust survivors. The students then created a "Children's Holocaust Memorial," which consisted of an authentic German rail car in which they housed 11 million of their paper clips. A news article about the project is available at http://www.acfnewsource.org/religion/paper_clip_project.html.

Survivor Interviews

TeenInk.com is a Web site of material by teens for teens. Michelle M. shares her interview with Hungarian Holocaust survivor Helen Handler, who, at age 10, survived three death marches http://teenink.com/Past/2004/January/17388.html. and Vicky S. interviews Polish Holocaust survivor Michael Zeiger (http://teenink.com/Past/2001/February/Interviews/MichaelZeiger.html). Founded in 1989 and supported by a nonprofit organization, Teen Ink also publishes a book series and a monthly magazine.

Oprah Winfrey's powerful *O Magazine* interview of 72-year-old Elie Wiesel, who's done so much to promote peace in the world, can be found at http://www.oprah.com/omagazine/200011/omag_200011_elie.jhtml, and features both archival and contemporary photos. Don't miss the related links to other survivor stories, to an excerpt from Wiesel's latest book, and to the "One-on-One with Elie Weisel," in which he and Oprah travel together to Auschwitz.

The Voice/Vision Holocaust Survivor Oral History Archive (http://holocaust.umd.umich.edu) was created in 1981 by Sidney Bolkosky, a professor in the social sciences and history at the University of Michigan–Dearborn. Since then, this archive has steadily grown and now contains more than 300 interviews. By accessing this Web site, students can select from more than 50 testimonies and can read the transcripts while listening to survivors' tell their stories in their own words.

The Shoah Foundation Institute Visual History Archive (http://www.usc.edu/libraries/archives/arc/libraries/sfa/index.php) is another great resource that includes both video and audio survivor testimonies, but the system requirements might be beyond what most schools can handle.

Journal Articles

"A Review of the Holocaust in Literature for Youth" by Lee Brown (2000).

This journal article reviews a book that not only provides a comprehensive bibliography of literature about the Holocaust but also rates and provides brief annotations for more than 600 print entries. Organized by genre, the book that is reviewed also provides a listing of journal articles, short stories, electronic resources, and strategies for teaching the Holocaust.

"Educating Without Overwhelming: Authorial Strategies in Children's Ho-
    locaust Literature" by S. D. Jordan (2004)
    For strategies and literature in addition to those mentioned in the chap-
ter, read this article, that "reviews a number of works of fiction about the
Holocaust intended for children and young adult readers and discusses the
strategies used by their authors to educate their readers without overwhelming them with highly emotional information."

"Making History Come Alive" by Howard Levin (2003)
    For an elective history class, high school students interviewed Holocaust
survivors and published their stories on the Web as part of a class project en-
titled "Telling Their Stories: Oral History of the Holocaust." The article may
also be accessed at http://www.tellingstories.org/about/1-1_large.pdf.

"Guidelines for Teaching the Holocaust: Avoiding Common Pedagogical Er-
    rors" by David H. Lindquist (2006)
    This article discusses how best to use *Anne Frank: The Diary of A Young
Girl* in the classroom and addresses common errors teachers make when
teaching about the Holocaust.

Video, Film, and Audio

Although the movies *Schindler's List* and *Sophie's Choice* are set during the
Holocaust, I question whether any teacher should show either of these intense films to their classes. Two films appropriate for teacher use and highly
recommended are *I Am David*, starring Ben Tiber (2003, Walden Media) and
Anne Frank: The Whole Story, starring Ben Kingsley and Brenda Blethyn (2001,
Walt Disney Video). You can learn more about *I Am David* by visiting the
Walden Media Web site (http://www.walden.com/walden/teach/david/
index.php). There you can download a free teaching guide for the film. Another appropriate but little known film is the documentary *The Last Seven
Months of Anne Frank* by Willy Lindwer (http://www.willylindwer.com/in-
dex.htm), which features interviews with 6 women who knew Anne.. Finally, 60 short video clips of concentration camps and other Holocaust-related
sites are available at http://fcit.usf.edu/holocaust/resource/VR.htm and
http:.//fcit.usf.edu/holocaust/resource/MOVIES.htm—and are invaluable
for their convenience.

    Alicia Keys performs her poem "P.O.W." (Prisoner of Words) in a poetry
slam at http://youtube.com/watch?v=ZLk_Q3Cq2Ns. The poem works as

a great segue for a discussion about the following classic quotation by Pastor Martin Niemöeller (1892-1984), a Protestant survivor of the Holocaust. Both talk about the consequences of silence:

> First they came for the communists and I did not speak out because I was not a communist. Then they came for the Jews and I did not speak out because I was not a Jew. Then they came for the trade unionists and I did not speak out because I was not a trade unionist. Then they came for the Catholics, and I did not speak out because I was a Protestant. Then they came for me, and by that time there was no one left to speak out.

After a teacher-led discussion, students can prepare for their own poetry slam by writing poems that deal with topics addressed in this unit.

Christian Z. Goering has developed LitTunes, a great resource for music that complements the teaching of classic literature, available at http://www.corndancer.com/tunes/tunes_main.html. LitTunes is a collaborative online community designed to serve three purposes: (a) to provide educators with a centralized source of materials and support for using popular music in the classroom; (b) to provide a forum for educators to share their successful experiences and research involving the use of popular music; and (c) to inspire educators to reach the disenfranchised with their own language—music. The site lists the following songs to complement *Anne Frank: The Diary of a Young Girl*:

- "Dear Anne" from *Swedish Sessions* by Ryan Adams (unreleased, 2001). The song was inspired by the artist's reading of the classic work, confirmed either through album liner notes or published interviews that specifically mention the artist's sources of inspiration.
- "Tattoo" from *Breaking the Silence* by Janis Ian (Morgan Creek, 1993)
- "Avinu Malkeinu" from *Higher Ground* by Barbara Streisand (Sony, 1997)

Chapter 5

The Struggle to Emerge: Exploring the Conflicts of Race and Family

Using *Crossing Jordan* as a Bridge to *A Raisin in the Sun*

April C. Templeton & Joan F. Kaywell

I look forward confidently to the day when all who work for a living will be one with no thought to their separateness as Negroes, Jews, Italians, or any other distinctions. This will be the day when we bring into full realization the American dream—a dream yet unfulfilled. A dream of equality of opportunity, of privilege and property widely distributed; a dream of a land where men will not take necessities from the many to give luxuries to the few; a dream of a land where men will not argue that the color of a man's skin determines the content of his character; a dream of a nation where all our gifts and resources are held not for ourselves alone, but as instruments of service for the rest of humanity; the dream of a country where every man will respect the dignity and worth of the human personality.

—Martin Luther King, Jr.

Introduction

"I have a boyfriend," I, April, announced, coming home from day one of kindergarten.

"Really, what's his name?" my mother asked.

"Willie." I beamed.

"*Willie?*" my mother questioned. She then slowly and carefully asked, "Honey, is Willie Black?"

"Uh-huh," I nodded.

"April, you can't have a Black boyfriend," my mother gently explained.

"Why not?" I asked, truly having no idea.

She paused. "Because Sissy doesn't have a Black boyfriend." She couldn't come up with anything else. But that was enough for me.

"Okay," I said, satisfied. My sister, 13 years older, was my guide. If she didn't have a Black boyfriend, then I didn't have one, either. I then probably went off to play with my Barbie thinking nothing more about it—until now.

When I look back on my childhood, this incident remains embedded in my mind as my first instructed moment in racism. I was 4 years old. A beautiful thing about children is that they come into this world without thoughts of discrimination or prejudice. These evils are *learned*. I learned it, and so did Cass Bodine in Adrian Fogelin's (2000) novel, *Crossing Jordan*. Such racism almost keeps Cass from becoming and remaining friends with Jemmie Lewis, her new African American neighbor. In Lorraine Hansberry's (1959-2004) classic play *A Raisin in the Sun*, the Younger family faces blatant racial discrimination: When the Youngers buy a home in an all-White neighborhood, their future neighbors try to prevent integration by offering to buy the Younger's new house from them at a higher price. For the Bodine and Lewis families in *Crossing Jordan* and for the Younger family in *A Raisin in the Sun*, the conflicts of race and family threaten each family's potential to emerge from the grips of inequities deeply rooted in society.

Years ago, a beloved English professor taught me to not simply read the novel or story or play, but to consider how the author's life experiences influenced his or her work. We've all heard that Ernest Hemingway "lived it up so he could write it down." Each of this unit's authors, Adrian Fogelin and Lorraine Hansberry, also wrote from personal experience.

For Hansberry, the Younger family's move into an all-White neighborhood echoes her own family's battle with housing discrimination based on racial identity. When she was 8 years old, her father, a prominent real estate broker, moved the family into an all-White neighborhood in legally segregated Chicago. When they faced legal opposition from their White neighbors, the Hansberry's case went all the way to the U.S. Supreme Court. As a result, *Hansberry v. Lee* helped overturn housing discrimination based on race in the state of Illinois (GradeSaver, 1999).

A very different incident involving racial discrimination inspired Adrian Fogelin to write *Crossing Jordan*. Fogelin writes on her Web site, "*Crossing Jordan* isn't a book that I planned to write. I was working on something entirely different when I had a conversation with the 9-year-old White girl who lived next door." The neighbor informed Fogelin that too many Blacks were moving into their neighborhood, so her family was going to move. The little girl feared Blacks because "they break into your house" and "they rob you and shoot you." Fogelin asked the girl if this had happened to her or to anyone she knows. The young neighbor admitted that no such incidents had occurred, but then said, "Oh, Miss Adrian, everyone knows it's true." Obviously, this child had been taught such racial prejudice. Because of this conversation, Fogelin felt compelled to write this story: "Sometimes an author writes a book because they [sic] feel they have to do something. *Crossing Jordan* is that kind of book. I wrote it for the girl next door and for any other kid who is being taught prejudice at home" (Fogelin, 2007).

Crossing Jordan's Cass and I were each raised by good parents who were good people, good people who sometimes held racist thoughts. Like Cass, I also heard "It's just better not to mix" (Fogelin, 2000, p. 14) and, even worse, such negative untruths as "for black people, stealing's as easy as breathing" (Fogelin, 2000, p. 15). Cass and Jemmie break through this negative cycle, but not without jumping some hurdles or—as Jemmie's grandmother, Nana Grace, sings—not without "crossing Jordan." Cass must deal with her racist father and her "I-don't-want-to-fight-with-your-father" mother; Jemmie must deal with the bitterness of her mother. On the girls' side stands Nana Grace, who somehow stays out of the battle yet dispenses a fountain of wisdom.

Plot Summary of *Crossing Jordan*

Cassie Bodine is a 12-year-old girl who lives in Tallahassee, Florida. Stuck at home with her two sisters, Cassie thinks she's in for another boring summer until new neighbors move into the house next door. When Cass's father discovers that the new neighbors are Black, he builds a fence between their properties. While peering through a knothole in the fence, Cass meets Jemmie, a girl her age with the same passion for reading and running. They challenge each other to a race, and a friendship is born. When Cass's father discovers the friendship between the two girls, he forbids Cass to have any contact with Jemmie—only because she is Black. The two girls can no longer run together or read their beloved *Jane Eyre* until they realize they can communicate through a "ghost" by placing notes on the gravestone of Cass's beloved Miss Liz, the previous owner of Jemmie's house. When Jemmie's mom, a pediatric nurse, saves the life of Cass's baby sister, the two families warm up to one another and start to actually mix. There is no fairy tale ending; the families make progress, but the reader is left to wonder if the fence, literally and figuratively, will ever come down. Nonetheless, these two girls—one Black and one White—teach their families and their community a valuable lesson on the importance of ignoring fences and overcoming prejudice.

Prereading Strategies for *Crossing Jordan*

Start this novel by asking students to describe an incident in which they were victims of or a witness to racism. A student who would rather avoid a personal response can describe an incident from a book, a movie, or a television show. Raichelle, an African American, wrote:

> I dated a biracial boy who was Puerto Rican and Irish. The school I went to wasn't racist, but biracial dating wasn't widely accepted. In middle school, breakups and new couples—the latest drama—were the talk of the school. So we constantly heard "Why are you two dating?" and "Why not date your own race?" There were a lot of different questions and curiosity.

Sometimes students write of powerful events—some horrific—about their parents' experiences growing up in the South during racial segregation. One student wrote about his mother's house being burned down by the Ku Klux Klan when she was just a child. Other students recall movies such as *Amistad* (1997, R) or *Remember the Titans* (2000, PG). Ask for volunteers to share their responses. If students are slow to volunteer, read what you have written as your response. Your sharing not only gets the ball rolling but also helps students got a little deeper into their teacher's world.

April Templeton Shares an Anecdote

I recently shared a story about going out to lunch with my old friend Keith, who is African American. The day we chose to catch up happened to be Valentine's Day. As you can imagine, the restaurant was filled with couples celebrating the holiday. I remember receiving second glances and odd stares from people not accustomed to seeing a White woman and a Black man dining together in my small Southern city. He sensed it, too, but we ignored the looks and enjoyed our time together.

The next time I spoke to Keith, he shared how a female African American friend of his who'd seen us together that day asked him why he had "gone to the other side." When Keith asked her what in the world she meant by that, she snapped, "I saw you dining with that *White woman* on Valentine's Day." Sadly, this is not the first such incident Keith and I have faced. In some societies, biracial dating or friendship is simply not accepted.

Lawrence Blum (2004) observed students' eagerness to discuss controversial topics like racism and race relations when given the chance. Although many teachers shy away from these topics, students welcome the opportunity to talk openly within a safe environment. Semi-structured class discussions not only provide an opportunity to talk about occurrences of racism and prejudice, they can also help sensitize students to where we have been and how far we still have to go.

Chapter Ideas for *Crossing Jordan*

Response-based activities for *Crossing Jordan* and *A Raisin in the Sun*. For *Crossing Jordan* are given below, see Figure 5.1 for questions about chapters 1–3 and Figure 5.2 for questions about chapters 7–9. In Figure 5.2, we have included student responses that demonstrate the powerful effect that this kind of unit can have on students. You can target questions so that students will have to think about specific issues. These questions are designed to replace the typical one-word-answer questions, which do not contribute to our goal of inspiring students to think critically. These questions may be few, but they ask students to *think*. The ensuing discussions are almost always enlightening.

Figure 5.1. Response Questions for Chapters 1–3 in *Crossing Jordan*

1. In chapter 1, Cass's father builds a fence after he learns that a Black family is moving in next door. "If they stay out of our business and we stay out of theirs," he reasons, "we'll get along just fine" (p. 1). Justify your thoughts about this?

2. In chapter 2, we get a glimpse of the new neighbors. When the mother sees the newly built fence separating the two properties and the two families, she tells her daughter, "This is what bigotry looks like" (p. 9). When have you seen examples of bigotry?

3. Nana Grace tells Jemmie's mother to let Jemmie "make up her own mind about all that" (p. 9). On the other hand, Cass's father has no problem teaching his family to be prejudiced. Can racism be learned or unlearned? Explain your thoughts.

Figure 5.2. Response Questions for Chapters 7–9 in *Crossing Jordan*

1. In chapter 7, while at the store, Andy accuses Jemmie of stealing. Cass then faces an internal conflict. She wants to believe Jemmie but wonders if Andy is right. Why didn't Cass completely trust Jemmie? What kind of friend is Cass?

2. In chapter 8, Cass and Jemmie go back to the store to buy bread. When Cass introduces Jemmie to Mr. G, the Indian store manager, he is very polite to Jemmie, saying he is pleased to meet her. Why do you think Mr. G is so kind to Jemmie when others are not?

3. In chapter 9, Jemmie tells Cass, "Y'all could get ahead if you wanted to. . . . You're white. You don't have a thing in the world stopping you." Cass replies, "Plenty of things stop people, not just the color of your skin. Not having money can stop you cold" (p. 56). Do you agree with Jemmie? Do you agree with Cass? Explain your thoughts.

Following is a response from an African American teenager:

> I think Cass didn't completely trust Jemmie because of her Daddy's prejudice. Being racist is not innate; it's learned. I think her Daddy's comments slowly influenced her way of thinking. He tells Cass she isn't allowed to socialize with blacks, then, when Cass questions him, he gives her a negative comment or belief about their character.
>
> I think Cass is a good friend. She isn't racist but, being young, her judgment and direction are led by her family and elders. I also think Cass may not have trusted her that much because she barely knew Jemmie's character or behavior. When Andy asked her to empty her pockets, she refused.

This student has thought deeply about what was asked, and her answer shows that she was also able to synthesize her response with what she has read. Response-based questions are an incredibly valuable tool to use in lieu of often unchallenging (and boring) knowledge-based questions.

A response letter is another valuable activity for students. Although response letters, which are half summary and half response, are often used as a comprehensive end-of-the-book activity, you can modify their use by asking students to write them throughout their reading. A response letter must prove that the student has entirely read the required sections of the book and that the student has thought deeply about what he or she has read and is making connections between the reading and personal experience. Students can approach the response letter as they would the response-based questions in Figures 5.1 and 5.2, but their responses should be lengthier. Students also have more freedom to choose what to write about, as long as the chapter basics are covered. Grade these informally, looking at content alone rather than at grammar and spelling mistakes. By noting students' writing mistakes in an informal manner, teachers can develop responsive mini-lessons on writing specific to their students' needs. Figure 5.3 shows an example of a response letter from chapters 1–7 in *Crossing Jordan*.

Figure 5.3. A Response Letter From Chapters 1–7 in *Crossing Jordan*

Chapters 1–7 Summary

Cass's neighbor Miss Liz dies and a Black family moves in. Cass's Daddy puts a fence up because the neighbors are Black. He states, "Good fences make good neighbors." While peeking through a hole in the wood and spying on the neighbors, Cass happens to meet Jemmie, and they become instant friends. They practice running, Cass starts going over to Jemmie's house, and they begin passing a book back and forth called *Jane Eyre* (left to Cass by Miss Liz when she died) to take turns reading.

One day, Nana Grace, Jemmie's grandmother, and Lou Anne, Cass's sister, catch them talking. In both families, being friends with someone from a different race wasn't widely accepted. Lou Anne scolded Cass and told her that Daddy wouldn't approve but agreed not to tell as long as their father didn't ask. Things are much different when Nana Grace and Cass meet. Nana Grace says that Cass could visit Jemmie and be her company on most days. Together they go to the store to buy groceries for Nana Grace, and the store clerk accuses Jemmie of stealing. Cass sticks up for her friend but notices afterwards that she has her own doubts; that fact bothers Cass and makes her think.

Chapters 1–7 Student's Response

I think the fact that Cass and Jemmie overlook society and what people have to say at the idea of them being friends is just amazing. It's great that they don't let the negativity influence them. They have a positive influence on each other, especially when it comes to reading. They build their vocabulary together. I congratulate Nana Grace on overlooking history and its racial issues that she lived through by the fact that she didn't stop Jemmie and Cass from hanging out. I think Cass's father is prejudiced to the extent that he wouldn't allow anything to change his mind.

At the conclusion of the unit, test the students on their knowledge of the novel by asking response-based questions in an open-book format. Figure 5.4 shows the essay test.

Figure 5.4. *Crossing Jordan* Essay Test

Directions: Choose any four (4) of the six (6) questions, and write approximately half summary and half response. Remember you must include at least one quote (and page number) to support each of your responses. Think of these as mini-response letters.

1. Do you agree that Jemmie and Cass have more similarities than differences? Explain how they are more similar or more different.

2. Jemmie and Cass disobey their parents and continue their friendship. Justify how—in this case—disobeying their parents was the right thing to do.

3. Explain the incident that brought the two families together. How did this help them overcome their differences?

4. During the race, Cass went back for Jemmie and refused to cross the finish line without her. What lesson did this teach everyone?

5. In the end of the novel, Cass's dad makes an effort to be social with the Lewis family, although his efforts are slow. Do you feel there is hope for Mr. Bodine to get over his prejudice?

6. Do you believe the author accurately depicts prejudice? Discuss at least two examples and explain.

A Literature-Composition (Lit-Comp) Activity is something you can use for any novel. The purpose of the activity is, once again, to get students to *think*. The beauty of the Lit-Comp Activity is that it can be used at any time and with any piece of literature. The idea is to use a poignant excerpt, making sure that the excerpt makes sense to someone who hasn't read the entire book. Answering a few questions based on the excerpt can get your students' creative juices flowing. You can stockpile Lit-Comp excerpts and questions to use at the beginning of class or when faced with an extra 15 minutes at the end of the period. Figure 5.5 shows an example of a Lit-Comp Activity for *Crossing Jordan*.

Figure 5.5. Lit-Comp Activity for *Crossing Jordan*

When there was no more danger that we'd drip paint on it, Nana Grace carried her own prize quilt from the hall. "This was made by my grandmother." She shook it out, and the bright quilt drifted down, dressing up Hattie's old bed. Nana Ivy was a seam-stress. Made all kind of fancy clothes for rich white folks. This quilt got little bits of ball dresses and wedding gowns in it, lawn-party dresses, and go-to-the-show getups." She stroked the slinky satins and mossy velvets like she was petting a cat.

"How about these?" I asked, pointing. Scattered among the fancy fabrics were scraps that were plain and worn.

"Family patches," she said.

Each family patch had something embroidered on it. Sometimes just a name, like Nesta Louise, or Uncle Henry Clay, but sometimes there were a few words along with the name. There was a pink patch that said Baby Dora Gone To Jesus and a blue one sprigged with red flowers that said Melba Owen married July 8, 1902. One scrap of gray flannel said Martin Clay a free man.

I fingered the patch. "What's this one mean?" I asked.

Nana Grace sat down in Hattie's chair and spread the edge of the quilt over her knees. "Martin Clay was born a slave, died a free man. Got a whole lotta history and a whole lotta family stitched into this quilt. What we forget, the quilt remembers." (Fogelin, 2000, p. 37)

Time to Write

1. Most families have a few special heirlooms that have been passed from genera-tion to generation, much like the quilt mentioned here. Describe one of your fam-ily heirlooms. What does it mean to you or to your family?

2. The family patches described in the passage honor the death of a baby and someone's wedding day. If your family had a quilt, what would five of the patches say? Explain each one.

3. Pretend you're the person who made this quilt and knew of the events that were mentioned. Write a narrative about one of the family patches.

Bridging *Crossing Jordan* with *A Raisin in the Sun*

Once students have used *Crossing Jordan* to examine prejudice in today's world and to think about how one's attitudes toward race can be influenced by family members, they are ready to dive into Lorraine Hansberry's *A Rai-sin in the Sun*, a brilliant, realistic play that catapults the reader into the lives of the Youngers, an African American family living in a tiny apartment in Chicago's South Side during the late 1940s and early 1950s.

Plot Summary of *A Raisin in the Sun*

In this play, five people live in a one-bedroom apartment. Mama, the matriarch of the family, has just lost her husband, and because of this, the family inherits his $10,000 life insurance policy. Her son, Walter Lee, who dreams of providing for his family by becoming a successful businessman, wants to invest it all in a liquor store. Her daughter, Beneatha, who dreams of becoming a doctor, wants some of that money for medical school. Mama's grandson, Travis, and her daughter-in-law, Ruth, round out the main cast of characters living in the dark apartment and prejudiced world in which African American's dreams rarely become realized.

Mama decides to use the insurance money to make a down payment on a house in an all-White neighborhood, prompting the neighborhood organization to bribe the family to not move in. The Youngers face prejudice—and a struggle within the family when the money disappears—as they battle society and one another in an attempt to fulfill dreams and claim what the world says was never, and never should be, theirs.

Prereading Strategies for *A Raisin in the Sun*

Students probably won't know the historical and literary significance of the play's title, *A Raisin in the Sun*. Introduce Langston Hughes's poem, "Harlem," also known as "A Dream Deferred," and point out these two lines: "What happens to a dream deferred? Does it dry up like a raisin in the sun?"

First, explain to students the meaning of the word *defer*—to put off, to postpone. Next, examine Hughes's opening questions and discuss examples of dreams that must be deferred. Typical responses include postponing a sports career due to an injury or not being able to afford college. Finally, ask students to think about the period in which Hughes wrote "Harlem"—the early 1950s—and discuss the dreams that African Americans might have had to defer at that time. It doesn't take long for students to realize that African Americans often had to defer everyday dreams simply because they were Black. Students' discussion about the poem provides a perfect segue to *A Raisin in the Sun*, set around the time the poem was written, deep in the heart of an era of racial discrimination and segregation.

In the following activity focusing on similes and metaphors, students respond to the imagery in Langston Hughes's "Harlem." Give students a large sheet of construction paper and six smaller squares of various colors. After a mini lesson on similes and metaphors, ask students to illustrate each of the poem's similes on one of the squares. Lines like *"Does it sag like a heavy load?"*

inspire many interpretive drawings, such as those showing a bulging book bag, tipped scales, or an overloaded weight bar. This activity allows students to explore the connections between these two brilliant pieces of literature, one of which, in a sense, gave birth to the other. Figure 5.6 shows one student's finished art.

Figure 5.6. Art Example

"Does it sag like a heavy load?" Simile Activity Result

In Act 1, Scene 2 of *A Raisin in the Sun*, the following exchange takes place between Mama and Walter:

Mama: Son—how come you talk so much 'bout money?

Walter: Because it is life, Mama!

Mama: Oh—so now it's life. Money is life. Once upon a time freedom used to be life – now it's money. I guess the world really do change. . . .

Walter: No—it was always money, Mama. We just didn't know about it.

Mama: No . . . something has changed. You something new, boy. In my time we was worried about not being lynched and getting to the North if we could and how to stay alive and still have a pinch of dignity too.

Some students may have studied the effects of Reconstruction on African Americans, but chances are that the topic was covered only superficially or that students have already forgotten what they've learned. "Strange Fruit," a powerful song about lynching, is, once heard, unforgettable. The song (Figure 5.7) was written by Abel Meerpol (under the pseudonym Lewis Allan) and performed by Billie Holiday, among others. Its harrowing lyrics help students better understand Mama when she says, "We was worried about not being lynched" in the excerpt.

Figure 5.7. Song

Strange Fruit by Abel Meerpol

Southern trees bear strange fruit

Blood on the leaves

Blood at the root

Black bodies swinging in the southern breeze

Strange fruit hanging from the poplar trees

Pastoral scene of the gallant South

The bulging eyes and the twisted mouth

The scent of magnolia sweet and fresh

Then the sudden smell of burning flesh

Here is a fruit for the crows to pluck

for the rain to gather

for the wind to suck

for the sun to rot

for the tree to drop

Here is a strange and bitter crop

Ideas for *A Raisin in the Sun*

Since plays are meant to be seen, not read, the entire play should be read aloud, with students volunteering for the parts. Just as you did with *Crossing Jordan*, use response letters as a primary tool for studying this play. As Figure 5.8 shows, this activity allows students to think deeply about what they have read. Students are not only allowed to express their opinions, they are analyzing, synthesizing, and evaluating various aspects of the play. Answering fill-in-the-blank questions requires low-level knowledge, but response letters require higher levels of thinking. A response letter can be done whenever you choose: after completing a scene, an entire act, or the entire play.

Figure 5.8. Response Letters for *A Raisin in the Sun*

Amina writes:

I noticed three main ideals in this play, such as the pride of a man, the wisdom of a mother, and the strength of a family. Everyone in the play is waiting for the check to come in. It's the life insurance from Walter's father's death. Walter expresses a great deal about what he could do with *all* that money and Ruth reminds him that it's Mama's, not his. He desires money and power and is a drunk. Beneatha wants to be a doctor but doesn't think she will be able to afford medical school. And Mama just wants everybody to be happy.

This book was awesome and inspiring. There was a lot of strength, love, and forgiveness in the hearts of Mama and Ruth. I'm glad everything worked out in the end. I only wish Walter would have seen what was most important earlier on in the play.

Allison writes:

The fact that they all had dreams was great. I think that kept the story moving. I almost felt bad for Walter because no one would support his dream. All it would have taken is for one person to believe in him, and I think he could have done it. Travis was a good character because he kept that innocence since he never really knew what was going on. Overall, I really enjoyed this play. It connects with everyone because everyone has dreams.

Amber writes:

I believe that this play helps people realize what hopes and dreams can do for people. They make them stronger people and give them something to hold on to. My favorite character in the play was Mama. I felt that she was the glue that ultimately held the family together. I feel that if she weren't there, the family would have separated and learned to dislike one another. I really enjoyed this play and how the author kept me guessing about what would happen next. For example, when Walter lost the money, Beneatha denied Walter as being her brother and said there was nothing to love about him. Mama replies by saying that there is always something to love. In the end, even though Walter lost $6,500.00, they still moved into their house and I think, in a way, became closer and stronger as a family.

Katie writes:

We finally got a happy ending. Now we get to see the Youngers getting a new beginning. I liked this play. It had plenty of close calls, almost putting an end to the Younger family but not quite. This play is about family—how they don't always make the best decisions but every decision they make is to better the others' lives. All Walter wants

---

cont.

is enough money to give his family a taste of the good life and to stop being a servant to the White man. Mama just wants to get her family to a better place, a place where they can function better and be happy. Ruth wants sunlight and her marriage back. Beneatha wants to help people and Travis wants to know what's going on and help out. They all want what's best for the others and themselves, but they just don't know quite how it's done. They have different views on how the money and their chance at a new life should be handled. Even though they quarrel a lot, in the end they show that they love each other and that they're family, an' no White man with money is gonna tell them that ain't good enough.

Another excellent activity is a performance-based response called *tableaux* (Purves, Rogers, & Soter, 1995, pp. 131–136). A tableau is a freeze-frame or still picture of a scene from a story or play. This alternative response allows students to "live" the play. Not only do tableaux demonstrate student response and emotion toward the play, they prompt class response and can be a wonderful tool for discussion.

Tableaux can be done in one of two ways. The first follows Purves, Rogers, and Soter's (1995) suggestion that you assign a particular moment in the story for a group of students to depict; on the count of three, the performing students "freeze" the moment of the scene. In the second option, students choose to present two or three moments from the act they are studying that day (or do the tableaux the next day as a review). Even if different groups choose to do tableaux for the same scenes, it is interesting for the class to compare and contrast each group's approach.

For assessment, use a response-based essay test. Figure 5.9 shows the essay test questions for *A Raisin in the Sun*, followed by examples of responses.

Figure 5.9. *A Raisin in the Sun* Essay Test

Directions: Choose any four (4) of the six (6) questions, and write approximately half summary and half response. In each response, be sure to include support from *Crossing Jordan* when possible as well as your own thoughts. Think of these as mini-response letters.

1. The main theme in this play revolves around dreams and dreams deferred. Explain how this theme relates to the play.

2. What does Mama's plant represent and how does the symbol evolve over the course of the play?

3. Often in life and in literature, a character searches for a better life. Show how this is true for two (2) characters from this play. Explain how each of those characters tries to improve his or her life.

4. Often in life, people either *make* things happen or *watch* things happen. How is this true for two (2) of the play's characters?

cont.

5. Discuss how another theme—the strength of family—is apparent in this play. Discuss the varying degrees of the family's strength in specific scenes.

6. From Act 1, Scene 2: Mama: Son—how come you talk so much 'bout money? Walter: Because it is life, Mama!

   Explain how this quote is relevant to the play. Be sure to discuss how it relates to the family's problems as well as to their dreams.

Anastasia Responds to Number 2:

Mama's plant represents the family. On page 16, Mama is talking to Ruth about the plant and about how the plant won't grow without the sun. If the Younger family didn't get out of the apartment and move somewhere else soon, they would fall apart and practically die. Like the plant, they have been sheltered from the light. In order to grow they had to move, which they did so the plant will begin to grow now that it has sunlight as will the family. Also, like the plant, it was Mama that took care of it. Mama took care of the family and kept it from falling apart by moving them.

Richard Responds to Number 3:

Walter Lee Younger is constantly trying to make life better for him and his family. The only problem is that he is so obsessed with money that it hinders his ability to see what is best for his family. In hopes of owning a liquor store, Walter invests all of his money in a person who Walter thinks is his friend. That man takes all of the money and runs, leaving Walter with nothing. Walter then tries to gain money from the White people who don't want the Youngers to move, but he soon realizes how wrong that is. Beneatha wants to take some of the money and put it toward her schooling to be a doctor.

Beneatha wanted to make a lot of money and marry somebody rich so that she would have a prosperous life. When the money was taken away, Beneatha changed her mind about being a doctor because her thoughts were clouded by everything that has happened to her family. Her conversation with Asagai finally opens her eyes to what matters most to her, trying to make a difference in others' lives.

Maria Responds to Number 6:

Money is the biggest subject in dreams and problems. Beneatha can't go to college without the money, the Youngers can't move out of the apartment without money, and money is what almost breaks this family down completely. When Walter invests the money and loses it, this brings out the worst in him. He believed that "money is life" and without it, he felt dead and so did most of the family. "Well, we are dead now. All the talk about dreams and the sunlight that goes on in this house. It's all dead now." When Walter finally realizes it's not money that makes life, but his family, we reach the climax of the story and the point is made.

Additional Resources for Teachers

Web Sites

Teaching Tolerance (http://www.teachingtolerance.org or http://www.splcenter.org/teachingtolerance/tt-index.html) is a National Education Project dedicated to helping teachers foster equity, respect, and understanding in the classroom and beyond. In 1990, research from the center's Intelligence Project and from other sources began to document both rising levels of intolerance among youth and the significant involvement of young people in hate crimes. Since its founding, Teaching Tolerance has continued to publish its self-titled magazine and has developed and distributed a series of award-winning curriculum packages to schools across the United States and abroad. The support of the center's donors has enabled Teaching Tolerance to provide its materials to schools and teachers for free. Its grants program, initiated in 1996, and its Web site, launched in 2001, demonstrate Teaching Tolerance's continued commitment to helping schools and teachers access and implement the best anti-bias strategies available. "Ten Ways To Fight Hate," available at http://www.tolerance.org/10_ways/index.html, should be posted in every classroom.

Journal Articles

"Don't Look and It Will Go Away: YA Books—A Key to Uncovering the Invisible Problem of Bullying" by C. J. Bott, Nancy Garden, Patrick Jones, and Julie Anne Peters (2007)

This is an adaptation from a panel presentation given at the 2006 ALAN Workshop in Nashville, Tennessee. The message is simple: We must be our students' role models and give them the tools necessary to stop bullying.

"The Bully in the Book and in the Classroom" by William Broz (2007)

Sometimes we are the enemy—the teachers who are obstacles to anti-bullying programs. Broz references YA novels that contain scenes of bullying behavior, includes an analysis of bullying, and lists pertinent articles and books.

"Opening Dialogue Amidst Conflict" by Kenan Metzger and Jill Adams (2007)

Metzger and Adams show how teachers can use YA literature to combat bullying. Statistics and titles are included.

Video, Film, and Audio

Teachers may want to use a clip or clips from *Save the Last Dance* (2001, PG-13), starring Julia Stiles and Sean Patrick Thomas. Sarah is a White girl from the suburbs who studies ballet. After her mother dies, Sarah must live with her father in Chicago's inner city. When her father meets Derek, her Black boyfriend, he doesn't even raise an eyebrow. Derek's friends and family are the ones who exhibit the racial prejudice. In one of the bar scenes (one of the reasons teachers need to preview and use *clips* of films), while Derek dances with his ex-girlfriend, his best friend walks up to Sarah and says, "You'll never look as good with him as she does. That's oil, you're milk, ain't no point in tryin' to mix." Derek's sister seems to speak for the entire Black female population when she tells Sarah, "White girls like you, creepin' up, takin' our men, the whole world ain't enough, you gotta conquer ours, too!"

Christian Z. Goering has developed LitTunes, a great resource for using popular music to complement the teaching of classic literature. LitTunes, available at http://www.corndancer.com/tunes/tunes_main.html, is a collaborative online community designed to serve three purposes: (a) to provide educators with a centralized source of materials and support for using popular music in the classroom; (b) to provide a forum for educators to share their successful experiences and research involving the use of popular music; (c) to inspire educators to reach the disenfranchised with their own language—music. The site lists the following song to complement *A Raisin in the Sun*: "The Cloud Song" from *Draw Them Near* by Jess Klein (Slow River, 2000).

Conclusion

Although our society has come a long way from the days of Jim Crow laws and "separate but equal" clauses, racism and prejudice still exist. Because of this, the lessons Cass and Jemmie teach us in *Crossing Jordan*—that the color of a person's skin does not determine anything other than his or her race—and what we learn from the Younger family in *A Raisin in the Sun*—that the conflicts of race and family can be overcome if we just stick together— must be taught.

In some families, the cycle of bigotry has existed for generations. However, as we learned from April's story in this chapter's introduction, this cycle can be broken. We cannot change our students' upbringing, but we can teach them to think for themselves. By doing so, we can instill in our students the value of PEACE—**P**eople **E**ncouraging **A** **C**hance for **E**veryone.

Chapter 6

Using Young Adult Literature to Develop a Comprehensive World Literature Course With Several Classics

Joan F. Kaywell

Introduction

More than a decade ago, Barbara Pace said that the literary "canon is not a chorus of multicultural voices" (Pace, 1992, p. 33). Today, many good world literature anthologies are available, such as *The Longman Anthology of World Literature* and *The Norton Anthology of World Literature*. However, many of these anthologies' selections are written only by authors of Western European descent and are beyond the skill level of most middle and high school students. Reading such selections may not help our students understand, let alone appreciate, other cultures beyond their own. Since September 11, 2001, it has become obvious that our students *must*.

The Reasons for Teaching Comprehensive World Literature

There are several reasons we must teach literature representative of cultures from both hemispheres. Years ago, I was greatly influenced by a presentation about demographics made by Dr. Harold Hodgkinson, director of the Center for Demographic Policy's Institute for Educational Leadership in Washington, DC. According to Dr. Hodgkinson (1993), "Demographic data don't lie. It's up to us to interpret them properly." Following are some of his claims:

- If the composition of the world were broken down to represent 1,000 people, this is what the world would look like: 564 Asians, 210 Europeans, 86 Africans, 80 South Americans, and 60 North Americans.
- The United States has two equally sized minority groups—Black and Hispanic—and a rapidly increasing Asian population.

- From 1985 to 2000, the U.S. youth population (newborn–18) increased by 4.5 million minority youths—2.4 million Hispanics; 1.7 million Blacks; 483,000 Asian or other--compared to 60,000 Whites.

- These states have "minority" populations that exceed more than half of the state's population: Hawaii, 79.5%; New Mexico, 76.5%; Texas, 56.9%; California, 56.9%; Florida, 53.0%; New York, 52.8%; and Louisiana, 50.3%.

After attending Dr. Hodgkinson's presentation, I decided to educate myself on world demographics at the Population Connection Training Institute in Washington, D.C. From my research at that highly regarded institute (http://www.populationeducation.org/index.php), I add this statistic:

- The combined population *in millions* of China (1.311) and India (1.122) is 2.433 million. Compare that to the U.S. population of 299 million and draw your own conclusions (Haub, 2006).

Now examine the data above in light of the following statistics relating to prejudice, violence, and our youth:

- The number of hate groups operating in America has increased by 48% since 2000. The number of identified hate groups rose to 888 in 2007, up 5% from 844 in 2006 (Southern Poverty Law Center).

- Klanwatch, a project of the Southern Poverty Law Center, documented more than 270 incidents of hate crimes in schools and colleges during 1992; more than half of them were committed by teenagers (O'Neil, 1993).

- In a 1990 Harris poll of 1,865 high school students, more said they would participate in or silently support a racial confrontation than condemn or try to stop one.

- The National Institute Against Prejudice and Violence estimates that 20%–25% of students of color are victims of physical or psychological harm every year (Downey & Stage, 1999).

My question to you is this: When was the last time you taught or read something written by a foreign writer?

According to Arthur Applebee (1993), the curriculum is "dominated by familiar selections drawn primarily from a white (99%), male (86%), Anglo-Saxon tradition . . . [and] the overall proportions of selections by minorities (1%) and women (14%) remain low in public schools" (pp. 60–64). Many middle and secondary school teachers hesitate to introduce literature by authors with whom—or about places with which—they're unfamiliar. In fact, Applebee's study revealed that 80% of teachers in the public school sample stated that when they select literature, the importance of "personal familiarity with the selection" is second only to "literary merit" (p. 79).

Reader Response Theory and Collaborative Groups

Current reader response theory suggests that rather than interpreting text for students, teachers need to teach students how to interpret text and make meanings for themselves. In many ways, the push for comprehensive world literature courses has presented a unique opportunity for teachers. As teachers themselves are developing their interpretations of this unfamiliar literature, they can model their own reader response process for their students, forgoing the usual "answer-the-questions-at-the-end-of-the-book" method of most anthologies.

As early as 1938, Louise Rosenblatt noted the importance of considering the reader's role when constituting meaning from a text. Later, she argued that it is more important that students experience literature for themselves than that they get "correct answers." Reader response theory is concerned with how readers make meaning from their transaction or experience with a text. According to Richard W. Beach (1993),

> Knowledge is perceived not as a fixed, external entity to be imparted from teacher to student; rather it is mutually constructed and verified through social interaction. And within the context of the classroom as an "interpretive community," students learn to share certain common assumptions and strategies specific to the classroom as a social community. (p. 118)

Carlsen and Sherrill (1988) posit that the best atmosphere for the study of literature is one in which students have a vehicle for sharing personal responses. As it is now used, the traditional book report is too restrictive. Required readings should include both modern and classic works that permit a variety of interpretations. Above all, such an atmosphere should include, to the greatest extent possible, opportunities for freedom of choice in selecting literary works: It is "not necessary for everyone in the class to read the same book at the same time" (Purves, Rogers, & Soter; 1990, p. 65). Thus, the organization of the comprehensive world literature course described here emphasizes students' abilities to select, develop, and defend their interpretations of various literary selections from around the world.

Setting Up the Class

The design of this world literature course may be a unique experience for both you and your students because you will not choose the literature nor will you tell students what it means. Instead, students will be learning how to select representative, quality pieces of literature and how to negotiate their interpretations with others. Since teachers will be unfamiliar with many of the students' selections, parents should help their children select appropriate texts. As indicated in the annotated bibliography provided in the appendix, some books are appropriate only for more mature students due to the nature of the hardships faced by the characters.

By using reader-response techniques and collaborative learning methods, students can broaden their understanding of themselves and of other cultures. The course described here emphasizes, but is not restricted to, the study of literature not considered Western European.

Objectives of the Course

Students will be able to do the following:
1. Choose, read, and discuss representative literature from different cultures
2. Engage in reader-response activities in order to enhance their own abilities to interpret literature
3. Negotiate their own interpretations with peers in order to see that some interpretations are more supported by the text than others
4. Better understand their own culture by comparing and contrasting it with others
5. Develop their multicultural perspectives by learning to appreciate our common experiences and value our differences
6. Acquaint themselves with literature from around the world
7. Improve their book-talking skills
8. Develop their creativity by preparing alternative book reports

Course Requirements

Individual Selection of a Country and Representative Literature

Students must choose to study one country other than their own unless they were born in another country. Because the United States is rich with people from different cultures, encourage your American-born students to talk to someone they know whose family is from a different country. Students should ask what literature—novels, poems, fairy tales or folktales, plays—is representative of that country, where one can purchase such literature, and why that culture values certain works more than others. If students don't know anyone from a different country and have no friends who know anyone from another country, advise them to note that fact and to consult the prepared bibliography for suggestions (see the appendix). For additional titles, refer students to Merri V. Lindgren's *The Multicolored Mirror: Cultural Substance Literature for Children and Young Adults* (1991), Lyn Miller-Lachmann's *Our Family, Our Friends, Our World: An Annotated Guide to Significant Multicultural Books for Children and Teenagers* (1992), and Hazel Rochman's *Against Borders: Promoting Books for a Multicultural World* (1993).

Students might choose a short story from Janet Bode's *New Kids on the Block: Oral Histories of Immigrant Teens* (1989) Don Gallo's *Join In: Multieth-*

nic Short Stories (1993), or Marilyn Singer's *Face Relations: Eleven Stories About Seeing Beyond Color* (2004). Bode presents the oral histories of 11 teenagers whose families immigrated to the United States from other countries, including Cuba, El Salvador, India, and Vietnam, often under harrowing circumstances. These teens talk about their dreams for the future and share their experiences of leaving loved ones behind, of feeling alone amid strangers, and of wanting to fit in without losing their cultural identity. Gallo includes 17 short stories, many written by well-known writers of YA literature, and has grouped them by theme: expectations, friendships, dilemmas, connections, and confrontations. Exposure to these stories is likely to inspire student interest in a particular country. Singer presents stories about American high school students' relationships with new immigrant students of Haiti, Mexico, and other cultures.

Once they have selected countries, group students to form learning teams according to the country chosen—not by student ability. Each individual is to view one film (PG-13 or less) and read three additional literary selections from the chosen country: (a) a fairy tale, folktale, or children's story, (b) a poem that would appeal to their peers, and (c) one novel—or the equivalent of one novel—featuring a young adult protagonist. Help students determine how many short stories equal a novel, how many combinations of poems and short stories equal a novel, and so on. Students are to decide among themselves the category from which they will read their "novel." To prepare for their group presentations, each student should select four outstanding works so that all categories are covered in each group.

1. Each individual views one film (rated PG-13 or lower), either set in the chosen country or featuring a character from the country.

2. Each member of the team reads one representative fairy tale or folktale or children's story illustrative of the country. Groups should read the best one to the class but should summarize all of them on a page.

3. Each member of the team reads one representative poem; students will read their chosen poems to the class and tell why they thought the class would enjoy their choice. Each student should provide a handout of that poem and any accompanying visuals.

4a. One member of the team reads one "novel" about that country's past: historical fiction.

4b. One member of the team reads one "novel" about that country's present: a contemporary piece about a character who is living in, has emigrated from, or whose family has emigrated from that country. For example, if the selected country is Vietnam, the novel might be written about a Vietnamese teenager or a Vietnamese American teenager.

4c. One member of the team reads one nonfiction work representative of that country.

Additionally, each student should search the Web to find one work of literature considered to be a classic of that country. Students will gain experience
doing more sophisticated Internet searches, and teachers can use this assignment to discuss what makes a classic a classic and to teach various styles
for citing sources. The Library of Congress has created a fabulous online resource called "A World of Books: International Classics," available at http://
www.loc.gov/rr/international/books00.html.

Students should type a plot summary for each of their chosen works—
film, historical novel, contemporary novel, nonfiction title, children's stories,
fairy tales, folktales—and the titles of classics—in two to three pages, making copies for the rest of the class. See Figure 6.1 for an example of a handout
developed by a three-person group.

Figure 6.1. Chinese or Chinese American Literature (Asia)

Film Titles (NOTE: In a three-person team, each individual watches and summarizes
a different film.)

Crouching Tiger, Hidden Dragon (2000, PG-13), starring Chow Yun-Fat, Michelle
Yeoh, Ziyi Zhang, Chang, Chen and Lung Sihung II (2 hrs.)

Set in ancient China with beautiful landscapes and stunning special effects, the
film follows the mystical journey of a warrior who has lost his way and must offer his
treasured weapon to a new owner. Martial arts fans will love this movie.

The Last Emperor (1987, PG-13), starring John Lone, Joan Chen, Peter O'Toole, Ying
Ruocheng, and Victor Wong (2 hrs. 40 mins.).

This movie follows the true story of Puyi, China's last imperial ruler, who took the
throne at the age of 3 and was forced to leave it at the age of 7. Puyi spends much
of his life trying to regain the throne given to him through divine right.

Mulan (1998, G), starring the voices of Ming-Na Wen (Mulan) and Eddie Murphy
(Mushu) (1 hr. 28 mins.)

This animated Disney movie is about Mulan, a Chinese tomboy who goes to fight
in the war against the Huns. This is done in response to the emperor's call that each
family must send one man to fight in the war. Rather than let her elderly father go,
Mulan dresses as a man to fight with the help of a dragon named Mushu.

Something Old or Historical Fiction (NOTE: In a three-person team, person 1 will
read from this category.)

Lady of Ch'iao Kuo: Warrior of the South, Southern China, A.D. 531 (The Royal Diaries) by Laurence Yep (300 pp.)

Set in 531 A.D., this fictionalized account of a real-life princess tells the story of Red Bird, the 16-year-old daughter of the Hsien tribe's king. Princess Red Bird confronts prejudice when she is sent away from the Great Forest to be educated in colonial China, where she's labeled a savage. The heroic princess must use her leadership skills to save the colonists and her own people when they are attacked by their common enemy, the vicious Dog Heads.

Something New or Contemporary (NOTE: In a three-person team, person 2 will read from this category.)

Infusion of Culture (Chinese American)

American Born Chinese by Gene Luen Yang (233 pp.)

This graphic novel tells the stories of three characters: Jin Wang, a Chinese American student who will do just about anything to fit in; Danny, an All-American kid who is on his third high school in 3 years, thanks to the antics of his Chinese cousin, Chin-Kee, who is intentionally portrayed stereotypically; and the ambitious Chinese folk hero, the Monkey King, a familiar character to Chinese children everywhere. In the end, the plot lines cleverly converge, and readers have explored the themes of stereotypes, racism, and conformity.

Something True or Nonfiction (NOTE: In a three-person team, person 3 will read from this category)

Red Scarf Girl: A Memoir of the Cultural Revolution by Ji Li Jiang (320 pp.)

Ji Li Jiang writes about her experiences as a teenager during Chairman Mao's Cultural Revolution in China. Many people were ruthlessly persecuted under the pretense of ridding the country of anticommunist influences. Jiang must make a huge decision that will affect her family no matter what she decides.

Children's Stories or Fairy Tales (NOTE: In a three-person team, each individual reads and annotates a different children's story, folktale, or fairy tale.)

Lon Po Po: A Red-Riding Hood Story from China translated and illustrated by Ed Young (32 pp.)

This winner of the 1990 Caldecott Medal for Most Distinguished Picture Book takes a familiar story and casts it with Chinese characters. Lon Po Po is the wolf disguised as the grandmother of three girls. See what happens when the eldest sister, Shang, suspects that Lon Po Po is not their grandmother.

The Song of Mulan by Jeanne M. Lee (40 pp.)

This beautifully illustrated story is based on a beloved Chinese poem about a brave girl named Mulan, the inspiration for the Disney movie. The author's father, Chan Bo Wan, reproduces the Chinese calligraphy, which corresponds to each page of English text.

The Sons of the Dragon King: A Chinese Legend written and illustrated by Ed Young
  (32 pp.)

  In this folktale, Dragon King helps his nine sons find their true calling in life because he understands that each son's shortcoming may actually be his gift. For example, the son who seems to do little more than stare into the distance is perfect for the job of sentinel; and another son who is noisy is perfect for playing musical notes that are loud and true.

Classic Titles (NOTE: In a three-person team, each individual finds and cites a different classic.)

Ch'eng-en, Wu. (ca. 1590). *Monkey: A Folk Novel of China*. New York: Grove Hill.

Confucius. (1995/ca. 551 BC). *The Analects*. Toronto: Dover.

Kuan-chung, Lo. (1976/ca. 1320 AD). *Three Kingdoms*. Translated by Moss Roberts. New York: Pantheon.

Poetry (NOTE: In a three-person team, each individual finds, reads, and explains a poem representative of their chosen country).

Tell students that their annotations should not tell too much about the plot or give away the ending. Teach students to give short book talks that will inspire their classmates to read at least one selection. Remind students that giving a book talk is similar to telling a friend about a really good movie. Having students find titles of classics gives you the opportunity to teach them about how to cite a reference. Having students view a film prior to their reading helps them to visualize some aspects of their reading. Having students view contemporary films after their reading can lead to meaningful critical thinking activities when they compare the authenticity of the movie to that of their books.

Each learning team tells why it selected its particular country (if pertinent), distributes the required handout to the class, gives a book talk on each of the literary works, and tells how they found representative literature. The best fairy tale or children's story, as well as each poem, should be read aloud. Students should share any information they might have about specialty stores or Web sites where classmates can purchase the literature if they desire.

Expanding the Experience: Reading and Responding to a Selection from Each Country

After a learning team presents its book talks, each individual in the class reads one of the books presented by that team and records his or her reactions to it in a reader response journal. Students must accomplish two primary tasks in their reader response journals: (a) They must prove that they read the material in its entirety, and (b) they must connect the material to their own lives in some meaningful way. For classes that are unfamiliar with reader response journals, provide starter questions such as the following:

- If the protagonist were your best friend, what advice would you give to him or her?
- Have you ever read, seen, or heard about someone in a similar circumstance?
- Whom in the novel would you like to have as a friend? Why?
- Copy into your journal and comment on any passages you especially like.

Learning teams should be prepared to share information that will heighten the class's ability to discuss the literature from that country. The class's experience can be enhanced through guest speakers, maps, food, music, film, newspaper clippings, or articles of clothing. The teacher and class should contribute as much as possible, but the learning team is responsible for creating a positive experience for the class.

Evaluation

For a grade of C, all students must do the following:

1. View one film, G to PG-13, and write a summary of it without giving away the ending.
2. Find, read, and summarize a fairy tale, a folktale, or a children's story and prepare to read it out loud.
3. Read and summarize one novel that fulfills the requirement so that all categories are addressed within your learning team. Prepare a book talk to give to the class.
4. Find a poem, type it on a page, include a fitting visual accompaniment, and prepare to read it aloud. Be sure to bring copies of the poem for your classmates, and prepare to explain why you thought they would enjoy the poem.
5. Using the format we agree upon in class—either APA or MLA—identify a work of literature considered a classic of that country.
6. Learning teams prepare a handout for the class, meeting the established criteria above.

For a grade of B, all students must complete 1–6 and the following:

7. Read and keep a reader-response journal on one additional novel chosen from another learning team's presentation.
8. Prepare an alternative book report (Carter and Rashkis, 1980) and present it to the class. This oral presentation about your novel can

replace a book talk. (See Figure 6.2, reprinted by permission of the publisher with some minor modifications.)

For a grade of A, all students must complete 1–8 in a superior manner and prepare a convention booth.

Figure 6.2. 34 Alternative Book Reports

1. Design an advertising campaign to promote the sale of the book. Include each of the following in your campaign: a poster, a radio or TV commercial, a magazine or newspaper ad, a bumper sticker, and a button.

2. Write a scene that could have happened—but did not happen—in the book. After you have written the scene, explain how it would have changed the outcome of the book.

3. Create a board game based on events and characters in the book. By playing your game, members of the class should learn what happened in the book. Your game must include the following: a game board, a rule sheet and clear directions, with events and characters from the story depicted on cards or on the game board.

4. Make models of three objects that were important in the book. On a card attached to each model, tell why the object was important in the book.

5. If the book involves a number of locations within a country or geographical area, plot the events of the story on a map. Make sure the map is large enough for us to read the main events clearly. Attach a legend to your map. Write a paragraph that explains the importance of each event indicated on your map.

6. Complete a series of five drawings that show five of the major events in the plot of the book. Write captions for each drawing so that the illustrations can be understood by someone who did not read the book.

7. Design a movie poster for the book. Cast the major characters in the book with real actors and actresses. Include a scene or dialogue from the book in the layout of the poster. Remember, you are trying to convince someone to see the movie version of the book, so your writing should be persuasive.

8. Make a test for the book. Include 10 true-false, 10 multiple choice, and 10 short-answer essay questions. After writing the test, provide answers to your questions.

9. Select one of the book's characters who has the qualities of a heroine or hero. List and explain why these qualities make someone heroic.

10. Imagine that you are about to make a feature-length film of the novel. Cast your English language arts classmates to play the major roles and tell why you selected each person for a given part. Consider both appearance and personality.

11. Plan a party for the characters in the book. To do this, complete each of the following tasks: (a) design a party invitation that would appeal to all of the characters, (b) imagine five of the characters in the book and tell what each would wear to the party and why, (c) tell what food you will serve and why, (d) tell what games or entertainment you will provide and why your choices are appropriate, and (e)

tell how three of the characters will act at the party.

12. List five of the main characters from the book. Give three examples of what each character learned or did not learn in the book and explain.

13. Obtain a job application from an employer in your area, and fill out the application as one of the characters in the book might do. Before you obtain the application, be sure that the job is one for which the character is qualified. If a résumé is required, write it. (A résumé is a statement that summarizes the applicant's education and job experience. Career goals, special interests, and unusual achievements are sometimes included.)

14. You are a prosecuting attorney, putting one of the characters from the book on trial for a crime or misdeed. Prepare your case on paper, giving all your arguments and supporting them with facts from the book.

15. Adapt the prosecuting attorney activity outlined above to a dual-role project: playing one role, present the prosecuting case and, playing the other, present the case for the defense. If a classmate has read the same book, you might make this a two-person project.

16. Make a shoebox diorama of a scene from the book. Write a paragraph explaining the scene and attach it to the diorama.

17. Pretend that you are one of the characters in the book. Tape a monologue (one person talking) of that character telling of his or her experiences. Be sure to write out a script before taping.

18. Make a television box show of 10 scenes in the order that they occur in the book. Cut a square from the front of a box to serve as a TV screen and make two slits on opposite sides of the box. Slide through the two slits a butcher paper roll on which you have drawn the scenes. Make a tape recording to go with your television show. Be sure to write out a script before taping.

19. Make a PowerPoint presentation or slide show picturing what happened in the book. You will have to work carefully on a script before making your presentation.

20. Tape an interview with one of the characters in the book. Pretend that this character is being interviewed by a magazine or newspaper reporter. You may do this project with a partner, but be sure to write a script before taping.

21. Make a book jacket for the book. Include the title, author, and publishing company of the book on the cover. Be sure the illustration relates to an important aspect of the book. On the inside flap or on the back of your book jacket, write a paragraph telling about the book. Explain why this book makes interesting reading when writing this blurb.

22. Write a letter to a friend about the book. Explain why you liked or did not like the book.

23. Make a "wanted" poster for a character in the book. Include the following: (a) a drawing of the character (you may use a magazine cutout), (b) a physical description of the character, (c) the character's misdeeds, (d) other information about the character that you think is important, (e) the reward offered for the capture of the character.

24. In *The Catcher in the Rye*, Holden Caulfield describes a good book as one that "when you're done reading it, you wish the author who wrote it was a terrific friend of yours and you could call him up on the phone whenever you felt like it." Imagine that the author of the book you read is a terrific friend of yours. Write out an imaginary telephone conversation between the two of you in which you discuss the book.

25. Imagine that you have been given the task of conducting a tour of the town in which the book is set. Make a tape describing the homes of the characters and the places where important events in the book took place. You may use a musical background for your tape.

26. Make a list of at least 10 proverbs or familiar sayings. Now decide which characters in the book should have followed the suggestions in the familiar sayings and why. Here are some proverbs to get you started: *He who hesitates is lost. All's fair in love and war. The early bird catches the worm. A stitch in time saves nine.*

27. Write copy for a newspaper front page that is devoted entirely to the book you read. The front page should look as much like a real newspaper page as possible. The articles on the front page should be based on events and characters in the book.

28. Using pictures and words cut from magazines, make a collage that represents major characters and events in the book.

29. Make a timeline of the major events in the book. Be sure the divisions on the timeline reflect the time periods in the plot. Use drawings or magazine cutouts to illustrate events along the time line.

30. Change the setting of the book. Tell how this change of setting would alter events and affect characters.

31. Make a paper doll likeness of one of the characters in the book. Design at least three costumes for this character. Next, write a paragraph commenting on each outfit; tell what the clothing reflects about the character, the historical period, and events in the book.

32. Pick a national issue. Compose a speech to be given on that topic by one of the major characters in the book. Be sure the contents of the speech reflect the character's personality and beliefs.

33. Retell the plot of the book as it might appear in a third-grade reading book. Be sure that the vocabulary you use is appropriate for that age group. Variation: Retell this story to a young child. Tape-record your storytelling.

34. Using what you've gained from your reading, complete each of these thoughts: This book made me wish that . . . , realize that . . . , decide that . . . , wonder about . . . , see that . . . , believe that . . . , feel that . . . , and hope that . . . .

Students can complete this project individually or with their learning teams. If a student decides to skip the two B project options but chooses to prepare a booth with his or her learning team, that student will earn a B, not an A.

Each convention booth must contain the following: a map, food, music, film or photos, newspaper articles, articles of clothing, and one "special something." As students visit your booth, you must be prepared to explain its contents and answer questions. A guest speaker from that country is acceptable and encouraged to assist with your booth.

When students add a "special something," they often generate ideas you might never have considered. My favorite ones to date are from learning teams that studied Polynesian and South African literature. The learning team that studied Polynesian literature obtained a film that highlighted the beauty of Hawaii. They turned off the sound and, while the class watched, read excerpts from the literature. It was just beautiful! Another learning team created a simulation of South Africa's apartheid, and then set up a conference call with an eloquent South African gentleman. His message: "Until everyone is free, no one is free."

Grading

I have found that grade contracts work well with this particular unit. Students know exactly what they are expected to do for an A, a B, or a C, and they can choose their own courses of action. I recommend grading all activities on a satisfactory and unsatisfactory basis. If they are deemed unsatisfactory, provide students with the opportunity to redo the assignment. Contracts determine their grades, but the teacher determines the quality. If students fulfill the requirements for an A, but the work is shoddy and they choose not to redo various assignments, then lower the grade by one or two letters. To keep things simple, encourage students to fulfill the requirements of each assignment to the best of their abilities and have them complete weekly self-evaluations of their progress. Because the success of this project depends on student participation, unexcused absences should have a negative effect on students' grades. In my experience, however, students usually exceed my expectations by reading way beyond the requirements; ownership has a way of getting people involved.

Conclusion

When you teach world literature using the model described here, "the reader seeks to participate in another's vision—to reap knowledge of the world, to fathom the resources of the human spirit, to gain insights that will make [the reader's] own life more comprehensible" (Rosenblatt, 1938, p. 7). Literature makes it possible to vicariously experience others' circumstances and to observe the many ways that people make meaning of their lives. In 1938, Rosenblatt said that "in a turbulent age, our schools and colleges must prepare the student to meet unprecedented and unpredictable problems. . . . Young people everywhere are asking, 'What do the things that we are offered in school and college mean for the life we are living or are going to live?'" (pp. 4–5). Students have been asking this question for so many years. Isn't it time we answer? I believe it is time for students to learn that what they study really can mean something: It can help them to create peace.

Additional Resources for Teachers

Web Sites

At the onset of the unit, show your students "Earth at Night," a panoramic view of the earth taken from the Space Station, available at http://ant wrp.gsfc.nasa.gov/apod/image/0011/earthlights_dmsp_big.jpg. The night photo allows viewers to clearly see lights, indicating the populated areas. You can scroll east–west and north–south, helping your students to make observations as they explore. Note that Canada's population is almost exclusively along the U.S. border. Moving east to Europe, note the high population concentration along the Mediterranean coast. It is easy to spot London, Paris, Stockholm, and Vienna. Check out the development of Israel compared to the rest of the Middle Eastern countries. Note the Nile River and Africa. After the Nile, the lights don't come on again until Johannesburg. Look at the Australian Outback and the Trans-Siberian Rail Route. Moving east, the most striking observation is the difference between North and South Korea and the density of Japan. Encourage your students to make other observations; for example, what can they observe about the world's energy consumption?

The International Children's Digital Library, http://www.childrens library.org, offers numerous picture books and children's literature organized by country that students may read online for free. Their mission is "to excite and inspire the world's children to become members of the global community—children who understand the value of tolerance and respect for diverse cultures, languages, and ideas—by making the best in children's literature available online." This is a must-use resource for any teacher interested in introducing cultural understanding to their students.

Although the Kwintessential Cross-Cultural Solutions Web site, http:// www.kwintessential.co.uk/resources/country-profiles.html, is designed for business travelers, it is a great reference source for facts about various countries around the world. The site includes an easy-to-use guide for developing understanding of another culture's language, etiquette, and taboos.

After a unit is completed, teachers might want to direct students to the Norton Anthology of World Literature's Web site, http://www.wwnorton. com/college/english/nawol/welcome.htm, where students can extend their exploration of world literature. This Web site includes maps, crossword puzzles, multiple-choices quizzes, and interactive timelines. An audio glossary enables students to hear the proper pronunciation of hundreds of glossary terms.

Journal Articles

"Finding Common Ground: Learning the Language of Peace" by Gerrit W.
    Bleeker, Barbara S. Bleeker, and Martha M. Bleeker (2006)
    The Bleekers studied YA literature's ability to positively affect students' attitudes. Twenty-three students from diverse backgrounds learned to promote self-respect, empathy, and peace in this pilot project that focused on the "language of peace."

"Can You Name One Good Thing That Comes Out of War?" by Wayne Brinda (2008)
    By asking five important questions and using nonfiction YA literature, teachers can help students find their own answers to the conflicts associated with war.

"Growing Up Female Around the Globe With Young Adult Literature" by
    Joan F. Kaywell, Patricia P. Kelly, Christi Edge, Larissa McCoy, and Narisa Steinberg (2006)
    Annotated YA booklists, facts, statistics, and sources for further exploration are included in this article, which examines the plight of females around the world. Topics include female genital mutilation, oppression, poverty, AIDS, depression, homosexuality, suicide, and war.

"Quantity and Quality: The Need for Culturally Authentic Trade Books in
    Asian American Young Adult Literature" by Virginia S. Loh (2006)
    This very informative article exposes the disconnect between what we know and what we practice in classrooms regarding multicultural YA literature, especially as it pertains to Asian American youth. An interview with Cynthia Kadohata is included.

"Making Time for Literature With Middle Eastern Perspectives" by Kristina
    V. Mattis (2007)
    Mattis presents young adult fiction, nonfiction, and poetry collections representative of the Middle East that point out the similarities in adolescent identity development across cultures.

"The Ever-Expanding Mexican American YA Canon" by René Saldaña Jr.
    (2007)
    To help teachers meet the needs of a growing Latino population, Saldaña comments on several novels, poetry collections, and nonfiction YA titles they may wish to add to their curriculum.

"The Power of Foreign Young Adult Literature" by Gretchen Schwarz (1996)

Schwarz suggests many books for young adults and makes a case for including foreign YA literature in the classroom. Topics include teaching tolerance, teaching across the curriculum, and building a world community.

Appendix

World Literature by Continent and Country

AFRICA

SUB-SAHARAN

Film Titles

Cry Freedom (1987, PG), starring Denzel Washington and Kevin Kline (2 hrs. 37 mins.)

Hotel Rwanda (2004, PG-13), starring Don Cheadle, Hakeem Kae-Kazim, and Nick Nolte (2 hrs.)

Lost Boys of Sudan (2004, Not rated), PBS documentary (1 hr. 27 mins.)

Out of Africa (1985, PG), starring Meryl Streep and Robert Redford (2 hrs. 30 mins.)

Fiction

Copper Sun by Sharon M. Draper (302 pp.)
Amari's just 15 years old when slave traders murder her family, take her from her homeland, and then sell her into slavery. This piece of historical fiction lets readers experience what slavery was like and can make the reader ashamed of what some did.

Waiting for the Rain by Sheila Gordon (224 pp.)
Tengo, who is Black, and Frikkie, a White Afrikaaner, grew up together on a farm in South Africa. As tensions over apartheid grow, the boys find their friendship in jeopardy. In the end, violence seems the only way to bring about the necessary changes to an unjust system.

Child of Dandelions by Shenaaz Nanji (214 pp.)
Fifteen-year-olds Zabine and Zena have been best friends for a long time, but all that changes when Ugandan President Idi Amin orders all non-citizen Indians to leave the country within 90 days. Zabine thinks her family will be spared because she was born and raised in Uganda and her father fought wild animals to build his business. She discovers, however, that when a dictator rules, no one is safe.

Nonfiction

Innocents Lost: When Child Soldiers Go to War by Ishmael Beah (240 pp.)
Beah was just like any other 12-year-old boy until rebel forces attacked his village in Sierra Leone in the early 1990s. Beah then becomes a child soldier, learning to shoot an AK-47 and kill without remorse until he receives rehabilitation at the age of 15. An estimated 10% of the soldiers in this region are children.

Kaffir Boy: The True Story of a Black Youth's Coming of Age in Apartheid South Africa by Mark Mathabane (368 pp.)
This is a very disturbing story about Mathabane's life growing up as a *kaffir*, or slave child, in apartheid South Africa. When Mathabane receives a tennis scholarship, he finds the opportunity to escape to America. His book chronicles many of the atrocities committed against people of color in South Africa. Mathabane's second book, *Kaffir Boy in America* (292 pp.), tells about his adult experiences in the United States.

Children's Story

A Promise in the Sun: An African Story by Mollel Tololwa (32 pp.)
This African story explains why bats come out only at night.

Poetry Resources

In the Country of the Heart: Love Poems From South Africa edited by Peter R. Anderson (148 pp.)

Basadzi Voices: An Anthology of Poetic Writing by Young Black South African Women compiled by Rose Mokhosi (86 pp.)

Classics

Things Fall Apart by Chinua Achebe (224 pp.)
A Lesson Before Dying by Ernest J. Gaines (272 pp.)

Cry, the Beloved Country by Alan Paton (283 pp.)

EGYPT

Film Titles

Caesar and Cleopatra (1945, Not rated), starring Claude Rains and Vivien Leigh (2 hrs. 18 mins.)

The Mummy Returns (1991, PG-13), starring Brendan Fraser, Rachel Weisz, and John Hannah (2 hrs. 10 mins.)

Raiders of the Lost Ark (1981, PG), starring Harrison Ford, Karen Allen, and Paul Freeman (1 hr. 55 mins.)

Stargate (1994, PG-13), starring Kurt Russell, James Spader, and Alexis Cruz (2 hrs. 1 min.)

Fiction

The Golden Goblet by Eloise Jarvis (256 pp.)
This Newbery Honor Book weaves the cultural beliefs of ancient Egypt into stories that deal with issues of abuse, fear, and loneliness, which span all times and places. Young Ranofer realizes that his half-brother is evil and must be stopped.

Pharaoh's Daughter: A Novel of Ancient Egypt by Julius Lester (192 pp.)
This is the story of Moses as a teenager as conceived by the author, who converted to Judaism and wrote this as a midrash, a Jewish tradition in which a person uses his or her imagination to explore sacred text.

Escape from Egypt by Sonia Levitin (272 pp.)
When Moses comes to lead the Israelites out of Egypt, a young slave named Jesse finds his faith and endurance challenged. He is a Hebrew slave, but he is interested in Jennat, an Egyptian-Syrian slave whose beliefs differ from his.

Land of Enchanters: Egyptian Short Stories From the Earliest Times to the Present Day edited by Bernard Lewis and Stanley Mayer Burstein (183 pp.)
This collection includes contemporary stories as well as stories dating back more than 4,000 years. Young and old should be able to find stories of interest in this treasure-trove collection of literature.

Nonfiction

A Border Passage: From Cairo to America—A Women's Journey by Leila Ahmed (336 pp.)

In her memoir, which covers the expanse of her life from childhood through adulthood, Ahmed shares her experiences as a child growing up in Cairo in the 1940s and 1950s. She then acquires her college education at Cambridge and journeys to America to teach.

Children's Stories

The Egyptian Cinderella by Shirley Climo and illustrated by Ruth Heller (32 pp.)

Young Rhodopis is stolen by pirates and sold into slavery in Egypt. Three servant girls treat her badly because "she is just a slave." Rhodopis makes friends with and dances for the animals that live in the forest. This sets off a chain of events that lead her to Pharaoh.

Zekmet the Stone Carver: A Tale of Ancient Egypt by Mary Stolz and illustrated by Deborah Nourse Lattimore. (32 pp.)

This is an imaginative story of how the stone carver of the Sphinx might have felt about creating this monument under orders from the Pharaoh.

Poetry Resource

Love Songs of the New Kingdom edited by John L. Foster (120 pp.)

Classic

Fountain and Tomb: Hakayat Haretna by Mahfouz Naguib and translated by James Kenneson (298 pp.)

ASIA (INCLUDING THE MIDDLE EAST)

AFGHANISTAN AND PAKISTAN

Film Titles

Afghan Stories (2003, Not rated), documentary (1 hr.)
Baran (2004, PG), starring Hossein Abedini and Zahra Bahrami (1 hr. 34 mins.)
Kandahar (2001, Not rated), starring Niloufar Pazira, Hassan Tantai, Niloufar Pazira, Hassan Tantai, and Hayatalah Hakimi (1 hr. 25 mins.).

Osama (2003, PG-13), starring Marina Golbahari and Arif Herati (1 hr. 23 mins.).

Fiction

Breadwinner by Deborah Ellis (170 pp.)
Due to the oppressive rule of the Taliban in Afghanistan, which prohibits girls from going to school or to market, 11-year-old Parvana must disguise herself as a boy when she needs to become the breadwinner for her family. The sequel, *Parvana's Journey* (176 pp.), picks up when Parvana, now 13, leaves Kabul to search for her mother and siblings, who disappeared during a Taliban takeover.

Mud City by Deborah Ellis (176 pp.)
Shauzia is an orphaned Afghani refugee who dreams of going to France. Like Parvana in the first book in the *Breadwinner* trilogy, she dresses as a boy in order to get food in Peshawar, Pakistan.

The Kite Runner by Khaled Hosseini (324 pp.)
Hosseini, an Afghani American medical doctor turned novelist, tells the story of Amir, a privileged boy who is best friends with Hassan, his father's servant's son and a member of an oppressed lower class. Hassan would give up his life for Amir, but Amir has some lessons to learn before he deserves such devotion.

Shabanu: Daughter of the Wind by Suzanne Fisher Staples (288 pp.)
Shabanu, the 11-year-old daughter of a camel breeder, survives the harsh desert of Pakistan. In a very male-dominated society, she must contend with issues surrounding her sister's upcoming wedding and her own betrothal. Readers who want to continue Shabanu's journey can read *Haveli* (336 pp.) which tells how, as an older teen, she becomes the fourth and favorite wife of Rahim. In *The House of Djinn* (224 pp.), Shabanu's story continues 10 years after her staged death. Shabanu's story highlights the cultural conflict between traditional and modern views.

Under the Persimmon Tree by Suzanne Fisher Staples (288 pp.)
Calling upon her experiences as a reporter in Afghanistan and Pakistan, Staples sets this post–9/11 novel in both of those countries and presents it from the points of view of two characters—a girl and a woman from very different worlds. Elaine (now Nusrat) moved from New York to Peshawar, Pakistan, to teach at a makeshift school for refugee children while her Afghani husband provides medical care for people in Afghanistan. Najmah,

who witnesses her family's demise at the hands of Afghanistan's Taliban, tries to make it to safety by crossing the border into Pakistan. The two meet and share their stories.

Refugees by Catherine Stine (288 pp.)
    After her foster mother leaves to work as a Red Cross doctor in a refugee camp on the Afghani-Pakistani border, 16-year-old Dawn runs away from her California home to New York City two days before 9/11. When Dawn tries to call her mother, she reaches Johar, a 15-year-old refugee. Through e-mail exchanges, the two help each other cope with the tragedy of the terrorist attacks and give readers two very different perspectives.

Nonfiction

Some Far and Distant Place by Jonathan S. Addleton (207 pp.)
    As an American child of missionary parents living in Pakistan, the author recounts his life as a child who visited the United States only 3 times in his first 18 years of life. This memoir couples Addleton's recollections with historical events, which makes an interesting read.

My Forbidden Face by Latifa (210 pp.)
    Latifa was only 16 when the Taliban took over her home city of Kabul as well as most of Afghanistan. Now Latifa and all of the other women have no rights, and she believes all Afghani women will be eliminated.

Children's Story

The Gifts of Wali Dad: A Tale of India and Pakistan by Aaron Shepard (32 pp).
    Wali Dad is an old grass cutter who lives a meager but happy life, always saving 10 of the 30 paisas he earns each day. After he saves more money than he could ever spend, he decides to buy something special to give away as a gift. He starts a chain reaction of gift giving that ends up in a marriage befitting a king.

Poetry Resources

Fifty Poems of Hafiz by A. J. Arberry (196 pp.)
A Cry in the Wilderness: Poetry from Pakistan by Munir Niazi (80 pp.)

Classic

The Blind Owl by Sadegh Hedayat (130 pp.)

CHINA

Film Title

Hero (2004, PG-13), starring Jet Li, Tony Leung Chiu Wai, and Maggie Cheung (1 hr. 39 mins.)

Fiction

It's Crazy to Stay Chinese in Minnesota by Eleanor Wong Telemaque (118 pp.)
    Ching's parents own the only Chinese restaurant in town, where she waits on tables, takes in cash, and dreams of attending the university. Ching is often torn between her traditional Chinese heritage and her progressive, nontraditional dreams; sometimes she wishes she were totally American. Through experiences with other Chinese American friends, Ching realizes that she can break from some of her family's traditions, and she learns to value how her heritage adds to her uniqueness.

Chu Ju's House by Gloria Whelan (240 pp.)
    Because the government forbids families to have more than one daughter, 14-year-old Chu Ju decides to take matters into her own hands by running away when her mother gives birth to another girl. What happens as a result of her leaving brings a significant message to her family.

Sea Glass by Laurence Yep (256 pp.)
    Craig Chin moved from China to San Francisco's Chinatown. He has a hard time adjusting to his peers' prejudice toward him until an uncle opens a whole new world to him—the sea.

The Star Fisher by Laurence Yep (160 pp.)
    Fifteen-year-old Joan Lee is caught between her family's traditional Chinese ways and the American way of doing things. Because she knows English, Joan understands the cruel and racist comments people make about her family, which force her to grow up faster than most.

Nonfiction

Chinese Cinderella: The True Story of an Unwanted Daughter by Adeline Yen Mah (199 pp.)
    Adeline Yen Mah's memoir details her childhood in both Tianjin and Shanghai. Because her mother died while giving birth to her, Mah must constantly fight for approval from the rest of her family—especially from her stepmother, Niang.

Children's Story

Yeh-Shen by Ai-Ling Louie (32 pp.)
This is possibly the oldest version of the Cinderella story known. It is based on ancient Chinese manuscripts written 1,000 years before the earliest European version. Yeh-Shen lives in a cave with her stepmother and stepsisters, and . . . (you know what happens).

Poetry Resources

Li Po and Tu Fu: Poems Selected and Translated With an Introduction and Notes by Arthur Cooper (256 pp.)

An English Translation of Poems of the Contemporary Chinese Poet Hai Zi by Hong Zeng and Hai Zi (177 pp.)

Classic

Dream of the Red Chamber by Tsao Hsueh-Chin (352 pp.)

INDIA

Film Titles

Bend It Like Beckham (2003, PG-13), starring Parminder Nagra, Keira Knightley, and Shaznay Lewis (1 hr. 52 mins.)

Lagaan: Once Upon a Time in India (2001, PG), starring Aamir Khan and Gracy Singh (3 hrs. 44 mins.)

The Namesake (2007, PG-13), starring Kal Penn, Zuleikha Robinson, and Irrfan Khan (2 hrs. 2 mins.)

Fiction

Tusk and Stone by Malcolm Bosse (252 pp.)
This work of historical fiction takes place during seventh-century India. When the caravan that Arjun and his family are traveling in comes under attack, his uncle is killed and his sister is kidnapped. Arjun, at 14, is sold to the army and becomes a *mahout*, or elephant driver. His quest to find his sister becomes legendary.

Sold by Patricia McCormick (264 pp.)
Based on the author's research in the red-light district of Calcutta, this

book presents the story of 13-year-old Lakshmi, who's sold into prostitution by her stepfather. This disturbing book will give readers an eye-opening view of adults' cruelty toward and brainwashing of these children.

The Not-So-Star-Spangled Life of Sunita Sen by Mitali Perkins (192 pp.)
Like any other eighth grader in America, Sunita Sen is caught between the two worlds of childhood and adulthood. She lives in the San Francisco area with her Indian-American family, but her Western world is shaken when her grandparents from India come for an extended visit.

Climbing the Stairs by Padma Venkatraman (247 pp.)
Set in India during World War II, 15-year-old Vidya dreams of one day attending college, but her plans are immediately put on hold when her father is beaten by the British police. She must go to live with her grandfather in a place where tradition holds that women are meant to be married off as soon as possible.

Homeless Bird by Gloria Whelan (240 pp.)
Koly's parents have been scrimping and saving for her dowry because it's time for her—at 13 years of age—to marry. As is customary, Koly goes to live with her new husband's family only to discover that he is very sickly. After he dies, her cruel mother-in-law abandons her, and Koly learns that widowed women are considered to be bad luck. The title comes from Rabindranath Tagore's famous poem in which a "homeless bird" represents these Hindu women who are without family, status, or financial security.

Nonfiction

Fodor's Exploring India (4th ed.) by Fiona Dunlop (288 pp.)
This book, produced by Fodor's, provides a complete traveler's guide to India. Indian life is categorized by food, clothing, architecture, religion, government, and music, both historic and contemporary. The pictures and maps really add to one's understanding of this country.

Karma Cola: Marketing the Mystic East by Gita Mehta (208 pp.)
This is the author's satirical look at how the Beatles actually changed the world by studying with the Maharishi Mahesh Yogi in the 1960s. In her opinion, Westerners were duped into believing that "enlightenment" could be had in an instant.

Jasmine by Bharati Mukherjee (256 pp.)
When Jasmine was very small, an astrologer predicted that she would be widowed and exiled. At 17, Jasmine Vidh is widowed and illegally im-

migrates to America, only to face more difficulty in rural Iowa.

Children's Stories

I Is for India by Prodeepta Das (32 pp.)
Each page of this realistic ABC book about Indian culture has a letter, a description of something that begins with that letter, and an accompanying photograph.

Folk Tales and Fairy Stories from India by Sudhin N. Ghose (144 pp.)
The 16 traditional tales in this collection include "How Princess Maya Got Her Deserts." Because Princess Maya is a smart girl who can speak the language of the animals, her father forces her to marry a beggar in front of the palace. Ah, but the beggar has a secret.

Poetry Resource

Second Sight: New Poetry in India by A. K. Ramanujan (89 pp.)

Classics

The Bhagvad Gita translated by Eknatt Easwaran (237 pp.)
The Ramayana translated by R. K. Narayan (171 pp.)
Swami and Friends by R. K. Narayan (190 pp.)

IRAN AND IRAQ

Film Titles

Arabian Nights (2001, Not rated), starring Mili Avital and Alan Bates (2 hrs. 55 mins.)

The Iran Hostage Crisis: 444 Days to Freedom (What Really Happened in Iran), (2006, Not rated), documentary narrated by William Shatner (1 hr. 36 mins.)

The Legend of a Sigh (1991, Not rated), starring Mahshid Afsharzadeh, Yarta Yaran, and Jahangir Almasi (1 hr. 45 mins.)

Leila (1999, PG), starring Leila Hatami, Ali Mosaffa, and Jamileh Sheikhi (2 hrs. 9 mins.)

Not Without My Daughter (1991, PG-13), starring Sally Field and Alfred Molina (1 hr. 54 mins)

Fiction

Suri and Co.: Tales of a Persian Teenage Girl by Mahshid Amirshahi (87 pp.)
Suri is an upper-class Iranian teenager living in Tehran when Western influence was at its height, just before the Islamic Revolution of 1979. Hers is a perspective that should not be forgotten.

Black Parrot, Green Crow: A Collection of Short Fiction by Hushange Gulshiri and Heshmat Moayyad (244 pp.)
This collection of three poems and 18 short stories captures the confusion that the Iranian people experienced during and following the Islamic Revolution. "My Little Prayer Room" tells the story of Hassan, a boy shamed by having six toes.

The Beast by Donna Jo Napoli (272 pp.)
Based on *The Beauty and the Beast*, this novel focuses on the beast's story. Orasmyn, a young Persian prince, angers a fairy who then casts a spell that turns him into a lion. He leaves the Middle East and goes to France, seeking redemption; there, he meets Belle, and the rest—as they say—is history.

Nonfiction

Funny in Farsi: A Memoir of Growing Up Iranian in America by Firoozeh Dumas (224 pp.)
In 1971, 7-year-old Dumas moved from Iran to the United States because of her father's job transfer. This memoir is more her coming-of-age story in America than one addressing the Islamic Revolution, but she does tell how her family was negatively affected by the Iranian hostage crisis.

Journey From the Land of No: A Girlhood Caught in Revolutionary Iran by Roya Hakakian (272 pp.)
This is the author's phenomenal account of being a young Jewish girl growing up during a war, seeing things that no child should ever see. Looking back at her childhood in Tehran during the overthrow of the Ayatollah Khomeini, she is able to paint the original beauty of her country, later darkened by the repressive government takeover.

Persepolis: The Story of a Childhood by Marjane Satrapi (160 pp.)
Satrapi was only 10 when the Islamic Revolution occurred in 1979. Her innocent misunderstanding of the dramatic transformations occuring in her society give the reader a picture of what a religious government can do to a culture, a country, and its people. This graphic novel's story is told through black-and-white illustrations, and so is its sequel, *Persepolis 2: The Story of a*

Return (192 pp.). Satrapi's parents send her away to be educated in Vienna, Austria, far away from religious police and war-torn Tehran. Now a teenager, Marjane tries but fails to fit in. She returns to Iran, where she must make more adjustments, trading freedom for a veil.

Children's Stories

The Legend of the Persian Carpet by Tomie de Paola (32 pp.)
This story tells how the Persian rug got its jeweled pattern. King Balash's beautiful giant diamond is stolen, and when the thief drops it on a rocky plain, it shatters into thousands of dazzling fragments. When the king is led to this location, he is overwhelmed by the beauty of this carpet of fragments. How will Payam, a young apprentice weaver, convince the beloved king to leave the shattered diamond behind and return to his kingdom? What other than the king's diamond can fill the palace with color and light?

The Persian Cinderella by Shirley Climo (32 pp.)
After her mother's death, a Persian girl with a heart of gold is treated poorly by her stepfamily, who is jealous of her beauty. When Settareh finds an ancient jug at a bazaar, events that follow are nothing like one would expect.

The Librarian of Basra: A True Story From Iraq by Jeanette Winter (32 pp.)
Little Alia Muhammad Baker loves her library and does not want to see it destroyed in war. She decides to take matters into her own hands to save 30,000 books.

Poetry Resources

Rubaiyat of Omar Khayyam translated by Edward Fitzgerald (128 pp.)

A World Between: Poems, Short Stories, and Essays by Iranian Americans edited by Persis M. Karim and Mohammad Mehdi Khorrami (67 pp.)

Classics

Shahnameh: The Persian Book of Kings by Abolqasem Ferdowsi (928 pp.)

Reading Lolita in Tehran: A Memoir in Books by Azar Nafisi (384 pp.)

Haft Paykar: A Medieval Persian Romance by Nizami (368 pp.)

ISRAEL AND THE PALESTIINIANS

Film Titles

Promises (2004, Not rated), documentary (1 hr. 46 mins.).
Wall (2005, Not rated), starring Simone Bitton and Amos Yaron (1 hr. 38 mins.).

Fiction

One More River by Lynn Reid Banks (256 pp.)
   The author shows the Arab-Israeli conflict during the Six-Day War through the eyes of Lesley, a 14-year-old Israeli girl. Lesley's father had moved his family from Canada to an Israeli kibbutz to reconnect with their Jewish heritage. Readers may wish to read the sequel, *Broken Bridge* (336 pp.), set 25 years later, in which an Israeli girl witnesses her cousin's murder by Arab terrorists.

Samir and Yonatan by Danielle Carmi and translated by Yael Lotan (192 pp.)
   Samir's brother was killed by an Israeli soldier. When an accident forces him to go to an Israeli hospital, this Palestinian boy dreads the very idea of it. When he meets Jewish children there and befriends a Jewish boy named Yonatan, more than his knee is healed.

Habibi by Naomi Shihab Nye (272 pp.)
   In this story, based on recollections of the author's childhood, 14-year-old Liyana must leave her home in St. Louis when her father, a doctor, decides to return to Jerusalem amid the Arab-Israeli conflict. Surrounded by her Palestinian relatives, things turn topsy-turvy when she falls for Omer, a Jewish boy.

Panther in the Basement by Amos Oz (160 pp.)
   Proffy, short for "Professor," is a 12-year-old boy growing up in Jerusalem in the late 1940s. Proffy and his friends pretend they are underground Israeli fighters and strategize how to kick the British out of Israel. While out past curfew one night, Proffy is caught by a British soldier. What happens next surprises everyone.

Nonfiction

Jerusalem Mosaic: Young Voices From the Holy City by I. E. Mozeson and Lois Stavsky (160 pp.)
   The authors, husband-and-wife English teachers, interview 36 teenag-

ers in Jerusalem during the summers of 1992 and 1993, showing that much of Israel's beauty lies in its mosaic of people from different religious backgrounds—Jewish, Muslim, and Christian.

Children's Stories

The Stone Lamp: Eight Stories of Hanukkah Through History by Karen Hesse (32 pp.)

Eight Jewish children tell the story of Hanukkah from the 12th through the 20th centuries. The children who tell the stories are from England, France, Turkey, Italy, Ukraine, Austria, Germany, and Israel.

Who Is the Builder? by Genendel Krohn (32 pp.)

While walking around his village, a little boy named Avraham notices the beautiful sights around him. After he asks the moon and many other aspects of nature if they built the world, a voice from heaven tells him who's responsible.

Sitti's Secrets by Naomi Shihab Nye (144 pp.)

Mona's father has decided to take his daughter to a remote Palestinian village to visit his birthplace and her paternal grandmother, or Sitti. Although Mona cannot speak Arabic, she and Sitti are able to communicate in a way that will last a lifetime.

Poetry Resources

Poems of Jerusalem and Love Poems by Yehuda Amichai (277 pp.)

Anthology of Modern Palestinian Literature edited by Salma Khadra Jayyusi (740 pp.)

The Space Between Our Footsteps: Poems and Paintings of the Middle East by Naomi Shihab Nye (144 pp.)

The Flower of Anarchy: Selected Poems by Meir Wieseltier (168 pp.)

JAPAN

Film Titles

Empires—Japan: Memoirs of a Secret Empire (2002, Not rated), documentary narrated by Richard Chamberlain (2 hrs. 40 mins.)

The Karate Kid (1984, PG), starring Ralph Macchio and Pat Morita (2 hrs. 6 mins.)

The Karate Kid, Part II (1986, PG), starring Ralph Macchio and Pat Morita (1 hr. 53 mins.)

Memoirs of a Geisha (2005, PG-13), starring Gong Li, Ken Watanabe, and Koji Yakusho (2 hrs. 25 mins.)

Pearl Harbor: The View From Japan (1994, Not rated), documentary (69 min.).

Fiction

Sadako and the Thousand Paper Cranes by Eleanor Coerr (80 pp.)
Coerr re-creates the story of Sadako Sasaki, a Japanese girl who was only 2 years old when the United States dropped the atom bomb on Hiroshima in 1945. No one ever thought that 10 years later she would become the victim of "bomb disease." Then Sadako's best friend recalls an old Japanese legend:"If a sick person folds one thousand cranes, the gods will grant her wish and make her healthy again." Sadako made 644 cranes before her death on October 25, 1955; her classmates finished them for her in her memory.

Pacific Crossing by Gary Soto (144 pp.)
Fourteen-year-old Lincoln Mendoza is a Mexican American teenager fascinated by the Japanese martial art of *shorinji kempo*. Selected to represent his school in a summer exchange program with a school in Japan, he's excited to practice *kempo* in an authentic dojo. His host family, Mr. and Mrs. Ono and their son, Mitsuo, teach him about Japanese culture and family values, showing him that people everywhere are more alike than different.

Nonfiction

Shipwrecked!: The True Adventures of a Japanese Boy by Rhoda Blumberg (80 pp.)
Set in anti-American 19th-century Japan, this is the true story of Manjiro Nakahama, a 14-year-old boy who, after his father dies, becomes the sole provider for his mother and five siblings. On a fishing expedition, he and four others are marooned for several months until rescued by an American vessel. Manjiro is the first Japanese person to set foot on American soil. He eventually returns to Japan and becomes an honored samurai.

Children's Story

A Tale of Two Tengu: A Japanese Folktale by Karen Kawamoto McCoy (28 pp.)

Kenji and Joji are both *tengu*, Japanese goblins who are quite proud of their magical noses. They have the ability to stretch their noses as far as they want, but they cannot decide whose nose is better. Finding out creates an awkward situation.

Grandfather's Journey by Allen Say (32 pp.)
Allen Say tells the story of his grandfather's enchantment with two countries: Japan and the United States. While in one, he longs for the other, which is often the case when someone leaves his or her homeland to make a home in another.

Poetry Resource

Festive Wine: Ancient Japanese Poems From the Kinkafu by Noah and William Elliott and translated by Brannen.

Classics

Hiroshima by John Hersey (152 pp.)
The Tale of Genji by Murasaki Shikibu (1,216 pp.)

KOREA

Film Titles

The Way Home (2002, PG), starring Yoo Seung-ho II, Kim Eul-boon II, and Min Kyung-Eun (1 hr. 20 mins.)

Welcome to Dongmakgol (2005, Not rated), starring Shin Ha-Kyun, Kang Hye-Jung, and Jung Jae-Young (2 hrs. 13 mins.)

Why Has Bodhi-Dharma Left for the East? (1989, Not rated), starring Yi Pan-Yong, Hae-Jin Huang, and Sin Won-Sop (2 hrs. 25 mins.)

Fiction

The Long Season of Rain by Helen Kim (237 pp.)
Young Junehee is ready for another long and uneventful *changma*, or rainy season, in her South Korean house while her father is away. But a mudslide brings a guest to Junehee's home, revealing family secrets and creating cultural tensions.

A Cab Called Reliable by Patti Kim (156 pp.)

Ahn Joo is only 8 years old when her family leaves Korea and moves to Arlington, Virginia. Because of her father's drinking, family life is far from harmonious. One day, Ahn Joo sees her mother and brother leaving in a cab that has the word *reliable* written on its door. Ahn Joo later finds a note from mother, who promises to return for her one day, but it seems that day will never come.

Finding My Voice by Marie G. Lee (224 pp.)

Ellen, a Korean American, struggles to find her identity as the only non-White teenager in a small town in Minnesota. Readers may be interested in its sequel, *Saying Goodbye* (240 pp.), in which Ellen confronts racism as a Harvard freshman. For a male character's perspective, consider Lee's *Necessary Roughness* (240 pp.), in which Chan and his family, the only Asian Americans in town, deal with similar issues.

A Single Shard by Linda Sue Park (148 pp.)

Set in 12th-century Korea in a potter's village, readers meet an orphan boy named Tree-ear who befriends and cares for an elderly man. Tree-ear is fascinated by Min, a local potter, and secretly watches him perform his craft. Eventually the potter notices Tree-ear and gives him an important mission.

When My Name Was Keoko by Linda Sue Park (208 pp.)

Based on her childhood experiences in Japanese-occupied Korea, the author tells the story from the perspectives of two children: a 10-year-old girl and a 13-year-old boy. Like all Korean families living under this strict fascist regime, the Kim family is stripped of its culture, permitted to learn only Japanese history and language. Koreans also had to convert their names to Japanese names. Sun-hee, now Keokoa, struggles to reconcile her Korean home life with her Japanese school and friends, but her brother Tae-yul, now Nobuo, wants to do more.

Nonfiction

The Aquariums of Pyongyang: Ten Years in the North Korean Gulag by Chol-hwan Kang and Pierre Rigoulot (238 pp.)

Chi-Hoon: A Korean Girl by Patricia McMahon and illustrated by Michael F. O'Brien (48 pp.)

Using colorful photographs, the author follows the daily life of 8-year-old Kim Chihhon and her family in Seoul, Korea. Beginning on Saturday and ending the following week on Sunday, the book is laid out in the form of journal entries that explain their lifestyle, clothes, housing, schools, foods, crafts, tourist attractions, and family relationships.

Remembering Korea, 1950: A Boy Soldier's Story by H. K. Shin (176 pp.)
The author was only 16 when he lied about his age in order to serve in the Republic of Korea army during the first months of the Korean War; he only did so for food, shelter, and water. Shin retains his humanity throughout the destruction of his country and provides us with a view on the war devoid of political bias.

Children's Stories

The Korean Cinderella by Shirley Climo (48 pp.)
In Korea, there are half a dozen versions of Cinderella. In Climo's rendition, Pear Blossom is visited by a Tokgabis, a benevolent goblin who rescues her from her jealous stepmother.

The Green Frogs: A Korean Folktale by Yumi Heo (32 pp.)
In Korea it is said that "children who don't listen to their mother are called *chung-gaeguri*, or green frogs." In this tale, two frog brothers always do the opposite of what their mother tells them. In the end, they learn their lesson the hard way.

Korean Children's Favorite Stories by Kim So-un (95 pp.)
This is an updated and newly illustrated version of 13 authentic Korean tales, originally published in 1955 as *Story Bag: A Collection of Korean Folk Tales*.

Poetry Resources

Sunset in a Spider Web: Sijo Poetry of Ancient Korea by Virginia Olsen Baron (82 pp.)

Notes From the Divided Country by Suji Kwock Kim and Sue Kwock Kim (80 pp.)
Anthology of Korean Poetry: From the Earliest Era to the Present edited by Peter H. Lee. (196 pp.)

Looking for the Cow: Modern Korean Poems edited by Kevin O'Rourke (168 pp.)

Classics

Kuunmong: The Cloud Dream of the Nine by Manjung Kim and translated by James S. Gale (252 pp.)

The Descendants of Cain by Hwong Sun-Won and translated by Suh Ji-Moon and Julie Pickering (181 pp.)

PHILIPPINES

Film Titles

Imelda (2004, Not rated), documentary with Imelda Marcos as herself (1 hr. 43 mins.)

Fiction

When the Rainbow Goddess Wept by Cecilia Manguerra Brainard (272 pp.)
     During the World War II Japanese invasion of the Philippines, 9-year-old Yvonne and her family escape to the jungle only to witness brutal killings. Her friend Laydan helps her cope by telling ancient Filipino folktales, which Yvonne commits to memory to help her sleep at night. Imagining herself as the strong woman in each tale helps her manage her fear when her father joins the resistance movement.

Beyond Paradise by Jane Hertenstein (165 pp.)

American Son by B. A. Roley (216 pp.)
     Gabe is a half Filipino and half Caucasian American who is torn between pleasing his mother and following the gangster path of his older brother. While Tomas engages in dangerous activities, Gabe's mother tries to ignore the letters from her brother, who wants the boys to return to a more disciplined life in the Phillipines. Eventually, Gabe takes a trip that changes his perception of himself and his relationship with his mother.

Nonfiction

The Laughter of My Father by Carlos Bulosan (152 pp.)
     This novel, considered by many a classic, may be hard to find. Written as a series of short tales, each of the 24 stories revolves around the author's father, Simeon. In many of the tales, the family finds humor in their struggles to survive in the economically unstable Philippines.

Nine Thousand Miles to Adventure: The Story of an American Boy in the Philippines by John P. Santacroce (210 pp.)
     John, whose family moves to the Philippines with his military father, describes his experiences in vivid detail. John's adventures include encounters with a python, kidnappers, and an unexploded bomb. This story will keep

readers turning the pages as they also learn more about the differences between American and Filipino cultures.

Children's Stories

Rockabye Crocodile: A Folktale from the Philippines by Jose Aruego and illustrated by Ariane Dewey (32 pp.)
This retelling of an old fable is about two boars, one who's considerate and the other who's selfish. Each separately attempts to help a crocodile and her baby, and each experiences very different results.

Filipino Children's Favorite Stories by Liana Elena Romulo and Joanne de Leon (94 pp.)
This collection of 13 classic Filipino folktales includes "The Hermit and the Two Worms," the tale of a hermit crab scolded by two magical worms for his lack of concern for the land. The hermit transforms the worms into people so that they can educate others about the need to preserve the land. The worms eventually have to decide for themselves between money and nature.

Poetry Resources

Returning a Borrowed Tongue: An Anthology of Filipino and Filipino American Poetry edited by Nick Carb (238 pp.)

Crossing the Snow Bridge by Fatima Lim-Wilson (105 pp.)

Classics

America Is in the Heart by Carlos Bulosan (327 pp.)

Noli Me Tangere [Touch Me Not] by Jose Rizal (480 pp.)

THAILAND

Film Titles

Anna and the King (2000, PG-13), starring Chow Yun-Fat, Jodie Foster, and Bai Ling (2 hrs. 27 mins.) This is a remake of the 1946 film *Anna and the King of Siam*, starring Irene Dunne and Rex Harrison.

Bridge on the River Kwai (1957, PG-13), starring William Holden, Jack Hawkins, and Alec Guinness (2 hrs. 41 mins.)

Return from the River Kwai (1989, PG-13), starring Nick Tate, Timothy Bottoms, and George Takei (1 hr. 41 mins.)

Fiction

Rice Without Rain by Minfong Ho (256 pp.)
Rural Thailand was in conflict with its military dictatorship during the 1970s. Seventeen-year-old Jinda and her father must pay half of their harvest for rent. Four university students from Bangkok visit the poor rice-farming villagers, telling them they must resist such payments. Jinda's father agrees, and his decision disrupts Jinda's life forever. The book is dedicated to those killed at Thammasart University on October 6, 1976.

Test by William Sleator (298 pp.)
Even though Lep is from Thailand and has limited English proficiency, he still must pass the XCAS high-stakes test or be destined for a life of poverty. With the help of another student, Lep discovers the truth about the test and helps expose its creators for the criminals they are.

Nonfiction

Thailand: The Golden Kingdom by William Warren and Luca Invernizzi Tettoni (96 pp.)
Although born and raised in the United States, William Warren has spent more than 30 years in Thailand. Using numerous photographs to help capture the beauty of the place and its people, Warren conveys Thailand's rich diversity.

Ten Lives of the Buddha by Elizabeth Wray, Clare Rosenfield, and Dorothy Bailey (153 pp.)
These authors use photographs of Siamese temple paintings to explain 10 of the most popular Jataka tales—stories of wisdom and morals based on the incarnations of Buddha.

Children's Story

Hush! A Thai Lullaby by Minfong Ho (32 pp.)
A mother asks many noisy animals, in turn, to keep quiet so that her baby can sleep. Once they all become quiet, the mother finally falls asleep, but the baby awakes.

Poetry Resource

A Promise for Siam by Tom Radzienda (105 pp.)

Classic

Four Reigns by Kukrit Pramoj and translated by Tulachandra (663 pp.)

TURKEY

Film Titles

The Accidental Spy (2001, PG-13), starring Jackie Chan and Eric Tsang (1 hr. 27 mins.)

Crossing the Bridge: The Sound of Istanbul (2006, Not rated), documentary (1 hr. 30 mins.)

Gallipoli (1981, PG), starring Mel Gibson, Mark Lee, and Harold Hopkins (1 hr. 50 mins.)

Fiction

Against the Storm by Gaye Hicyilmaz (200 pp.)
　　Based on a story reported in the Turkish Press. The author tells about Mehmet and his parents' quest for a better life in the capital city of Ankara. As they soon find out, things aren't any better there than in their home village and are, in some ways, worse because they become beholden to a mean uncle.

Nonfiction

The Other Side of the Mountain by Erendiz Atasu and translated by Elizabeth Malsen (283 pp.)
　　From memoirs, poems, love letters, and journals left by her mother, Atasu pieces together the history of her family. As she learns about her heritage Atasu sees how the country's history shaped her family's belief system. This work earned Turkey's most valued literary prize.

Children's Stories

The Hungry Coat by Demi (40 pp.)
　　Nasrettin Hoca (1208–1284) was a teacher who's often a main character in Turkish folktales. In this tale, while en route to a banquet, Nasrettin soils his coat when he helps some villagers who are having problems with a goat. Shunned by people at the banquet, Nasrettin leaves, bathes, and returns in a clean coat, which he stuffs with food. Readers will enjoy his witty replies.

Folk Tales of Turkey by Somnath Dhar (124 pp.)

This collection of 12 traditional Turkish folktales includes "Orhan and Ayesha." Orhan, a young Turkish prince, falls in love with Ayesha and asks for her hand in marriage. When Orhan disappears, the dishonorable Kara Kaptan takes advantage of the situation and tries to take Ayesha as his own bride.

Poetry Resource

Nightingales and Pleasure Gardens: Turkish Love Poems edited by Talat S. Halman and Jayne L. Warner (159 pp.)

Classics

The Book of Dede Korkut: A Turkish Epic by Anonymous (168 pp.)

Memed My Hawk by Kemal Yashar (392 pp.)

VIETNAM

Film Titles

Mai's America (2002, Not rated), PBS documentary (1 hr. 12 mins.)
Three Seasons (1999, PG-13), starring Don Duong, Nguyen Ngoc Hiep, and Tran Manh Cuong (II) (1 hr. 50 mins.)

Fiction

Monkey Bridge by Lan Cao (272 pp.)

This semi-autobiographical novel is told by Mai Ngyuen, who was already safely in the United States when the Communists invaded Saigon on April 30, 1975, the day her mother was flown out. Her mother decides they will live in Washington, D.C., because she believes it is the "safest place on earth" and does her best to surround them with everything she can from Vietnam. Unfortunately, Mai doesn't feel part of either culture.

Shadow of the Dragon by Sherry Garland (314 pp.)

Sixteen-year-old Danny Vo lives with his extended family in the United States. Life changes dramatically when Sang Le, a cousin who spent time as a prisoner in a Vietnamese reeducation camp and then as a refugee in Hong Kong, comes to America to live with them. Sang Le gets involved with a dangerous Vietnamese gang, whereas Danny is more interested in getting involved with Tiffany Schultz. Unbeknown to Danny, however, Tiffany's older brother is a member of a White supremacist skinhead gang. Fans of Garland might want to read *Song of the Buffalo Boy* (288 pp.), about the aftereffects of the Vietnam War.

Jason's Women by Jean Davies O'Kimoto (224 pp.)
Awkward and shy 16-year-old Jason answers a newspaper ad and goes to work for an eccentric 80-year-old woman named Bertha Jane Filmore. Thao Nguyen, a young Vietnamese refugee girl who is staying with Bertha, helps Jason stretch his ability to communicate.

Goodbye, Vietnam by Gloria Whelan (144 pp.)
Thirteen-year-old Mai and her family leave their small Vietnamese rice village by taking a rickety boat to Hong Kong in the hope of finding a better life there. They seem to be jumping out of the frying pan and into the fire as they endure a harsh sea voyage only to be placed in a detention camp when they reach land.

Nonfiction

When Heaven and Earth Changed Places by Le Ly Hayslip (400 pp.)
Le Ly was 12 years old when the Vietnam War began. By the time Le Ly was 16, she'd survived starvation, imprisonment, torture, rape, and the deaths of family members. Le Ly tells her tragic story in flashbacks as she returns to visit her family in Vietnam 20 years later.

Vietnam: Journeys of Body, Mind, and Spirit edited by Nguyen Van Huy and Laurel Kendall (303 pp.)
This book takes readers on a journey through 21st century Vietnam, devoting chapters to art, literature, pottery, dress, architecture, celebrations, holidays, and traditions.

Children's Story

Children of the Dragon: Selected Tales From Vietnam by Sherry Garland (64 pp.)
An introduction to the history of Vietnam is followed by six traditional folktales and an explanation of how each tale relates to Vietnamese culture.

Poetry Resource

Black Dog, Black Night: Contemporary Vietnamese Poetry by Nguyen Do and Paul Hoover (272 pp.)

Classics

Dumb Luck by Vu Trong Phung and translated by Nguyen Nguyet Cam (189 pp.)

The Tale of Kieu by Du Nguyen and translated by Huynh Sanh Thong (256 pp.)

CARIBBEAN ISLANDS

BAHAMAS, BARBADOS, CAYMAN ISLANDS, AND ST. LUCIA

Film Titles

After the Sunset (2004, PG-13), starring Pierce Brosnan, Salma Hayek, and Woody Harrelson (1 hr. 37 mins.)

Casino Royale (2006, PG-13), starring Daniel Craig and Judi Dench (2 hrs. 24 mins.)

Hurricane Ivan: A Cayman Experience (2004, Not rated), documentary (50 mins.)

Pirates of the Caribbean: Curse of the Black Pearl (2003, PG-13), starring Johnny Depp, Keira Knightley, Geoffrey Rush, Orlando Bloom, (2 hrs. 13 mins.)

Fiction

A Caribbean Mystery by Agatha Christie (227 pp.)
    Written in 1964, this classic murder mystery features Miss Marple, who is trying to find out who killed Major Palgrave.

The Cay by Theodore Taylor (144 pp.)
    The Cay, pronounced "The Key" by islanders, is about the adventures of young, privileged Phillip, who has always looked down on dark-skinned people. Things change, however, when he is stranded on a small Caribbean Island with a Black man.

Cayman Gold by Richard Trout (212 pp.)
    Three teenagers—Chris, R. O., and Heather MacGregor—are visiting the Cayman Islands because their father, a zoologist, is working to protect the islands' environment. When the courageous scuba-diving teens discover pirates whose search for gold is destroying the reef, it's survival of the fittest.

Nonfiction

A History of the Cayman Islands by Neville Williams (96 pp.)
Williams writes about pirates hiding their gold in the bluffs of Cayman Brac and tells how the islands got their name. He also describes the significance of the turtle to their culture and how the islanders have survived so many hurricanes.

Children's Stories

An Evening in Guanima: A Treasury of Folktales From the Bahamas (2nd ed.) by Patricia Glinton-Meicholas (159 pp.)
Bahamian folktales, derived primarily from the islanders' African heritage, are meant to be performed. In this collection of tales that feature magical drums, ghosts, obedient and disobedient children, heroes, tricksters, and birds that assume human form, poetic justice prevails.

My Grandpa and the Sea by Katherine Orr (32 pp.)
Grandpa lives on the Caribbean Island of St. Lucia and teaches his granddaughter Lila lessons about appreciation. He's an island fishermen who makes his living the old way—the nongreedy way.

CUBA

Film Titles

American Experience: Fidel Castro (2005, Not rated), documentary (2 hrs.).

Cuba Story, 1953 (2002, Not rated), documentary (50 mins.)

Dirty Dancing: Havana Nights (2004, PG-13), starring Romola Garai and Diego Luna (1 hr. 26 mins.)

Fidel: The Untold Story (2003, Not rated), starring Fidel Castro and Harry Belafonte (1 hr. 31 mins.)

Thirteen Days (2001, PG-13), starring Bruce Greenwood and Kevin Costner (2 hrs. 27 mins.)

Fiction

Raining Sardines by Enrique Flores-Galbis (176 pp.)
Set in pre-Castro Cuba, this is the story of two girls determined to protect

wild horses from a wealthy landowner who's running the horses off the land to make way for a coffee plantation—or so he says.

From Amigos to Friends by Pelayo "Pete" Garcia (242 pp.)
Set during the Cuban Revolution and based on historical fact, this coming-of-age story tells how three friends--David, Carlos, and Luis--grow up quickly when they must go into exile and become refugees.

Heat by Mike Lupica (220 pp.)
Michael Arroyo is the star pitcher of his little league team. Jealous rivals start a rumor that he is older than 12, which causes a big problem when Michael cannot produce a birth certificate. Because his Papi died of a heart attack after they fled Cuba, Michael must take care of his younger brother. What will social services do?

Cuba 15 by Nancy Osa (304 pp.)
The daughter of a Cuban father and a Polish mother, Violat Paz knows her 15th birthday is going to be different. Her Cuban grandparents are coming to visit, so Violet's having a *quinceanera* party, even though she's not familiar with Cuban traditions.

Cubanita by Gaby Triana (208 pp.)
Seventeen-year-old Isabel Díaz is ready to leave her Miami home to attend college in the fall and be the American girl she is, but her Mami pushes her to focus on her Cuban heritage and home—in its truest sense!

Flight to Freedom by Ana Veciana-Suarez (224 pp.)
This novel is based on 13-year-old Yara's actual diary accounts of fleeing from Castro's Cuba and transitioning to the American way of life in the late 1960s.

Nonfiction

Next Year in Cuba: A Cubano's Coming of Age in America by Gustavo Pérez Firmat (213 pp.)
Gustavo Perez Firmat and his entire family escaped from Cuba when Castro came into power in 1959. The book starts when he is 11 years old and living in Dade County, Florida, and continues through his graduation from college, his marriage, and their rearing of his "ABCs"—American Born Cubans!

Hemingway in Cuba by Hilary Hemingway and Carlene Brennan (288 pp.)
Ernest Hemingway's niece Hilary partners with Carlene Brennan to give

readers a view of the life Hemingway lived in Cuba from 1928 to 1954.

Exiled Memories: A Cuban Childhood by Pablo Medina (135 pp.)
    Pablo Medina arrived in the United States at age 12 when his family fled the Castro regime in 1960. As an adult, he recalls his ideal childhood in Cuba in an effort to make sense of its revolution.

Children's Stories

Cuban Kids by George Ancona (40 pp.)
    Photos of kids in their regular routines make this nonfiction book about life in Cuba meaningful.

Martina the Beautiful Cockroach: A Cuban Folktale by Carmen Agra Deedy and
    illustrated by Michael Austin (32 pp.)
    It's time for Martina Josefina Catalina Cucaracha, a beautiful 21-day-old cockroach living in Old Havana, to marry. She's told that hot coffee will lure a husband, but nothing turns out right until Perez the mouse responds.

Poetry Resources

Cool Salsa: Bilingual Poems on Growing Up Latino in the United States (Sandra M. Castillo, Oscar Hijuelos, Carolina Hospital, Pablo Medina, Berta G. Montalvo, & E. J. Vega, poets) edited by Lori M. Carlson (160 pp.)

Cubanisimo!: The Vintage Book of Contemporary Cuban Literature edited by Cristina Garcia (400 pp.)

Classics

Jose Marti: Selected Writings translated by Esther Allen (496 pp.)

Islands in the Stream by Ernest Hemingway (448 pp.)

HAITI

Film Titles

The Agronomist (2001, PG-13), documentary (1 hr. 30 mins.)

The Man by the Shore (1993, Not rated), starring Jennifer Zubar, Toto Bissainthe, Jean-Michel Martial, Patrick Rameau, and Mireille Metellus (1 hr. 45 mins.)

Port-au-Prince Is Mine (2000, Not rated), documentary (57 mins.)

Fiction

Anacaona: Golden Flower, Haiti, 1490 by Edwidge Danticat (192 pp.)
   In 15th century Haiti, there lived a young, beautiful queen named Anacaona who gracefully ruled the Tainos until the Spanish conquistadors arrived and brought much devastation.

Behind the Mountains by Edwidge Danticat (166 pp.)
   Celine's father left the family in Haiti to make a better life for all of them in New York. After 5 years, the family is finally reunited. Thirteen-year-old Celine records in her diary her experiences adjusting to a new way of life.

Fresh Girl by Jaira Placide (216 pp.)
   Mardi, a Haitian American 14-year-old, is dealing with an awful lot these days. She can handle the teasing and a certain boy, but it's what happened to her while she was living in Haiti with her grandmother during a military coup that's making her behave strangely.

Tonight, by Sea by Frances Temple (160 pp.)
   Paulie is a young girl living in Belle Fleuve with her uncle and Grann Adeline. After the military overthrow of Jean-Bertrand Aristide, the Macoutes, or bad men, are wreaking terror all across the country. Her uncle decides to build a boat—rather than so many coffins—so that they can flee to "Mee-ay-mee" (Miami) for safety.

Nonfiction

Restavec by Jean-Robert Cadet (304 pp.)
   Parents who agreed to let their child read Mathabane's (1986) *Kaffir Boy* might consider allowing their child to read this book, which tells a story just as horrifying. *Restavecs* are young Haitian slaves who are denied education, dignity, and love. Jean-Robert escaped his life as a *restavec* and lived to tell about it in this autobiography that shows the importance of education.

Children's Stories

The Magic Orange Tree and Other Haitian Folktales edited by Diane Wolkstein (224 pp.)
   This collection of 27 folktales includes "The Magic Orange Tree," a story about a girl and her evil stepmother.

Selavi, That Is Life: A Haitian Story of Hope by Landowne Youme (40 pp.)

     Selavi is a homeless boy living on the streets of Port-au-Prince. With the help of a church, he and other street children build a "home" and radio station, where they can care for themselves and others.

Poetry Resources

Open Gate: An Anthology of Haitian Creole Poetry edited by Paul Laraque and Jack Hirschman (235 pp.)

When the Tom-Tom Beats: Selected Prose and Poetry by Jacques Roumain (109 pp.)

Classics

Krik? Krak! by Edwidge Danticat (240 pp.)

Masters of the Dew by Jacques Roumain (188 pp.)

JAMAICA

Film Titles

Bob Marley and The Wailers: The Bob Marley Story (1984, Not rated), documentary (1 hr. 4 mins.)

Cool Runnings (1993, PG), starring John Candy, Doug E. Doug, Leon, Malik Yoba, and Rawle Lewis (1 hr.38 mins.)

Marcus Garvey: Look for Me in the Whirlwind (2001, Not rated), documentary (1hr. 30 mins.)

Fiction

A Jamaican Storyteller's Tale by Lorrimer Burford (164 pp.)

     Cecil and his family leave Jamaica and go to Florida to work in the sugarcane fields around Okeechobee. Cecil loves to hear his father's storytelling, but his mother wants him to learn proper English and attend school.

Abeng by Michelle Cliff (176 pp.)

     Twelve-year-old Clare Savage begins to consider what it means to be raised by multiracial parents in Jamaica. Her father is White and extremely prejudiced; her mother is mixed, but yields to her husband's opinions. Because Clare is light, she is treated differently than her darker best friend.

Pirates! by Celia Rees (340 pp.)

This award-winning novel will keep the most reluctant reader turning the pages with its swashbuckling adventures of two girls. One the daughter of a rich merchant and the other a daughter of a Jamaican plantation slave, the girls disguise themselves as pirates for an 18th-century adventure of a lifetime.

Every Time a Rainbow Dies by Rita Williams-Garcia (176 pp.)

For mature readers only, this is the story of 16-year-old Thulani, who witnesses a rape and assists the victim. Thulani is also dealing with the fact that his mother, ill with cancer, has decided to leave their New York home and return to their native Jamaica to die.

Nonfiction

Slipstream: A Daughter Remembers by Rachel Manley (304 pp.)

Michael Manly was the prime minister of Jamaica for 11 years during the 1970s and 1980s and is associated with Jamaica's independence. This is his story as told by his daughter, Rachel, whose recollections begin when she is 8 years old and continue through her adulthood.

The Gathering of the Healers by Robert and Julia Roskind (304 pp.)

Don't let the length of this book intimidate you. In response to Jamaica's increase in violence, these authors challenged all Jamaicans to embrace Bob Marley's message of One Love. After encouraging Jamaica to heal itself with love and forgiveness, they watched the murder rate in Jamaica drop by 20%.

Children's Stories

Doctor Bird: Three Lookin' Up Tales From Jamaica by Gerald Hausman and Ashley Wolff (40 pp.)

These three tales feature Doctor Bird, a rainbow-winged hummingbird found only in Jamaica and revered in the Jamaican culture. Jamaica's national bird, Doctor Bird is believed to have magical powers and to use tricks to teach lessons to animals.

Anancy the Spider Man by Philip M. Sherlock and illustrated by Marcia Brown (96 pp.)

This collection includes 15 Jamaican folktales about Anancy, a clever arachnid who is the protagonist of many Jamaican folktales. It is believed that these stories were brought to Jamaica by storytelling African slaves.

J Is for Jamaica by Benjamin Zephaniah (32 pp.)
   In this ABC book about Jamaican culture, C is for "cricket" and U is for "ugli fruit."

Poetry Resource

Selected Poems of Claude McKay by Claude McKay (110 pp.)

Classics

Brother Man by Roger Mais (191 pp.)
The Hills Were Joyful Together by Roger Mais (304 pp.)

PUERTO RICO

Film Titles

Boricua Beisbol (Major League Baseball): The Passion of Puerto Rico (2003, Not rated), documentary (1 hr. 25 mins.)
Memories of Puerto Rico (2007, Not rated), video and photos (1 hr. 11 mins.)

Fiction

Call Me Maria by Judith Ortiz Cofer (144 pp.)
   Born and raised in Puerto Rico, Maria finds her world gets rattled when she joins her father in a New York barrio where she's introduced to a new language—Spanglish.

The Meaning of Consuelo by Judith Ortiz Cofer (185 pp.)
   Consuelo, whose name means comfort and consolation, is the elder of two girls growing up in Puerto Rico in the 1950s. Consuelo constantly has to take care of her little sister Milagros, who actively brings drama into their lives. Their mother tries to live by tradition, and their father is enamored by the glamour of the United States. Both Consuelo and her country must learn independence.

Going Home by Nicholasa Mohr (192 pp.)
   Although Felita is Puerto Rican by blood, she is American by birth. When the opportunity arises for her to spend an entire summer with her uncle in Puerto Rico, Felita jumps at the chance. Felita is both glad and sad when she must return to New York. Readers might want to read its prequel, *Felita* (112 pp.), in which she must adjust to a new American neighborhood where she

gets teased for her ethnicity.

Emily Goldberg Learns to Salsa by Micol Ostow (288 pp.)
Years before Emily was born, her mother left Puerto Rico to pursue an education in New York and never looked back. There was no reason for her to return to her homeland until her mother—the grandmother that Emily has never known—passes away. Emily accompanies her mother to the funeral and spends a life-changing summer in Puerto Rico, learning about the culture and her family's secrets, past and present.

Nonfiction

Silent Dancing: A Part Remembrance of a Puerto Rican Childhood by Judith Ortiz
Cofer (168 pp.)
Ortiz Cofer uses essays and poems to tell her story. Because her father is in the U.S. Navy, Judith and her family shuttle between a village in Puerto Rico and a high-rise "barrio" in Paterson, New Jersey. Such is the life of young Judith as she dances between two cultures.

When I Was Puerto Rican by Esmeralda Santiago (288 pp.)
In this memoir, Esmeralda recollects growing up in rural Puerto Rico with her discontented parents and seven siblings. Seeking a better economic life in America, the family moves to its *abuela's* (grandmother's) house in New York City. Esmeralda attends a school where teachers don't know how to teach a teenager who knows no English. Its sequel, *Almost a Woman* (336 pp.), picks up where she left off, covering her early teen years to just days before her 21st birthday.

Pride of Puerto Rico: The Life of Roberto Clemente by Paul Robert Walker (176 pp.)
Walker captures the country's pride in a boy who becomes a great baseball player in spite of growing up having to use a stick as a bat and a ball made of rags. While touring with the Pittsburgh Pirates, all was not fun and games for Roberto as he experienced prejudice for the first time.

Children's Stories

The Golden Flower: A Taino Myth From Puerto Rico by Nina Jaffe and illustrated by Enrique O. Sanchez (32 pp.)
A Taino Indian tells the story of how Puerto Rico was created. There was nothing until a boy planted a seed on top of a mountain,.

Juan Bobo and the Horse of Seven Colors: A Puerto Rican Legend by Jan Mike and illustrated by Charles Reasoner (32 pp.)

According to the author, "Juan Bobo stories were told by the jibaros to make fun of the often pompous and silly behavior of the aristocratic Spanish rulers and the Puerto Ricans who imitated them." In this case, Juan Bobo (John Fool) captures a magical horse of seven colors. In exchange for his freedom, the horse gives Juan Bobo seven magical tail hairs that have the power to grant wishes. How Juan Bobo uses his wishes will make even a princess laugh.

Poetry Resources

Cool Salsa: Bilingual Poems on Growing Up Latino in the United States (Judith Ortiz Cofer, Pedro Pietri, & Johanna Vega) edited by Lori M. Carlson (160 pp.)

The Year of Our Revolution: New and Selected Stories and Poems by Judith Ortiz Cofer (128 pp.)

Classics

The Labyrinth by Enrique A. Laguerre (275 pp.)
Down These Mean Streets by Piri Thomas (352 pp.)
La Charca [*The Pond*] by Manuel Zeno-Gandia (216 pp.)

EUROPE

BOSNIA

Film Title

Grbavica (Esma's Secret): The Land of My Dreams (2007, Not rated), starring Mirjana Karanovic (II), Luna Mijovic, and Leon Lucev (1 hr. 30 mins.) . English subtitles.

Fiction

Under the Sun by Arthur Dorros (224 pp.)
While reading about 13-year-old Ehmet's struggle to survive in war-torn Sarajevo in the early 1990s, readers might make the connection between this war and the Holocaust.

Nonfiction

Zlata's Diary by Zlata Filipovic (208 pp.)

Zlata Filipovic starts her diary in the fifth grade and continues making entries for 2 years. Beginning in September 1991, she writes about what life is like for her and her family during the war.

Sarajevo Days, Sarajevo Nights by Elma Softic (200 pp.)
Sarajevo native Elma Softic writes her first entry in April 1992 and continues chronicling what life is like for her and her family during the war.

Children's Stories

A Bosnian Family by Robin Landew Silverman (64 pp.)
Many pictures illustrate this true story about the Duspers, a Bosnian family that leaves its country to seek refuge in Grand Forks, North Dakota. The Yugoslavian fairy tale "Bas Celik" is also included.

Gleam and Glow by Eve Bunting (32 pp.)
Based on a true story. Bunting tells of 8-year-old Viktor and how two little goldfish offer hope in a country torn by civil war.

Poetry Resources

Heart of Darkness: Poems by Ferida Durakovic (109 pp.)

Sarajevo Blues by Semezdin Mehmedinovic (122 pp.)

The Horse Has Six Legs: An Anthology of Serbian Poetry edited by Charles Simic (224 pp.)

Classic

Sarajevo Marlboro by Miljenko Jergovic (180 pp.)

CZECHOSLOVAKIA

Film Titles

Kafka (1991, PG-13), starring Jeremy Irons, Theresa Russell, and Joel Grey (1 hr. 45 mins.)

Prague Spring (1999, Not rated), documentary (1 hr. 21 mins.)

The White Dove (Bila Holubice) (1960, Not rated), starring Gustav Puttjer (1 hr. 7 mins.)

Fiction

The Book of Jude by Kimberly Heuston (217 pp.)
Jude is not your typical American teenager. She is as brilliant as her mother, who, after receiving a fellowship to study in Prague, decides to relocate the entire family. Jude feels isolated and threatened and is fighting the onset of mental illness. The story is set against the backdrop of the Soviet invasion in August 1968.

Rivka's Way by Teri Kanefield (137 pp.)
Set in 1778, this is the story of 15-year-old Rivka Liebermann, who wants to see more than the Jewish ghetto. After she finds out about her arranged marriage to Oskar Kara, she decides to risk everything by disguising herself as a Christian boy and venturing into Prague by herself.

The Three Golden Keys by Peter Sis (64 pp.)
The author is magically transported to Prague, but his old home is locked by three huge padlocks. As he tries to find the keys, he is told three ancient tales: one about the knight Bruncvik, one about the Golem, and one about the clockmaker Master Hanus.

Nonfiction

The Twelve Little Cakes by Dominika Dery (349 pp.)
In this memoir, the author pens her life's story beginning at age 4, when she sees a performance of *Swan Lake* and dreams of becoming a ballet dancer. She also tells about her family's difficult life during the Communist Revolution in Prague, where her parents are considered outlaws .

The Czech Americans: The Immigrant Experience by Stephanie Saxon-Ford (106 pp.)
This simply written book is about the Czechs who emigrated from their country beginning in the 1800s and follows their struggles and triumphs adjusting to a new life in North America.

The Wall: Growing Up Behind the Iron Curtain by Peter Sis (56 pp.)
Using drawings to help tell his story, Sis writes about growing up in Prague under Communist rule.

Children's Stories

Madlenka's Dog by Peter Sis (32 pp.)
Little Madlenka wants a dog more than anything in the whole world.

When she figures her parents won't let her have one, she decides to take her imaginary dog for a walk around her block and comes home with a few surprises.

Golem by David Wisniewski (32 pp.)
The Jews of 16th-century Prague are being mercilessly persecuted as a result of the blood lie. During that time, hostile gentiles claimed that Jews mixed the blood of Christian children with the flour and water of matzo. To save his people, a rabbi uses magical powers to conjure from clay a *golem*, an artificial human being in Hebrew folklore that is endowed with life. This story is believed to be the inspiration for Mary Shelley's *Frankenstein*.

Poetry Resources

The Poetry of Jaroslav Seifert edited by George Gibian (255 pp.)
I Never Saw Another Butterfly by Hana Volavkova (128 pp.)

Classics

My Antonia by Willa Cather (298 pp.)

The Metamorphosis by Franz Kafka (224 pp.)

Valerie and Her Weeks of Wonders by Vitezslav Nezval and translated by David Short (185 pp.)

IRELAND

Film Titles

The Bells of St. Mary's (1946, G), starring Bing Crosby and Ingrid Bergman (2 hrs. 6 mins.)

The McCourts of New York (1999, Not rated), starring the McCourt brothers: Malachy, Frank, Alphie, and Mike (1 hr. 16 mins.)

Waking Ned Devine (1998, PG), starring Ian Bannen, David Blake Kelly, and Fionnula Flanagan (1 hr. 31 mins.)

Fiction

Reading in the Dark by Seamus Deane (213 pp.)
An Irish boy begins his story in 1945 by telling a family secret: his mother sees ghosts. In reality, his mother is haunted by the memory of her brother,

Uncle Eddie, an Irish Republican Army gunman who was blown up in a distillery in 1922 for being an informer. The narrator's quest is to find out the truth about his uncle's death.

The Commitments by Roddy Doyle (176 pp.)
   Inspired by James Brown and Otis Redding recordings, a group of Irish teenagers decide to bring "soul" to Dublin by starting their own band. After a brief period of fame, they pay a heavy price, which begs the question—was it worth it? (Note: There is an R-rated movie version of this book.)

Paddy Clarke, Ha Ha Ha by Roddy Doyle (288 pp.)
   Ten-year-old Patrick is adept at getting into mischief in this humorous coming-of-age story set in Dublin. Paddy's explanations for his working-class parents' arguments are both moving and poignant.

The Gift of the Pirate Queen by Patricia Reilly Giff (192 pp.)
   Since Grace O'Malley's mother passed away, she's been in charge of caring for her father and her diabetic little sister. Cousin Fiona is coming all of the way from Ireland to help, but Grace doesn't want things to change, even if things aren't going so well.

Nonfiction

Angela's Ashes by Frank McCourt (288 pp.)
   Frank McCourt had a rough childhood, growing up with an alcoholic father who had many mouths to feed. Excerpts from the film version (released in 2000, rated R for profanity and nudity) could be shown, using your own discretion.

Children's Story

Tales for the Telling: Irish Folk and Fairy Stories by Edna O'Brien (127 pp.)
   Twelve classic Irish tales are included, among them "Two Giants." Finn was the biggest and bravest giant in all of Ireland, but he used his brains to trick Scotland's giant McConigle to leave without a fight. What he does will amuse readers.

Poetry Resources

An Anthology of Irish Literature edited by David H. Greene (288 pp.)
Ireland in Poetry edited by Charles Sullivan (208 pp.)

Classics

The Dubliners by James Joyce (190 pp.)
Dracula by Bram Stoker (336 pp.)
Gulliver's Travels by Jonathan Swift (336 pp.)
The Importance of Being Earnest by Oscar Wilde (76 pp.)

NETHERLANDS

Nonfiction

The Last Seven Months of Anne Frank by Willy Lindwer (256 pp.)
While making the documentary film of the same name, Lindwer interviews six people who met Anne Frank either during childhood, at school, or in the concentration camps. These interview transcripts give readers a glimpse of Anne as those who knew her saw her.

POLAND

Film Titles

Ladies in Lavender (2005, PG-13), starring Maggie Smith and Judi Dench (1 hr. 44 mins.)

Louder Than Bombs (2001, Not rated), starring Rafal Mackowiak, Sylwia Juszckzak, Madalena Schejbal (1 hr. 32 mins.)

Fiction

A Coal Miner's Bride: The Diary of Anetka Kaminska by Susan Campbell Bartoletti (224 pp.)
This fictional account of a 13-year-old girl's life in the late 1800s gives an accurate account of Polish immigration to Pennsylvania's coal-mining towns. Anetka's Tata (her father) has promised her hand in marriage to an old coal miner who can bring her family to America for a better life.

Rodzina by Karen Cushman (215 pp.)
In the late 1800s, Rodzina Clara Jadwiga Anastazya Brodski escapes Poland at the age of 2 with her parents. Later, orphaned and living in streets in Chicago, she is herded into an orphan train headed west. To comfort the worried children, Rodzina tells them Polish folktales and stories about her family.

Eva Underground by Dandi Daley Mackall (256 pp.)

After her mother's death, Eva Lott must make a drastic change during her senior year. Her father has decided to move the family from the comfort of the Chicago suburbs to behind the Iron Curtain in Poland. Set in 1978, this novel gives readers interesting historical information about Nobel Peace Prize winner Lech Walesa, the Solidarity Movement, and the election of Pope John Paul II, the first Polish Pope. Others will enjoy reading about Eva's romance, which makes her want to stay in this foreign land.

Nonfiction

Alicia: My Story by Alicia Appleman-Jurman (448 pp).

This autobiography is Alicia's account of Germany's invasion of Poland during World War II. As a young Jewish girl growing up in Buczacz, Poland, Alicia's life goes from normal to horrific; She survived the deaths of her entire family.

The Cage by Ruth Minsky Sender (224 pp.)

Riva Minska recalls growing up in the Lodz ghetto in Poland during the Holocaust. First her mother, then Riva and her younger brothers are taken to the death camps. Riva survives. For readers interested in how Riva rebuilds her life and immigrates to America, read the sequel, *To Life* (240 pp.)

Behind the Secret Window: A Memoir of a Hidden Childhood During World War Two by Nelly S. Toll (161 pp.)

Nelly went into hiding at the age of 6 when the Nazis took over her home town of Lvov, Poland, in 1941. Her artwork and journal are what saved her.

Poland in Pictures by Jeffrey Zuehlke (80 pp.)

This book of photographs of Poland is replete with images of its stunning cathedrals and landscapes. The book also provides information about the country's land, history, government, and people.

Children's Stories

Rechenka's Eggs by Patricia Polacco (32 pp.)

An old woman, known for painting beautiful eggs for the Easter Festival, finds a wounded goose that she names Rechenka. As Rechenka gains her strength, she accidentally destroys the old woman's creations and lays special eggs as a way to make amends for her mistake. One egg gives the old woman a very special gift.

Always Remember Me: How One Family Survived World War II by Marisabina Russo (48 pp.)

Poetry Resource

View With a Grain of Sand: Selected Poems by Wislawa Szymborska (224 pp.)

Classics

The Chosen by Chaim Potok (304 pp.)
Poland by James A. Michener (640 pp.)
Notes From the Warsaw Ghetto by Emmanuel Ringelblum (359 pp.)
On the Field of Glory by Henryk Sienkiewicz (255 pp.)

RUSSIA

Film Titles

Dr. Zhivago (2001, 1965, PG-13), starring Omar Sharif and Julie Christie (3 hrs. 20 mins.)

The Fiddler on the Roof (1971, G), starring Topol, Norma Crane, and Leonard Frey, (3 hrs.).

Fiction

One Way to Ansonia by Judie Angell (196 pp.)
Rose Olshansky is 10 years old when she leaves Russia to join her father in New York. Her father surprises his new wife with Rose and her four siblings on his wedding day! Only Rose's younger sister, Celia, is welcomed into his American home, and the rest are separated and sent to live with four different families. Set in the 1890s, the story follows Rose as she learns to make a better life for herself in this new country.

Sworn Enemies by Carol Matas (132 pp.)
Aaron is revered in his Russian community for his academic ability; Zev is jealous of Aaron's success. The two Russian Jews have numerous confrontations until both are forced to work together to escape forced military service.

Burying the Sun by Gloria Whelan (224 pp.)
As German troops approach Russia in 1941, 15-year-old Georgi and his family do all that they can to protect Leningrad and the beautiful artwork at

the Hermitage Museum. Readers who enjoy Whelan's writing might enjoy two other of her novels set in historic Russia, *Angel on the Square* (304 pp.) and *The Impossible Journey* (256 pp.), both of which have teen girls as protagonists.

Nonfiction

A Calendar of Wisdom by Leo Tolstoy (378 pp.)
    For 15 years, Tolstoy dreamed of collecting "the wisdom of the centuries in one book" for a general audience. Tolstoy draws on the greatest works of religion, philosophy, and literature to write a practical spiritual guide on how to find inner peace and live a life filled with kindness, satisfaction, and happiness. (Not a YA title.)

Children's Stories

The Frog Princess by Patrick J. Lewis (32 pp.)
    A tsar instructs each of his three sons to find a bride by shooting an arrow "deep into the heart of Russia." The arrow leads two of the brothers to find brides who are beauties, but the youngest son's arrow is found by a frog. As one might predict, the frog is actually a beautiful maiden who is under a spell that the tsar's youngest son must break. The art in the book captures the spirit of Russian folklore's Vasilisa the Wise, who was famed for her exquisite household skills, particularly her embroidery.

The Sea King's Daughter: A Russian Legend by Aaron Shepard (40 pp.)
    While playing his gusli (a type of harp) to keep the rich noble's guests dancing, poor Sadko is noticed by the Sea King, who asks him to play at the underwater palace. The Sea King is so impressed that he offers Sadko an amazing gift. However, if Sadko accepts the gift, it will cost him what he loves most in the world.

Poetry Resource

Stories and Prose Poems by Alexander Solzhenitsyn (267 pp.)

Classics

Crime and Punishment by Fyodor Dostoevsky (576 pp.)
A Day in the Life of Ivan Denisovich by Aleksandr Solzhenitsyn (160 pp.)
War and Peace by Leo Tolstoy (1,472 pp.)
We by Yevgeny Zamyatin (256 pp.)

SPAIN

Film Titles

Ascent to Heaven (1951, PG), starring Esteban Marquez and Victor Perez (1 hr. 15 mins.)

The Sea Inside (2004, PG-13), starring Javier Bardem, Belen Rueda, and Lola Duenas, (2 hrs. 5 mins.)

Fiction

The Alchemist: A Fable About Following Your Dream by Paulo Coelho (208 pp.)
   An Andalusian shepherd boy named Santiago dreams one night of treasure hidden in the Egyptian pyramids. He decides to leave his happy life in Spain and travel to Egypt to literally follow his dream. The author is Brazilian, and this fable has had huge appeal in Latin American countries.

Returning to A by Dorien Ross (168 pp.)
   This semi-autobiographical novel is the story of 16-year-old Loren. She wants Andalusian Gypsies to teach her to play flamenco guitar, which she thinks will help her deal with her brother's death. As she tries to master this classical musical form usually denied to women, this New Yorker must also sort out her almost immediate attraction to a certain Spaniard.

Nonfiction

Driving Over Lemons: An Optimist in Andalucia by Chris Stewart (272 pp.)
   Although not a young adult work, this humorous book by a former drummer of the rock band Genesis will appeal to teens. Chris and his wife leave their English home and move to a remote farmhouse in Granada, Spain.. What they expect to find and what they actually find are two very different things.

Children's Stories

The Three Golden Oranges by Alma Ada Flor and illustrated by Reg Cartwright (32 pp.)
   Three brothers—Santiago, Tomas, and Matias—visit an old woman to seek her advice about how to find brides. She gives them very specific directions to obtain three golden oranges and to work together to make their dreams come true. Their quest illustrates the value of loyalty and the consequences of being selfish. The author's note explains how oranges are a part

of Spain's history.

The Story of Ferdinand by Munro Leaf and illustrated by Robert Lawson (72 pp.)
This classic Spanish children's story is about a bull named Ferdinand who doesn't act like a bull is supposed to: He'd rather smell flowers than fight with a matador. During an unfortunate encounter with a bee, Ferdinand displays what the crowd has been waiting for.

Poetry Resources

Introduction to Spanish Poetry edited by Eugenio Florit (160 pp.)

Poet in New York: A Bilingual Edition by Federico Garcia Lorca and translated by Greg Simon and Steven F. White (288 pp.)

Classics

Don Quixote by Miguel de Cervantes and translated by Tobias Smollett (1,168 pp.)

The Sun Also Rises by Ernest Hemingway (256 pp.)

Tales of the Alhambra by Washington Irving (308 pp.)

The Celestina: A Fifteenth-Century Spanish Novel in Dialogue by Fernando de Rojas and translated by Lesley Byrd Simpson (162 pp.)

NORTH AMERICA
MEXICO

Film Titles

All the Pretty Horses (2002, PG-13), starring Matt Damon, Penélope Cruz, and Henry Thomas, (1 hr. 57 mins.)

Fun in Acapulco (1963, PG), starring Elvis Presley and Ursula Andress (1 hr. 37 mins.)

The Three Amigos (1986, PG), starring Chevy Chase, Steve Martin, and Martin Short (1 hr. 45 mins.)

Fiction

Bless Me, Última by Rudolfo Anaya (262 pp.)

Antonio Marez is growing up in New Mexico during the 1940s. He is torn between the traditions of his family and the American ways of his classmates. Ultima, a *curandera* (a traditional folk healer or shaman), mentors him in this coming-of-age story.

Leaving Tabasco by Carmen Boullosa (244 pp.)

Demira Ulloa is coming of age in Mexico during the politically charged 1960s. The author uses a memoir format to weave together a story about a girl's search for self. The story is told using magical realism, a style made famous by many Latin American authors, most notably Gabriel Garcia Marquez.

The House on Mango Street by Sandra Cisneros (128 pp.)

In a beautiful and intense series of vignettes and poems, Esperanzo shares her coming-of-age trials and tribulations as a Mexican American girl growing up in a poor area of Chicago. She describes her Hispanic neighborhood and shares her dreams of a real house in which to live.

Esperanza Rising by Pam Muñoz Ryan (288 pp.)

After her wealthy father's murder, 13-year-old Esperanza and her mother leave their estate in Mexico and flee to California during the Depression of the 1930s. In this "riches to rags" coming-of-age story, Esperanza must overcome many of her own prejudices.

Becoming Naomi Leon by Pam Muñoz Ryan (246 pp.)

Naomi and her brother Owen happily live with their Gram in a close-knit community in California. When their mother, an alcoholic woman who abandoned them years before, wants custody of just Naomi, Gram takes the children go to Oaxaca, Mexico, to seek help from their biological father.

The Jumping Tree: A Novel by René Saldaña (192 pp.)

Readers share in the experiences of Rey Castanada during his middle school years when he is living in Texas, across the border from his Mexican relatives. As Rey matures, he begins to understand how those on each side of the border are treated differently and have very different opportunities in life.

Help Wanted: Stories by Gary Soto by Gary Soto (224 pp.)

This collection contains ten short stories about Mexican-American teenagers growing up in California.

Nonfiction

Living Up the Street by Gary Soto (176 pp.)

The author recounts growing up in the barrios of Fresno, California. Soto experiences many hardships on his way to becoming a successful author and poet, and he shares how he overcomes those obstacles. In *Small Faces* (126 pp.), Soto continues his recollections, which begin with his marriage to his Japanese wife and continue through the raising of their daughter.

Children's Stories

The Lizard and the Sun: A Folktale in English and Spanish by Alma Flor Ada and illustrated by Felipe Davalos (48 pp.)

Once upon a time in ancient Mexico, the sun suddenly disappeared. All of the animals search and search for the sun, but all eventually give up—all except for the lizard.

Big Bushy Mustache by Gary Soto (32 pp.)

Everyone tells Ricky that he looks like his mother until he wears one of the costumes his teacher passes out for the Cinco de Mayo celebration.

Poetry Resource

Cool Salsa: Bilingual Poems on Growing Up Latino in the United States (Alicia Gaspar de Alba, Ana Castillo, Sandra Cisneros, Pat Mora, Amado Nervo, Trinidad Sanchez, Gary Soto, and Gina Valdes) edited by Lori M. Carlson (160 pp.)

Classics

The Underdogs: A Novel of the Mexican Revolution by Mariano Azuelo (149 pp.)

Like Water for Chocolate by Laura Esquivel (256 pp.)

The Monkey Grammarian by Octavio Paz (176 pp.)

NATIVE AMERICANS (UNITED STATES)

Film Titles

Dances with Wolves (1990, PG-13), starring Kevin Costner, Mary McDonnell, Graham Greene, and Tantoo Cardinal (3 hrs. 56 mins.)

The Education of Little Tree (1997, PG), Joseph Ashton, James Cromwell, Tantoo Cardinal, Leni Parker, and Rebecca Dewey II (1 hr. 55 mins.)

Smoke Signals (1998, PG-13), starring Adam Beach and Evan Adams (1 hr. 29 mins.)

Song of Hiawatha (1996, PG), starring Graham Greene II and Litefoot (1 hr. 54 mins.)

Spirit Rider (2001, Not rated), starring Michelle St. John and Tom Jackson (2 hrs.).

Squanto: A Warrior's Tale (1994, PG), starring Adam Beach and Sheldon Peters Wolfchild (1 hr. 42 mins.)

Fiction

The Absolutely True Diary of a Part-Time Indian by Sherman Alexie (240 pp.)
This semi-autobiographical novel is the story of Arnold Spirit, better known as Junior, who's told that the only way he'll make it in the world is to leave the Indian reservation and get educated in the White school. This 14 year old survives being an outcast at school and begins to discover what really makes a community.

The Journal of Jesse Smoke, a Cherokee Boy by Joseph Bruchac (203 pp.)
This work of historical fiction, researched and written by an author who's Cherokee, tells about the forced relocation of the Cherokee nation to the area now known as Oklahoma, a journey called the Trail of Tears. Through his diary entries, 16-year-old Jesse Smoke allows us to view this tragic chapter of U. S. history from his perspective.

Living Stories of the Cherokee by Barbara R. Duncan (272 pp.)
Various storytellers share traditional and contemporary stories of the Cherokee in authentic voices. Many of these stories have been passed down through many generations, but readers will see their relevance today.

Sing Down the Moon by Scott O'Dell (128 pp.)
In this story, based on a real event—the 1864 forced removal of the Navahos from their original homeland—15-year-old Bright Morning tells about her capture by Spanish slave traders, her escape, her return to her clan, and the spirit-breaking effects of the relocation.

Nonfiction

Growing Up Native American by Bill Adler, Ines Hernandez, and Patricia Riley (336 pp.)

Twenty-two Native American writers, many of whom faced and overcame hardships, tell about their lives. In "Grace," Jodi Ann and Billie Jim are placed in an orphanage and treated as indentured servants.

Rising Voices: Writings of Young Native Americans edited by Arlene B. Hirschfelder and Beverly R. Singer (144 pp.)

The editors have compiled several short essays and poems written by young Native Americans. These 19th- and 20th-century literary pieces are personal in nature, yet reflect concerns—such as identity, family, prejudice, and oppression—that are relevant to readers today.

Children's Stories

Yonder Mountain: A Cherokee Legend by Robert H. Bushyhead, Jean L. Bushyhead and Kay Thorpe Bannon (32 pp.)

An old chief wants to find someone who can lead his tribe after he's gone, so he sends three men to the top of a mountain, instructing them to bring something back. Two return with items that will help their people, one returns with nothing in hand, but with his heart in the right place.

Seminole Diary: Remembrances of a Slave by Dolores Johnson (32 pp.)

Written in journal form, a young slave named Libby recounts her family's escape from slavery and how the Seminole Indians helped them along the way.

Poetry Resources

Broken Flute: The Native Experience in Books for Children by Doris Seale (480 pp.)

The Cherokee Lottery: A Sequence of Poems by William Jay Smith (72 pp.)

Classics

Wildcat, the Seminole by Electa Clark (192 pp.)
House Made of Dawn by N. Scott Momaday (198 pp.)

CENTRAL AMERICA

PANAMA

Film Title

A Man, a Plan, a Canal—Panama (2004, 1987, Not rated), documentary with author David McCullough (1 hr.).

Fiction

Marisol and Magdalena: The Sound of Our Sisterhood by Veronica Chambers (176 pp.)
Marisol's and Magdalena's mothers grew up together in Panama, and now their 13-year-old daughters are best friends, or *mejores amigas*, growing up together in Brooklyn. Because Marisol and Magdalena don't speak much Spanish or know much about their heritage, Marisol's mother decides to send her daughter to live with her grandmother, or *abuela*, in Panama. Magdalena wonders if she's forever lost her *mejor amiga*.

Come Together, Fall Apart by Christina Henriquez (306 pp.)
This highly praised collection of eight short stories and a novella presents Panama before and after Manuel Noriega's expulsion from office. In the title novella, through journal entries written by a 15-year-old boy, readers see a family falling apart, facing eviction while bracing for America's planned invasion.

Nonfiction

The Building of the Panama Canal in Historic Photographs by Ulrich Keller (176 pp.)
100 historic photographs tell the story of the construction of the Panama Canal.

Magnificent Molas: The Art of the Kuna Indian by Michael Perrin and translated by Deke Dusinberre (201 pp.)
This is a beautiful book that tells the story of the Kuna (Cuna) Indians and their culture. Kuna is the name given by Whites to the Indians who live on the archipelago of the San Blas Islands, which are off of Panama's Atlantic Coast to the south of the canal. The title refers to the pieces of bright cloth the Kuna women use to make clothes. The book includes many pictures of these "fabric paintings."

Children's Story

Mola: Cuna Life Stories and Art by Maricel E. Presilla (32 pp.)
   The Cuna Indians have a unique way of making *molas*, the elaborately designed front and back panels of the Cuna women's traditional blouse. These *molas* are composed of several layers of cloth embellished using a technique called reverse appliqué. Each page shows a detail or full panel of a *mola* to enhance the text, which describes the Cuna's lives and customs with quotes and songs.

Poetry Resource

Locks, Crocs, and Skeeters: The Story of the Panama Canal by Nancy Winslow
   Parker (32 pp.)

SOUTH AMERICA
ARGENTINA

Film Titles

Tango (Saura) (1998, PG-13), starring Miguel Ángel Solá, Cecilia Narova, and
   Mía Maestro (1 hr. 52 mins.)

Valentin (2004, PG-13), starring Julieta Cardinali, Rodrigo Noya, and Carmen
   Maura (1 hr. 26 mins.)

Fiction

The Dirty War by Charles Slaughter (166 pp.)
   Atre and his best friend Chino are two young boys living in a suburb of Buenos Aires. The story is set during the "Dirty War" of the mid-1970s, a time of civil unrest when people mysteriously disappear after being questioned by the government. The boys' carefree lifestyle ends when Arte's father goes missing.

Nonfiction

Hunger of Memory: The Education of Richard Rodriguez by Richard Rodriguez
   (224 pp.)
   Originally published in 1983, this book is still available and worth reading. The author grows up in a Latin-American household and speaks only Spanish until he starts school. Richard feels alienated from his family when he becomes a "scholarship boy" and writes about dealing with school, reli-

gion, his dark complexion, and affirmative action.

Children's Story

"Juan Bobo and the Three-Legged Pot" In *Senor Cat's Romance and Other Favorite Stories From Latin America* by Lucia M. Gonzalez and illustrated by Lulu Delacre (5 pp.)
   Juan Bobo is one of Latin America's famous folk heroes, and this story is about his confrontation with a three-legged pot, which ought to be able to walk faster than a child, who has only two legs.

Poetry Resources

Cool Salsa: Bilingual Poems on Growing Up Latino in the United States edited by Lori M. Carlson (160 pp.)

An Anthology of Contemporary Latin-American Poetry edited by Dudley Fitts (667 pp.)

Classics

The Honorary Consul by Graham Greene (310 pp.)
The Gaucho Martin Fierro by Jose Hernandez (99 pp.)

BRAZIL

Film Titles

Black Orpheus (1958, PG), starring Breno Mello and Marpessa Dawn (1 hr. 47 mins.)

Chronically Unfeasible (2000, Not rated), starring Umberto Magnani and Cecil Thiré (1 hr. 41 mins.)

God Is Brazilian (2003, Not rated), starring Antônio Fagundes and Wagner Moura (1 hr. 50 mins.)

Hour of the Star (1987, Not rated), starring Marcelia Cartaxo and José Dumont (1 hr. 36 mins.)

Fiction

Asphalt Angels by Ineke Holtwijk (184 pp.)

After his mother dies, 13-year-old Alex is thrown out of the house by his stepfather. Alex tries to remain clean, but life on the streets of Brazil is hard, especially when the "Asphalt Angels" are your new family. This novel was inspired by a young boy whom the author met in a homeless shelter in Rio de Janeiro.

Jaguar by Roland Smith (256 pp.)

Fourteen-year-old Jake has a restless dad who takes him on wild journeys to save endangered species all over the world. When Jake leaves his home in New York to follow his dad to Brazil, he soon realizes his dad is planning to stay because of his work in the Amazon Rain Forest.

Nonfiction

An Invisible Minority: Brazilians in New York City by Maxine Margolis (141 pp.)

The author explains the whys and hows of Brazilian immigration to the United States, especially to New York.

Children's Stories

The Sea Serpent's Daughter: A Brazilian Legend by Margaret H. Lippert (32 pp.)

Bonita, the daughter of the Great Sea Serpent who lives at the bottom of the dark ocean, tells how nightfall became part of the lives of the people of the Amazon Rain Forest.

So Say the Little Monkeys by Nancy van Laan (40 pp.)

Based on a Brazilian folktale, this rhythmic story is about the playfulness of monkeys and all of their jabbering along the Rio Negro (black river) in Brazil.

Poetry Resources

An Anthology of Twentieth-Century Brazilian Poetry edited by Elizabeth Bishop and Emanuel Brasil (203 pp.)

Looking for Poetry: Poems by Carlos Drummond de Andrade and Rafael Alberti and Songs from the Quechua translated by Mark Strand (192 pp.)

Classics

Iracema by Jose Martiniano de Alencar and translated by Clifford E. Landers (148 pp.)

Memoirs of a Militia Sergeant by Manuel Antonio de Almeida (208 pp.)

Dom Casmurro by Joaquim Maria Machado de Assis and translated by John Gledson (288 pp.)

CHILE

Film Titles

Machuca (2004, PG-13), starring Matías Quer, Ariel Mateluna, and Manuela Martelli (2 hrs. 1 min.). English subtitles.

Fiction

City of the Beasts by Isabel Allende (406 pp.)
    Fifteen-year-old Alexander goes to live with his eccentric grandmother, who's on a quest to find "the Beast" that lives in the far corners of the Amazon jungle. On his journey, Alex meets 12-year-old Nadios Santos, a girl raised in the Amazon, who helps him help the People of the Mist.

Nonfiction

Travels in a Thin Country: A Journey Through Chile by Sara Wheeler (302 pp.)
    While on a cruise ship, Sara Wheeler meets a Chilean worker who tells her she should write a book about his country. She travels through Chile for 6 months, going from north to south, and learns about the people, the land, and the politics.

Children's Story

The Enchanted Raisin by Jacqueline Balcells (104 pp.)
    Chilean author Blacells gives us seven original short stories for children. The title story is about three mischievous boys whose antics wear their mother down into a shriveled raisin.

Poetry Resource

Pablo Neruda: Selected Poems by Pablo Neruda (512 pp.)

Classics

The House of the Spirits by Isabel Allende (448 pp.)

COLOMBIA

Film Titles

Clear and Present Danger (1994, PG-13), starring Harrison Ford, Willem Dafoe, and Anne Archer (2 hrs. 21 mins.)

Missing Peace: The Kidnapping of Ingrid Betancourt (2005, Not rated), documentary (1 hr. 32 mins.)

Romancing the Stone (1984, PG), starring Michael Douglas, Kathleen Turner, and Danny DeVito (1 hr. 45 mins.)

Fiction

Celebrating the Hero by Lyll Becerra de Jenkins (192 pp.)
     Camila Draper's Colombian heritage has always fascinated her, so she jumps at the chance to go to Santander, Colombia, to attend a celebration to honor her late grandfather. This 17 year old finds out more than she'd care to know about her family and a culture she thought she knew.

The Treasure of Diogenes Sampuez by James Munves (186 pp.)
     Diogenes' father has died and Uncle Mauricio is selling off everything on the family farm. With his younger sister and a friend, Diogenes sets off on a journey across the Sierra Nevada Mountains in northern Columbia to find an older brother in Cartagena.

Stories of Life and Death / Historias De Vida Y Muerte by the Students of Fundacion Creando Cambio (96 pp.)
     Students from 10 to 16 years of age write their own fictional stories about living in a poor town in Soacha, Columbia. Black-and-white photographs add to this troubling glimpse into the lives of impoverished kids who have dreams of doing things that we in the United States take for granted. Both the Spanish and the English translation are presented.

Boy Kills Man by Matt Whyman (152 pp.)
     Sonny is a 13-year-old grade school dropout living in an impoverished barrio in Colombia. El Fantasma offers Sonny and his best friend Alberto money in exchange for their souls.

Nonfiction

Out of War: True Stories From the Front Lines of the Children's Movement for Peace in Colombia by Sara Cameron (186 pp.)

In nine gripping narratives, Columbian teenagers detail their experiences, which include death threats, killings, gang violence, and poverty and tell how the Children's Movement for Peace in Columbia has helped them overcome these difficulties—one voice at a time.

Secrets of Colombian Cooking by Patricia McCausland-Gallo (251 pp.)

If food is a way to a man's heart, it can also be a way into the heart of a country The author's narrative, which accompanies many recipes, provides an additional Colombian flavor.

Presidential Homes of Colombia by Benjamin Villegas and Juan Gustavo Cobo Borda, and translated by Andrew Alexander Reid (160 pp.)

One of Colombia's most prominent poets, Juan Gustavo Cobo Borda, describes three presidential homes, two in Bogota and one in Cartegena. The book is illustrated with beautiful photographs of Colombian architecture and landscapes.

Children's Story

The Monkey People: A Colombian Folktale by Eric Metaxas and illustrated by Diana Bryan (32 pp.)

Imagine moving every time your house gets too dirty. That's what this Amazon tribe does until an old man turns leaves into monkeys who do all the tribe's chores.

Poetry Resources

Colombia International Poetry Web.

Cool Salsa: Bilingual Poems on Growing Up Latino in the United States (Daniel Jacome Roca, poet) edited by Lori M. Carlson (160 pp.)

Classics

Love in the Time of Cholera by Gabriel Garcia Marquez (368 pp.)
One Hundred Years of Solitude by Gabriel Garcia Marquez (464 pp.)

PERU

Film Titles

The Bridge of San Luis Rey (2005, PG), starring Robert De Niro, Gabriel Byrne, and Kathy Bates (2 hrs. 4 mins.)

Galapagos (1999, Not rated), starring Kenneth Branagh and David Pawson (39 mins.)

Master and Commander: The Far Side of the World (2003, PG-13, starring Russell Crowe, Paul Bettany, and James D'Arcy (2 hrs. 18 mins.)

Secrets of Lost Empires: Inca (1997, Not rated), documentary (1 hr.).

Fiction

Go and Come Back by Joan Abelove (192 pp.)
    The author of this novel, who lived in the Amazon jungle for 2 years, shows how behaviors of one culture can be misunderstood by another when a young teenager named Alicia instructs "two old fat ladies from New York" about her village's culture.

Secret of the Andes by Ann Nolan Clark (128 pp.)
    Cusi, a young Inca Indian, only knows the hidden valley in Peru, where he has always lived with Chuto, the Old One. The day comes when Cusi decides to leave with his pet llama to go to Cuzco, the Holy Place of the Ancients, to discover who he is.

A Gift for Ampato by Susan Van de Grier and illustrated by Mary Jane Gerber
    (112 pp.)
    Inspired by the 1995 discovery of a girl's mummified body on the slopes of Nevado Ampato, the author explores Incan culture through the story of young woman named Tinta. When crops fail, the Incas offer human sacrifices to appease the gods. It is considered a great honor to be selected, but when Timta is chosen, she has different ideas.

Evil Star: Book Two of the Gatekeepers by Anthony Horowitz (320 pp.)
    Matt is one of five special teenagers chosen to save the world from evil. In this book, Matt meets up with Pedro, a street kid in Peru, and together they must close the second gate. They run into trouble when language barriers get in the way of their efforts. Interested students may want to read the first book in the series, *Raven's Gate* (272 pp.), which is set in Yorkshire, England, or the third book, *Nightrise* (368 pp.), set in Nevada, but neither is necessary for understanding this book.

Nonfiction

Insight Guide Peru edited by Pam Barrett (267 pp.)
    This guide informs the reader of ancient and recent Peruvian history and

serves as an excellent source for the enrichment of the Peruvian literature experience.

Children's Stories

Llama and the Great Flood: A Folktale From Peru by Ellen Alexander (39 pp.)
   A llama dreams of a great rain that will flood the world. He tells his master, a farmer, who then moves his family and his belongings up to the highest peak in the Andes, where every animal in the world has gathered. The story goes that, because no one other than the farmer's family survived the flood, we are all his descendants.

Moon Rope by Lois Ehlert (32 pp.)
   Based on an ancient Peruvian tale and presented in both English and Spanish, this wonderful picture book explains the face we see in the moon and why moles live in the ground.

Poetry Resource

The Complete Poetry: A Bilingual Edition by César Vallejo (732 pp.)

Classics

Letters from a Peruvian Woman by Francoise de Graffigny (174 pp.)
Birds without a Nest: A Novel by Clorinda Matto de Turner (205 pp.)

References

Applebee, A. N. (1993). *Literature in the secondary school: Studies of curriculum and instruction in the United States.* Urbana, IL: National Council of Teachers of English.

Barrett, P. (Ed.). (2005). *Insight guide Peru.* New York: Insight Guides.

Beach, R. (1993). *A teacher's introduction to reader-response theories.* Urbana, IL: National Council of Teachers of English.

Bleeker, G. W., Bleeker, B. S., & Bleeker, M. M. (2006). Finding common ground: Learning the language of peace. *The ALAN Review, 33* (3), 7–12.

Blum, L. (2004, Summer). A high school class on race and racism. *Radical Teacher,* n.p.

Bontempo, B. T. (1995, Spring). Exploring prejudice in young adult literature through drama and role play. *The ALAN Review, 22* (3), 31–33.

Bott, C. J., Garden, N., Jones, P., & Peters, J. A. (2007). Don't look and it will go away: YA books—a key to uncovering the invisible problem of bullying. *The ALAN Review, 34* (2), 44–51.

Bowman, C. A. (Ed.). (2000). *Using literature to help troubled teenagers cope with health issues.* Westport, CT: Greenwood Press.

Brinda, W. (2008). Can you name one good thing that comes out of war? *ALAN Review, 35* (2), 14–23.

Brown, L. H. (2000). A review of the Holocaust in literature for youth. *The ALAN Review, 27* (3), 56–57.

Broz, W. (2007). The bully in the book and in the classroom. *The ALAN Review, 34* (2), 34–43.

Bushman, J. H., & Haas, K. P. (2006). *Using young adult literature in the classroom* (4th ed.). Upper Saddle River, NJ: Pearson.

Carlsen, R. G., & Sherrill, A. (1988). *Voices of readers: How we come to love books.* Urbana, IL: National Council of Teachers of English.

Carter, C., & Rashkis, Z. (Eds.). (1980). *Ideas for teaching English in the junior high and middle schools.* Urbana, IL.: National Council of Teachers of English.

Christenbury, L., & the Committee on the Senior High School Booklist. (1995).

Books for you: An annotated booklist for senior high students (pp. 151–157). Urbana, IL: National Council of Teachers of English.

Coencas, J. (2007, March). How movies work for secondary students with special needs. *English Journal, 96* (4), 67–72.

Delahunty, A., Dignen, S., & Stock, P. (2003). *The Oxford dictionary of allusions.* New York: Oxford University Press.

Downey, J. P., & Stage, F. K. (1999). Hate crimes and violence on college and university campuses. *Journal of College Student Development, 40* (1), 3–9.

Duncan, B. R. (1998). *Living stories of the Cherokee.* Chapel Hill: University of North Carolina Press.

Dunlop, F. (2007). *Fodor's exploring India* (4th ed.). New York: Fodor.

Easwaran, E. (Trans.). (1993). *The Bhagvad Gita.* Tomales, CA: Nilgiri Press.

Elliott, N., & Elliott, W. (1969). *Festive wine: Ancient Japanese poems from the Kinkafu* (Brannen, Trans.). New York: Walker/Weatherhill.

Engel, E. (1986). *The genius of Mark Twain.* Raleigh, NC: LITE Learning.

Fogelin, A. (2007). *Adrian Fogelin.* Retrieved August 2, 2008, from http://www.adrianfogelin.com/book_cross_jordan.htm.

Franek, M., & NiiLampti, N. (2005). Shoot the author, not the reader. *English Journal, 94* (6), 20–22.

Gallo, D. R., & the Committee on the Senior High School Booklist. (1985). *Books for you: A booklist for senior high students.* Urbana, IL: National Council of Teachers of English.

George, M. A. (2002). Living on the edge: Confronting social injustices. *Voices From the Middle, 4* (9), 39–44.

George, M. A. (2006). Promoting social justice through historical young adult literature: An action research project. *SIGNAL Journal, 30* (1), 7–10.

Goering, C. Z. *LitTunes.* Retrieved March 13, 2008, from http://www.corndancer.com/tunes/tunes_man.html.

GradeSaver (1999). *Biography of Lorraine Hansberry.* Retrieved August 2, 2008, from http://www.gradesaver.com/classicnotes/authors/about_lorraine _hansberry.html.

Harste, J. (2000). Supporting critical conversation in classrooms. In K. M. Pierce (Ed.) *Adventuring with books: A booklist for pre-K–grade 6* (pp. 507–554). Urbana, IL: National Council of Teachers of English.

Haub, C. (2006). *The 2006 world population data sheet.* Washington, DC: Population Reference Bureau.

Hillesum, E. (1996). *Etty Hillesum: An interrupted life—the diaries 1941–1943 and letters from Westerbork* (A. J. Pomerans, Trans.). New York: Holt.

Hinton, K. (2004). Sturdy black bridges: Discussing race, class and gender. *English Journal, 94* (2), 61–64.

Hodgkinson, H. (1993, April). American education: The good, the bad, and the task. *Phi Delta Kappan, 74* (8), 619–623.

Jordan, S. D. (2004). Educating without overwhelming: Authorial strategies in children's Holocaust literature. *Children's Literature in Education, 35* (3), 199–218.

Kaywell, J. F. (1993a). *Adolescent literature as a complement to the classics* (Vol. 1, pp. 37–59). Norwood, MA: Christopher-Gordon.

Kaywell, J. F. (1993b). *Adolescents at risk: A guide to fiction and nonfiction for young adults, parents, and professionals.* Westport, CT: Greenwood Press.

Kaywell, J. F. (1995). *Adolescent literature as a complement to the classics* (Vol. 2, pp. 37–59). Norwood, MA: Christopher-Gordon.

Kaywell, J. F. (1997). *Adolescent literature as a complement to the classics* (Vol. 3, pp. 37–59). Norwood, MA: Christopher-Gordon.

Kaywell, J. F. (2000). *Adolescent literature as a complement to the classics* (Vol. 4, pp. 37–59). Norwood, MA: Christopher-Gordon.

Kaywell, J. F., Kelly, P. P., Edge, C., McCoy, L., & Steinberg, N. (2006). Growing up female around the globe with young adult literature. *The ALAN Review, 33* (3), 62–69.

Landrum, J. (2001). Selecting intermediate novels that feature characters with disabilities. *The Reading Teacher, 55* (3), 252–258.

Landt, S. M. (2006). Multicultural literature and young adolescents: A kaleidoscope of opportunity. *Journal of Adolescent and Adult Literacy, 49* (8), 690–697.

Levin, H. (2003). Making history come alive. *Learning and leading with technology, 31* (3), 22–26.

Lindgren, M. V. (Ed.). (1991). *The multicolored mirror: Cultural substance literature for children and young adults.* Fort Atkinson, WI: Highsmith Press.

Lindquist, D. H. (2006). Guidelines for teaching the Holocaust: Avoiding common pedagogical errors. *Social Studies, 97* (5), 215–217.

Loh, V. S. (2006). Quantity and quality: The need for culturally authentic trade books in Asian American young adult literature. *The ALAN Review, 34* (1), 36–53.

Mason, K. (2008). Creating a space for YAL with LGBT content in our personal reading. *The ALAN Review, 35* (3), 55–61.

Mathabane, M. (2001, August 21). Interracial myths still nag couples. *USA Today,* n.p.

Matthews, D., & the Committee to Revise "High-Interest Easy Reading." (1988). *High-interest easy reading for junior and senior high school students.* (5th ed.). Urbana, IL: National Council of Teachers of English.

Mattis, K. V. (2007, January). Making time for literature with Middle Eastern perspectives. *English Journal, 96* (3), 110–113.

Metzger, K., & Adams, J. (2007). Opening dialogue amidst conflict. *The ALAN*

Review, 34 (3), 61–66.

Miller-Lachmann, L. (Ed.). (1992). *Our family, our friends, our world: An annotated guide to significant multicultural books for children and teenagers.* New Providence, NJ: Bowker.

Narayan, R. K. (Trans.). (1998). *The Ramayana.* New York: Penguin.

Nilsen, A. P., & the Committee on the Junior High and Middle School Booklist. (1991). *Your reading: A booklist for junior high and middle school students* (8th ed.). Urbana, IL: National Council of Teachers of English.

O'Neil, J. (1993, May). A new generation confronts racism. *Educational Leadership, 50* (8), 60–63.

Pace, B. G. (1992, September). The textbook canon: Genre, gender, and race in U.S. literature anthologies. *English Journal, 81* (5), 33–38.

Pajka-West, S. (2007). Perceptions of deaf characters in adolescent literature. *The ALAN Review, 34* (3), 39–45.

Perry, A. E. (2003). PowerPoint presentations: A creative addition to the research process. *English Journal, 92* (4), 64–69.

Plous, S. (2002). *Understanding prejudice and discrimination.* New York: McGraw-Hill.

Purves, A. C., Rogers, T., & Soter, A. O. (1990). *How porcupines make love II: Teaching a response-centered literature curriculum.* White Plains, NY: Longman Press.

Purves, A. C., Rogers, T., & Soter, A. (1995). *How porcupines make love III: Readers, texts, cultures in the response-based classroom.* White Plains, NY: Longman Press.

Rochman, H. (1993). *Against borders: Promoting books for a multicultural world.* Chicago: American Library Association.

Rosenblatt, L. (1938). *Literature as exploration.* New York: Modern Language Association.

Saldaña, R., Jr. (2007, November). The ever-expanding Mexican American YA canon. *English Journal, 97* (2), 110–113.

Salend, S. J. (2005). Using technology to teach about individual differences related to disabilities. *Teaching Exceptional Children, 38* (2), 32–38.

Samuels, B. G., Beers, K., & the Committee on the Middle School and Junior High Booklist. (1996). *Your reading: An annotated booklist for middle school and junior high, 1995–96 edition* (pp. 147–209). Urbana, IL: National Council of Teachers of English.

Schwarz, G. (1996). The power of foreign young adult literature. *The ALAN Review, 23* (3), 10–12.

Seale, D. (2005). *Broken flute: The Native experience in books for children.* Lanham, MD: AltaMira Press.

Stephens, E. C., Brown, J. E., & Rubin, J. E. (1995). *Learning about the Ho-*

locaust: Literature and other resources for young people. North Haven, CT: Library Professional Publications.

Stover, L., Zenker, S. F., & the Committee on the Senior High School Booklist. (1997). *Books for you: An annotated booklist for senior high* (pp., 206–211). Urbana, IL: National Council of Teachers of English.

Ward, M. (2002). *Voices from the margins: An annotated bibliography of fiction on disabilities and differences for young people.* Westport, CT: Greenwood Press.

Zuidema, L. A. (2005). *Myth education: Rationale and strategies for teaching against linguistic prejudice.* Urbana, IL: National Council of Teachers of English.

Young Adult and Classics Bibliography

Abells, C. (1986). *The children we remember*. New York: Greenwillow Books.

Achebe, C. (1994). *Things fall apart*. New York: Anchor Books. (Original work published 1958)

Ada, A. F. (1999). *The lizard and the sun: A folktale in English and Spanish* (F. Davalos, Illus.). Albuquerque, NM: Dragonfly Books.

Addleton, J. S. (1997). *Some far and distant place*. Athens: University of Georgia Press.

Adler, B., Hernndez, I., & Riley, P. (1995). *Growing up Native American*. New York: Harper.

Ahmed, L. (2000). *A border passage: From Cairo to America—a woman's journey*. New York: Penguin.

Aiken, J. (1999). *Dangerous games*. New York: Delacorte Press.

Akhmatova, A. (2006). *Selected poems of Anna Akhmatova* (D. M. Thomas, Trans.). New York: Penguin. (Original work published 1963)

Alencar, J. M. de (2000). *Iracema* (C. E. Landers, Trans.). New York: Oxford University Press. (Original work published 1865)

Alexander, E., (1989). *Llama and the great flood: A folktale from Peru*. New York: Crowell.

Alexander, S. H. (1997). *On my own: The journey continues*. New York: Farrar, Straus & Giroux.

Alexander, S. H., & Alexander, R. (2008). *She touched the world: Laura Bridgman, deaf-blind pioneer*. New York: Clarion Books.

Alexie, S. (2007). *The absolutely true diary of a part-time Indian*. New York: Little, Brown.

Allende, I. (1986). *The house of the spirits*. New York: Bantam Books.

Allende, I. (2002). *City of the beasts*. New York: HarperCollins.

Almeida, M. A. de. (2000). *Memoirs of a militia sergeant*. New York: Oxford University Press. (Original work published 1854)

Amichai, Y. (1992). *Poems of Jerusalem and love poems*. Riverdale-on-Hudson, NY: Sheep Meadow.

Amirshahi, M. (1995). *Suri and Co.: Tales of a Persian teenage girl*. Austin: University of Texas Press.

Anaya, R. (1994). *Bless me, Ultima*. New York: Grand Central.

Ancona, G. (2000). *Cuban kids*. Tarrytown, NY: Marshall Cavendish.

Anderson, P. R. (Ed.). (2005). *In the country of the heart: Love poems from South Africa*. Auckland Park, South Africa: Jacana Media.

Andrews, V. C. (2006). *Girl in the shadows*. New York: Pocket Star.

Angell, J. (2001). *One way to Ansonia*. Bloomington, IN: iUniverse.

Anonymous. (1974). *The book of Dede Korkut: A Turkish epic* (G. Lewis, Trans.). New York: Penguin.

Appleman-Jurman, A. (1990). *Alicia: My story*. New York: Bantam Books.

Arberry, A. J. (1993). *Fifty poems of Hafiz*. London: Rowe.

Aruego, J. (1993). *Rockabye crocodile: A folktale from the Philippines* (A. Dewey, Illus.). New York: HarperTrophy.

Atasu, E. (2000). *The other side of the mountain* (E. Malsen, Trans.). London: Milet.

Atkins. C. (2003). *Alt Ed*. New York: Putnam.

Axelrod, T. (2002). *Rescuers defying the Nazis: Non-Jewish teens who rescued Jews (teen witnesses to the Holocaust)*. Irvine, CA: Saddleback.

Ayer, E. H. (with Waterford, H., & Heck, A.). (2000). *Parallel journeys*. New York: Aladdin Books.

Azuelo, M. (1976). *The underdogs: A novel of the Mexican Revolution*. Cutchogue, NY: Buccaneer Books.

Bagdasarian, A. (2000). *Forgotten fire*. New York: Random House.

Balcells, J. (1988). *The enchanted raisin* (E. G. Miller, Trans.). Pittsburgh, PA: Latin American Literary Review Press.

Banks, L. R. (1993). *One more river*. New York: HarperTrophy.

Banks, L. R. (1996). *Broken bridge*. New York: HarperTeen.

Baron, V. O. (1974). *Sunset in a spider web: Sijo poetry of ancient Korea* (S. P. Chung, Trans.). New York: Holt, Rinehart & Winston.

Bartoletti, S. C. (2003). *A coal miner's bride: The diary of Anetka Kaminska*. New York: Scholastic.

Bartoletti, S. C. (2005). *Hitler Youth: Growing up in Hitler's shadow*. New York: Scholastic.

Beah, I. (2007). *Innocents lost: When child soldiers go to war*. New York: Farrar, Straus & Giroux.

Beals, M. P. (1994). *Warriors don't cry: A searing memoir of the battle to integrate Little Rock's Central High*. New York: Pocket Books.

Benedict, H. (2008). *The opposite of love*. New York: Viking.

Bennett, C., & Gottesfeld, J. (2001). *Anne Frank and me*. New York: Putnam.

Bernstein, S. T. (1999). *The seamstress: A memoir of survival*. New York: Berkley.

Bildner, P. (2006). *Playing the field*. New York: Simon & Schuster.

Bishop, E., & Brasil, E. (Eds.). (1997). *An anthology of twentieth-century Brazilian poetry*. Middletown, CT: Wesleyan.

Bitton-Jackson, L. (1999). *I have lived a thousand years: Growing up in the Holocaust*. New York: Simon Pulse.

Blackman, M. (2005). *Naughts and crosses*. New York: Simon & Schuster.

Blatchford, C. H. (2000). *Nick's secret*. Minneapolis: Lerner

Bloor, E. (2001). *Tangerine*. New York: Scholastic.

Bloor, E. (2006). *London calling*. New York: Knopf.

Blumberg, R. (2003). *Shipwrecked! The true adventures of a Japanese boy*. New York: HarperTrophy.

Boas, J. (1996). *We are witnesses: Five diaries of teenagers who died in the Holocaust*. New York: Scholastic.

Bode, J. (1989). *New kids on the block: Oral histories of immigrant teens*. New York: Franklin Watts.

Bosse, M. (2004). *Tusk and stone*. Asheville, NC: Front Street Books.

Boullosa, C. (2001). *Leaving Tabasco* (G. Hargroves, Trans.). New York: Grove Press.

Brainard, C. M. (1995). *When the rainbow goddess wept*. New York: Plume.

Bruchac, J. (2001). *The journal of Jesse Smoke, a Cherokee boy*. New York: Scholastic.

Bryant, J. (2004). *The trial*. New York: Knopf.

Bulosan, C. (1946). *The laughter of my father*. New York: Bantam Books.

Bulosan, C. (2001). *America is in the heart*. Seattle: University of Washington Press. (Original work published 1946)

Bunting, E. (2001). *Gleam and glow* (P. Sylvada, Illus.). New York: Harcourt.

Bunting, E. (2007). *A sudden silence*. San Diego: Harcourt.

Burford, L. (2005). *A Jamaican storyteller's tale*. Kingston, Jamaica: LMH.

Bushyhead, R. H., Bushyhead, J. L., & Bannon, K. T. (2002). *Yonder mountain: A Cherokee legend* (K. Rodanas, Illus). Tarrytown, NY: Marshall Cavendish.

Cadet, J. R. (1998). *Restavec*. Austin: University of Texas Press.

Cameron, S. (2001). *Out of war: True stories from the front lines of the Children's Movement for Peace in Colombia*. New York: Scholastic.

Cao, L. (1998). *Monkey bridge*. New York: Penguin.

Carb, N. (Ed.). (1995). *Returning a borrowed tongue: An anthology of Filipino and Filipino American poetry*. Minneapolis, MN: Coffee House Press.

Carlson, L. M. (1995). *Cool salsa: Bilingual poems on growing up Latino in the*

United States. New York: Fawcett Juniper.

Carmi, D. (2000). *Samir and Yonatan* (Y. Lotan, Trans.). New York: Levine Books.

Carpentier, A. (2001). *The lost steps*. (H. De Onis, Trans.). Minneapolis, MN: University of Minnesota Press. (Original work published 1956)

Cather, W. (1994). *My Antonia*. New York: Bantam. (Original work published 1918)

Cervantes, M. de. (2001). *Don Quixote* (T. Smollett, Trans.). New York: Modern Library.

Chambers, V. (2001). *Marisol and Magdalena: The sound of our sisterhood*. New York: Hyperion Books.

Chang, P. M. (1997). *Bound feet and Western dress: A memoir*. New York: Anchor Books.

Ch'eng-en, Wu. (1994). *Monkey: A folk novel of China*. New York: Grove Press.

Christie, A. (2001). *A Caribbean mystery*. New York: Signet Books.

Cisneros, S. (1991). *The house on Mango Street*. New York: Vintage Books.

Clark, A. N. (1976). *Secret of the Andes*. New York: Puffin Books.

Clark, E. (1956). *Wildcat, the Seminole*. New York: Aladdin Books.

Cliff, M. (1995). *Abeng*. New York: Plume.

Climo, S. (1992). *The Egyptian Cinderella* (R. Heller, Illus.). New York: Harper Trophy.

Climo, S. (1993). *The Korean Cinderella* (R. Heller, Illus.). New York: HarperCollins.

Climo, S. (1999). *The Persian Cinderella* (R. Florczak, Illus.). New York: HarperCollins.

Coelho, P. (1998). *The alchemist: A fable about following your dream*. New York: HarperCollins.

Coerr, E. (1999). *Sadako and the thousand paper cranes* (R. Himler, Illus.). New York: Putnam.

Cofer, J. O., (1990). *Silent dancing: A partial remembrance of a Puerto Rican childhood*. Houston, TX: Arte Publico Press.

Cofer, J. O. (1998). *The year of our revolution: New and selected stories and poems*. Houston: Piñata Books.

Cofer, J. O. (2003). *The meaning of Consuelo*. New York: Farrar, Straus, & Giroux.

Cofer, J. O. (2006). *Call me Maria*. New York: Scholastic.

Confucius. (1995) *The analects*. Toronto, Ontario, Canada: Dover.

Connor, L. (2008). *Waiting for normal*. New York: Tegen Books.

Cooper, A. (1973). *Li Po and Tu Fu: Poems selected and translated with an introduction and notes*. New York: Penguin.

Cooper, M. (2000). *Fighting for honor: Japanese Americans and World War II.* New York: Clarion Books.

Cooper, M. (2002). *Remembering Manzanar: Life in a Japanese relocation camp.* New York: Clarion Books.

Crowe, C. (2002). *Mississippi trial, 1955.* New York: Dial.

Crowe, C. (2003). *Getting away with murder.* New York: Dial.

Crutcher, C. (2002). *Whale talk.* New York: Laurel-Leaf.

Crutcher, C. (2003). *The crazy horse electric game.* New York: HarperTempest.

Curry, C. (1995). *Silver rights.* Chapel Hill, NC: Algonquin Books.

Curtis, C. P. (1997). *The Watsons go to Birmingham.* New York: Yearling.

Curtis, C. P. (2007). *Elijah of Buxton.* New York: Scholastic.

Cushman, K. (2003). *Rodzina.* New York: Clarion Books.

Damrosch, D. (2003). *The Longman anthology of world literature* (Vol. F). White Plains, NY: Longman Press.

Danticat, E. (1996). *Krik? Krak!* New York: Vintage Books.

Danticat, E. (2002). *Behind the mountains.* New York: Orchard Books.

Danticat, E. (2005). *Anacaona: Golden flower, Haiti, 1490.* New York: Scholastic.

Das, P. (2004). *I is for India.* Frances London: Lincoln.

Davis, P. A. (2000). *Brian's bird.* Morton Grove, IL: Whitman.

Deane, S. (1997). *Reading in the dark.* New York: Vintage Books.

Deedy, C. A. (2007). *Martina the beautiful cockroach: A Cuban folktale* (M. Austin, Illus.). Atlanta: Peachtree.

Demi. (2004). *The hungry coat.* New York: McElderry Books.

dePaola, T. (1993). *The legend of the Persian carpet.* New York: Putnam.

Dery, D. (2005). *The twelve little cakes.* New York: Riverhead Books.

Dhar, S. (1996). *Folk tales of Turkey.* New Delhi, India: Learners Press.

Do, N., & Hoover, P. (2008). *Black dog, black night: Contemporary Vietnamese poetry.* Minneapolis, MN: Milkweed.

Dorris, M. (1999). *Sees behind trees.* New York: Hyperion.

Dorros, A. (2004). *Under the sun.* New York: Abrams.

Dostoevsky, F. (1996). *Crime and punishment.* New York: Bantam. (Original work published 1864)

Doyle, R. (1989). *The commitments.* New York: Vintage Books.

Doyle, R. (1994). *Paddy Clarke, ha ha ha.* New York: Vintage Books.

Draper, S. M. (2006). *Copper sun.* New York: Atheneum.

Draper, S. M. (2007). *Fire from the rock.* New York: Dutton's Children's Books.

Dumas, F. (2004). *Funny in Farsi: A memoir of growing up Iranian in America.* New York: Random House.

Duncan, B. R. (1998). *Living stories of the Cherokee*. Chapel Hill: University of North Carolina Press.

Dunlop, F. (2007). *Fodor's exploring India* (4th ed.). New York: Fodor's Travel.

Durakovic, F. (1999). *Heart of darkness: Poems* (A. Simic & Z. Mutic, Trans.). White Plains, NY: White Plains Press.

Ehlert, L., (2003). *Moon rope*. Harpers Ferry, WV: Voyager Books.

Elliott, L. M. (2003). *Under a war-torn sky*. New York: Hyperion Books.

Ellis, D. (2001). *Breadwinner*. Toronto Ontario, Canada: Groundwood Books.

Ellis, D. (2003). *Parvana's journey*. Toronto Ontario, Canada: Groundwood Books.

Ellis, D. (2004). *Mud city*. Toronto Ontario, Canada: Groundwood Books.

English, K. (1999). *Francie*. New York: Farrar, Straus & Giroux.

Esquivel, L. (1995). *Like water for chocolate*. New York: Anchor Books.

Ferdowsi, A. (2006). *Shahnameh: The Persian book of kings* (D. Davis, Trans.). New York: Viking.

Ferris, J. (2001). *Of sound mind*. New York: Farrar, Straus, and Giroux.

Filipovic, Z. (2006). *Zlata's diary: A child's life in wartime Sarajevo*. New York: Penguin.

Fitts, D. (1942). *An anthology of contemporary Latin-American poetry*. Norfolk, CT: New Directions.

Fitzgerald, E. (Trans.). (1997). *Rubaiyat of Omar Khayyam*. London: Wordsworth.

Flake, S. (2000). *The skin I'm in*. New York: Jump at the Sun.

Flake, S. (2007). *Money hungry*. New York: Jump at the Sun.

Fleischman, P. (1999). *The mind's eye*. New York: Holt.

Flor, A. A. (1999). *The three golden oranges* (R. Cartwright, Trans.). New York: Atheneum.

Flores-Galbis, E. (2007). *Raining sardines*. New York: Roaring Brook Press.

Florit, E. (Ed.). (1991). *Introduction to Spanish poetry*. Mineola, NY: Dover.

Fluek, T. K. (1990). *Memories of my life in a Polish village, 1930–1949*. New York: Knopf.

Fogelin, A. (2000). *Crossing Jordan*. Atlanta: Peachtree.

Foster, J. L. (Ed. & Trans.). (1992). *Love songs of the New Kingdom*. Austin: University of Texas Press.

Fox, P. (1997). *The slave dancer*. New York: Laurel-Leaf.

Fradin, D. (1997). *Louis Braille: The blind boy who wanted to read*. Englewood Cliffs, NJ: Silver Burdett Press.

Frank, A. (1993). *Anne Frank: The diary of a young girl*. New York: Bantam Books. (Original work published 1942)

Frazier, S. T. (2007). *Brendan Buckley's universe and everything in it*. New York:

Delacorte Press.

Friedman, I. R. (1995). *The other victims: First-person stories of non-Jews persecuted by the Nazis.* Boston: Houghton Mifflin.

Fritz, J. (1999). *Homesick: My own story.* New York: Putnam.

Gaines, E. J. (1997). *A lesson before dying.* New York: Vintage Books.

Gallo, D. (Ed.). (1993). *Join in: Multiethnic short stories.* New York: Delacorte Press.

Gallo, D. (2008). *Owning it: Stories about teeens with disabilities.* Cambridge, MA: Candlewick Press.

Garcia, C. (Ed.). (2003). *Cubanisimo!: The Vintage book of contemporary Cuban Literature.* New York: Vintage Books.

Garcia, P. (1997). *From amigos to friends.* Houston, TX: Piñata Books.

Garden, N. (2006). *Endgame.* New York: Harcourt.

Garland, S. (1993). *Shadow of the dragon.* New York: Harcourt.

Garland, S. (1994). *Song of the buffalo boy.* San Diego, CA: Harcourt.

Garland, S. (2001). *Children of the dragon: Selected tales from Vietnam* (T. Schart Hyman, Illus.). New York: Harcourt.

Ghose, S. N., (1986). *Folk tales and fairy stories from India.* Mineola, NY: Dover.

Gibian, G. (Ed.). (1998). *The poetry of Jaroslav Seifert.* North Haven, CT: Catbird Press.

Gibran, K. (1970). *The prophet.* New York: Knopf. (Original work published 1923)

Gibson, W. (2002). *The miracle worker.* New York: Pocket Books. (Original work published 1956)

Giff, P. R. (1983). *The gift of the pirate queen.* New York: Yearling.

Giff, P. R. (1997). *Lily's crossing.* New York: Delacorte Press.

Glinton-Meicholas, P. (1994). *An evening in Guanima: A treasury of folktales from the Bahamas* (2nd ed.). Nassau, Bahamas: Guanima Press.

Gonzalez, L. M. (1997). Juan Bobo and the three-legged pot. In *Senor cat's romance and other favorite stories from Latin America* (pp. 15–19). New York: Scholastic.

Gordon, S. (1996). *Waiting for the rain.* New York: Laurel-Leaf.

Graffigny, F. de (1997). *Letters from a Peruvian woman* (D. Kornacker, Trans.). New York: Modern Language Association.

Greene, B. (1999). *Summer of my German soldier.* New York: Puffin Books. (Original work published 1973)

Greene, G. (1973). *The honorary consul.* New York: Simon & Schuster.

Grimes, N. (2001). *Bronx masquerade.* New York: Dial.

Gruenwald, M. M. (2005). *Looking like the enemy: My story of imprisonment in Japanese-American internment camps.* Eugene, OR: New Sage Press.

Hakakian, R. (2005). *Journey from the land of no: A girlhood caught in revolutionary Iran*. New York: Three Rivers Press.

Halman, T. S., & Warner, J. L. (Eds.). (2005). *Nightingales and pleasure gardens: Turkish love poems*. Syracuse, NY: Syracuse University Press.

Hansberry, L. (2004). *A raisin in the sun*. New York: Vintage Books. (Original work published 1959)

Harlow, J. H. (2003). *Shadows on the sea*. New York: McElderry Books.

Harrison, L. (2004). *The clique*. New York: Random House.

Harrison, L. (2005). *Invasion of the boy snatchers* (Vol. 4). New York: Little, Brown.

Hartinger, B. (2003). *The geography club*. New York: HarperTempest.

Hartinger, B. (2007). *Split screen*. New York: HarperTempest.

Hausman, G., & Wolff, A. (1998). *Doctor bird: Three lookin' up tales from Jamaica*. New York: Philomel Books.

Hayslip, L. L. (1993). *When heaven and earth changed places*. New York: Plume.

Heck, A. (1985). *Child of Hitler: Germany in the days when God wore a swastika*. New York: Renaissance House.

Heck, A. (1988). *The burden of Hitler's legacy*. New York: Renaissance House.

Hedayat, S. (1957). *The blind owl* (D. P. Costello, Trans.). New York: Random House.

Hemingway, H., & Brennan, C. (2003). *Hemingway in Cuba*. New York: Rugged Land.

Henriquez, C. (2006). *Come together, fall apart*. New York: Penguin.

Heo, Y. (2004). *The green frogs: A Korean folktale*. Boston: Houghton Mifflin.

Hermes, P. (2004). *Summer secrets*. Tarrytown, NY: Marshall Cavendish.

Hernández, J. (1975). *The gaucho Martin Fierro*. New York: State University of New York Press.

Hernández, J.A.Y. (1997). *White bread competition*. Houston, TX: Pinata Books.

Hersey, J. (1995). *Hiroshima*. New York: Scholastic. (Original work published 1946)

Hertenstein, J. (1999). *Beyond paradise*. New York: Morrow.

Hesse, K. (2001). *Witness*. New York: Scholastic.

Hesse, K. (2003a). *Aleutian sparrow*. New York: McElderry Books.

Hesse, K. (2003b). *The stone lamp: Eight stories of Hanukkah through history* (B. Pinkey, Illus.). New York: Hyperion Books.

Heuston, K. (2008). *The book of Jude*. Honesdale, PA: Front Street Books.

Heyes, E. (1993). *Children of the swastika: The Hitler youth*. Brookfield, CT: Millbrook Press.

Hicyilmaz, G. (1993). *Against the storm*. New York: Yearling.

Hirschfelder, A. B., & Singer, B. R. (Eds.). (1993). *Rising voices: Writings of young Native Americans*. New York: Ivy Books.

Hirschmann, M. A. (1982). *Hansi, the girl who loved the swastika*. Wheaton, IL: Tyndale House.

Ho, M. (1990). *Rice without rain*. New York: HarperCollins.

Ho, M. (2000). *Hush! A Thai lullaby* (H. Meade, Illus.). New York: Scholastic.

Ho, M. (2003). *The stone goddess*. New York: Orchard Books.

Hobbs, W. (2004). *Bearstone*. New York: Aladdin Books.

Holm, A. (2004). *I am David* (L. W. Kingsland, Trans.). New York: Harcourt.

Holt, K. W. (2000). *My Louisiana sky*. New York: Yearling.

Holtwijk, I. (2004). *Asphalt angels*. Asheville, NC: Front Street Books.

Horowitz, A. (2006). *Raven's gate: Book one of the gatekeepers*. New York: Scholastic.

Horowitz, A. (2007a). *Evil star: Book two of the gatekeepers*. New York: Scholastic.

Horowitz, A. (2007b). *Nightrise: Book three of the gatekeepers*. New York: Scholastic.

Hosseini, K. (2003). *The kite runner*. New York: Penguin.

Houston, J. W., & Houston, J. D. (2002). *Farewell to Manzanar*. Boston: Houghton Mifflin.

Howe, J. (2003). *The misfits*. New York: Aladdin Books.

Hsueh-Chin, T. (1958). *Dream of the red chamber*. New York: Anchor Books.

Ingold, J. (2003). *The window*. San Diego: Harcourt.

Irving, W. (1982). *Tales of the Alhambra*. Madrid, Spain: Marques de Mondejar.

Isaacs, A. (2000). *Torn thread*. New York: Scholastic.

Jaffe, N. (2005). *The golden flower: A Taino myth from Puerto Rico* (E. O. Sanchez, Illus.). Houston, TX: Piñata Books.

Jarvis, E. (1986). *The golden goblet*. New York: Puffin Books.

Jayyusi, S. K. (Ed.). (1992). *Anthology of modern Palestinian literature*. New York: Columbia University Press.

Jenkins, L. B. de. (1995). *Celebrating the hero*. New York: Puffin Books.

Jergovic, M. (2004). *Sarajevo Marlboro* (S. Tomasevic, Trans.). New York: Archipelago Books.

Jiang, J. L. (1998). *Red scarf girl: A memoir of the cultural revolution*. New York: HarperCollins.

Johnson, D. (1994). *Seminole diary: Remembrances of a slave*. New York: Atheneum Books.

Johnson, H. M. (2006). *Accidents of nature*. New York: Holt.

Jones, P. (2006). *Nailed*. New York: Walker Books.

Joyce, J. (2006). *The Dubliners*. Clayton, DE: Prestwick House. (Original work published 1914)

Juby, S. (2003). *Alice, I think*. New York: HarperTempest.

Kadohata, C. (2006). *Weedflower*. New York: Atheneum Books.

Kafka, F. (1972). *The metamorphosis*. New York: Bantam. (Original work published 1915)

Kanefield, T. (2001). *Rivka's way*. Chicago: Cricket Books.

Kang, C., & Rigoulot, P. (2002). *The aquariums of Pyongyang: Ten years in the North Korean gulag*. New York: Basic Books.

Karim, P. M., & Khorrami, M. M. (Eds.). (1999). *A world between: Poems, short stories, and essays by Iranian Americans*. New York: Braziller.

Keller, H. (1990). *The story of my life*. New York: Bantam. (Original work published 1904)

Keller, U. (1984). *The building of the Panama Canal in historic photographs*. Mineola, NY: Dover.

Kerr, M. E. (2001). *Gentlehands*. New York: HarperTeen.

Kertesz, I. (1996). *Fateless* (K. Wilson, Trans.). Evanston, IL: Hydra Books.

Kertesz, I. (2004). *Fatelessness* (T. Wilkinson, Trans.). New York: Vintage Books.

Keys, A. (2004). P.O.W. In *Tears for water: Songbook of poems and lyrics* (pp. 11–14). New York: Putnam.

Kherdian, D. (1995). *The road from home: A true story of courage, survival and hope*. New York: HarperTeen.

Kim, H. (1997). *The long season of rain*. New York: Fawcett Juniper.

Kim, M. (2003). *Kuunmong: The cloud dream of the nine* (J. S. Gale, Trans.). Fukuoka, Japan: Kurodahan Press. (Original work published 1687)

Kim, P. (1998). *A cab called reliable*. New York: St. Martin's Griffin.

Kim, S. K., & Kim, S. K. (2003). *Notes from the divided country*. Baton Rouge, LA: Louisiana State University Press.

Klein, G. W. (1999). *All but my life: A memoir*. New York: Hill and Wang. (Original work published 1957)

Klise, K. (2005). *Deliver us from Normal*. New York: Scholastic.

Kluger, S. (2008). *My most excellent year: A novel of love, Mary Poppins, and Fenway Park*. New York: Dial.

Koja, K. (2005). *Talk*. New York: Foster Books.

Korman, G. (2007). *Schooled*. New York: Hyperion Books.

Krisher, T. (2001). *Spite fences*. New York: Delacorte Press.

Krohn, G. (2000). *Who is the builder?* (T. Pelleg, Illus.). Jerusalem: Feldheim.

Kuan-Chung, L. (1976). *Three kingdoms* (M. Roberts, Trans.). New York: Pantheon.

Laguerre, E. A. (1960). *The labyrinth* (W. Rose, Trans.). New York: Americas.

Lamming, G. (1994). *In the castle of my skin*. Ann Arbor, MI: University of Michigan Press. (Original work published 1927)

Laraque, P., & Hirschman, J. (Eds.). (2001). *Open gate: An anthology of Haitian Creole poetry*. Willimantic, CT: Curbstone Press.

Latifa. (2001). *My forbidden face*. New York: Hyperion Books.

Lawall, S. (2003). *The Norton anthology of world literature* (2nd ed.). New York: Norton.

Leaf, M. (1977). *The story of Ferdinand* (R. Lawson, Trans.). New York: Puffin Books. (Original work published 1936)

Le Carre, J. (1996). *The tailor of Panama*. New York: Knopf.

Lee, H. (2006). *To kill a mockingbird*. New York: Harper. (Original work published 1960)

Lee, J. M. (1991). *The song of Mulan*. Arden, NC: Front Street Books.

Lee, M. G. (1994). *Saying goodbye*. Boston: Houghton Mifflin.

Lee, M. G. (1998). *Necessary roughness*. New York: HarperTeen.

Lee, M. G. (2001). *Finding my voice*. New York: HarperTeen.

Lee, P. H. (Ed.). (1974). *Anthology of Korean poetry: From the earliest era to the present*. New York: Day.

Leitner, I., & Leitner, I. A. (1990). *Fragments of Isabella: A memoir of Auschwitz*. New York: Dell Laurel.

Lester J. (2002). *Pharaoh's daughter: A novel of ancient Egypt*. New York: Harper-Trophy.

Levitin, S. (1996). *Escape from Egypt*. New York: Puffin Books.

Levitin, S. (2003). *Room in the heart*. New York: Dutton Books.

Lewis, B., & Burstein, S. M. (2002). *Land of enchanters: Egyptian short stories from the earliest times to the present day*. Princeton, NJ: Markus Wiener.

Lim-Wilson, F. (1995). *Crossing the snow bridge*. Columbus: Ohio State University Press.

Lingard, J. (1992). *Tug of war*. New York: Puffin Books.

Lippert, M. H. (1993). *The sea serpent's daughter: A Brazilian legend*. New York: Troll.

Lobel, A. (1998). *No pretty pictures: A child of war*. New York: Greenwillow Books.

Lorca, F. G. (2007). *Poet in New York: A bilingual edition* (P. Medina & M. Statman, Trans.). New York: Grove Press.

Louie, A. L. (1996). *Yeh-Shen*. New York: Putnam.

Lowry, L. (1998). *Number the stars*. New York: Dell Laurel-Leaf.

Lowry, L. (2004). *The messenger*. Boston: Houghton Mifflin.

Lowry, L. (2006).*Gathering blue*. New York: Delacorte Press.

Lupica, M. (2006). *Heat*. New York: Philomel Books.

Lynch, C. (1996). *Slot machine*. New York: HarperTeen.

Machado de Assis, J. M. (1998). *Dom Casmurro* (J. Gledson, Trans.). New York: Oxford University Press. (Original work published 1899)

Mackall, D. D. (2005). *Love rules*. Carol Stream, IL: Tyndale House.

Mackall, D. D. (2006). *Eva underground*. New York: Harcourt.

Maguire, G. (1999). *The good liar*. New York: Clarion Books.

Mah, A. Y. (1999). *Chinese Cinderella: The true story of an unwanted daughter*. New York: Laurel-Leaf.

Mairs, N. (1997). *Waist-high in the world: A life among the nondisabled*. Boston: Beacon Press.

Mais, R. (1974). *Brother man*. Portsmouth, NH: Heinemann. (Original work published 1954)

Mais, R. (1981). *The hills were joyful together*. Portsmouth, NH: Heinemann. (Original work published 1953)

Manley, R. (2002). *Slipstream: A daughter remembers*. New York: Vintage Books.

Margolis, M. (1998). *An invisible minority: Brazilians in New York City*. Needham Heights, MA: Allyn & Bacon.

Marquez, G. G. (1989). *Love in the time of cholera* (E. Grossman, Trans.). New York: Penguin.

Marquez, G. G. (1998). *One hundred years of solitude* (G. Rabassa, Trans.). New York: Perennial.

Marti, J. (2002). *Jose Marti: Selected writings* (E. Allen, Trans.). New York: Penguin.

Matas, C. (1994). *Sworn enemies*. New York: Laurel-Leaf.

Matas, C. (1999). *In my enemy's house*. New York: Simon & Schuster.

Mathabane, M. (1986). *Kaffir boy: The true story of a Black youth's coming of age in apartheid South Africa*. New York: Plume.

Mathabane, M. (1989). *Kaffir boy in America*. New York: Collier Books.

Matlin, M. (2002). *Deaf child crossing*. New York: Aladdin Books.

Matto de Turner, C. (1996). *Birds without a nest: A novel* (J. G. H., Trans.). Austin: University of Texas Press.

Mazer, H. (1999). *The last mission*. Minneapolis: Tandem Library.

McCausland-Gallo, P. (2004). *Secrets of Colombian cooking*. New York: Hippocrene Books.

McCormick, P. (2006). *Sold*. New York: Hyperion Books.

McCourt, F., (1999). *Angela's ashes*. New York: Scribner.

McCoy, K. M. (1993). *A tale of two tengu: A Japanese folktale* (K. Fossey, Trans.). Morton Grove, IL: Whitman.

McDonald, J. (2003). *Twists and turns.* New York: Farrar, Straus & Giroux.

McElfresh, L. E. (1999). *Can you feel the thunder?* New York: Atheneum Books.

McKay, C. (1969). *Selected poems of Claude McKay.* New York: Harvest/HBJ Books.

McKissack, P. C. (2007). *A friendship for today.* New York: Scholastic.

McMahon, P. (1998). *Chi-Hoon: A Korean girl* (M. F. O'Brien, Illus.). Arden, NC: Boyds Mill Press.

McMahon, P. (2000). *Dancing wheels.* Boston: Houghton Mifflin.

Mead, A. (2007). *Dawn and dusk.* New York: Farrar, Straus & Giroux.

Medina, P. (2002). *Exiled memories: A Cuban childhood.* New York: Persea Books.

Mehmedinovic, S. (1998). *Sarajevo blues.* San Francisco: City Lights Books.

Mehta, G. (1994). *Karma cola: Marketing the mystic East.* New York: Vintage Books.

Metaxas, E. (1995). *The monkey people: A Colombian folktale* (D. Bryan, Illus.). New York: Rabbit Ears.

Meyer, C. (1995). *Drummers of Jericho.* New York: Harcourt Brace.

Michener, J. A. (1983). *Poland.* New York: Ballantine.

Mikaelsen, B. (2000). *Petey.* New York: Hyperion.

Mike, J. (2001). *Juan Bobo and the horse of seven colors: A Puerto Rican legend* (C. Reasoner, Illus.). Mahwah, NJ: Troll.

Miklowitz, G. D. (1999). *The war between the classes.* New York: Tandem Library.

Miller, K. (2007). *New Caribbean poetry: An anthology.* Manchester, England: Carcanet Press.

Miller, S. (2007). *Miss Spitfire: Reaching Helen Keller.* New York: Atheneum Books.

Mohr, N. (1999a). *Felita.* New York: Puffin Books.

Mohr, N. (1999b). *Going home.* New York: Puffin Books.

Mokhosi, R. (Ed.). (2007). *Basadzi voices: An anthology of poetic writing by young Black South African women.* Durban, South Africa: University of Natal Press.

Millel, T. M. (1992). *A promise to the sun: An African story.* Boston: Little, Brown.

Momaday, N. S. (1999). *House made of dawn.* New York: Harper Perennial.

Moore, M. (1993). *In the dark.* Washington, DC: Young Playwrights Program.

Moore, P. (2004). *Blind sighted.* New York: Puffin Books.

Morrison, T. (1998). *Beloved.* New York: Plume.

Moses, S. P. (2003). *The legend of Buddy Bush.* New York: Simon Pulse.

Moses, S. P. (2005). *The return of Buddy Bush.* New York: McElderry Books.

Moses, S. P. (2007). *The baptism.* New York: McElderry Books.

Moskin, M. D. (1999). *I am Rosemarie.* Bridgewater, NJ: Replica Books.

Mowat, F. (2004). *And no birds sang.* Mechanicsburg, PA: Stackpole Books.

Mozeson, I. E., & Stavsky, L. (1994). *Jerusalem mosaic: Young voices from the Holy City.* New York: Simon & Schuster.

Mukherjee, B. (1999). *Jasmine.* Union Grove, NY: Grove Press.

Munves, J. (1979). *The treasure of Diogenes Sampuez.* New York: Atheneum Books.

Myers, W. D. (2001). *Bad boy: A memoir.* New York: HarperCollins.

Myers, W. D. (1999). *Monster.* New York: Amistad/HarperCollins.

Myracle, L. (2005). *Rhymes with witches.* New York: Amulet Books.

Na, A. (2006). *Wait for me.* New York: Putnam.

Nafisi, A. (2003). *Reading Lolita in Tehran: A memoir in books.* New York: Random House.

Naguib, M. (1988). *Fountain and tomb: Hakayat haretna* (J. Kenneson, Trans.). Washington, DC: Three Continents Press.

Nanji, S. (2008). *Child of dandelions.* Honesdale, PA: Front Street Books.

Napoli, D. J. (1999). *Friends everywhere.* New York: Aladdin Books.

Napoli, D. J. (2000). *The beast.* New York: Atheneum Books.

Narayan, R. K. (1994). *Swami and friends.* Chicago: University of Chicago Press. (Original work published 1935)

Neruda, P. (1990). *Pablo Neruda: Selected poems* (A. Kerrigan, Trans.). Boston: Houghton Mifflin.

Neufeld, J. (1998). *Gaps in stone.* New York: Aladdin Books.

Nezval, V. (2005). *Valerie and her weeks of wonders* (D. Short, Trans.). Prague, Czechoslovakia: Twisted Spoon Press. (Original work published 1935)

Nguyen, D. (2002). *The tale of Kieu* (H. S. Thong, Trans.). New Haven, CT: Yale University Press.

Niazi, M. (2002). *A cry in the wilderness: Poetry from Pakistan.* New York: Oxford University Press.

Nizami. (1995). *Haft Paykar: A medieval Persian romance* (J. Scott Meisami, Trans.). New York: Oxford University Press.

Nye, N. S. (1997). *Sitti's secrets* (N. Carpenter, Illus.). New York: Aladdin Books.

Nye, N. S. (1998). *The space between our footsteps: Poems and paintings of the Middle East.* New York: Simon & Schuster.

Nye, N. S. (1999). *Habibi.* New York: Simon Pulse.

O'Brien, E. (1986). *Tales for the telling: Irish folk and fairy stories* (M. Forman, Illus.). New York: Atheneum Books.

O'Dell, S. (1997). *Sing down the moon*. New York: Laurel-Leaf.

O'Kimoto, J. D. (2000). *Jason's women*. Bloomington, IN: iUniverse.

Oppenheim, J. (2006). *Dear Miss Breed: Stories of the Japanese American incarceration during World War II and a librarian who made a difference*. New York: Scholastic.

O'Rourke, K. (Ed). (1999). *Looking for the cow: Modern Korean poems*. Dublin, Ireland: Dedalus Press.

Orr, K. (1991). *My grandpa and the sea*. Minneapolis, MN: Carolrhoda Books.

Orr, W. (1997). *Peeling the onion*. New York: Holiday House.

Osa, N. (2005). *Cuba 15*. New York: Delacorte Press.

Ostow, M. (2006). *Emily Goldberg learns to salsa*. New York: Razorbill/Penguin.

Oz, A. (1998). *Panther in the basement*. New York: Harvest Books.

Park, L. S. (2002). *When my name was Keoko*. New York: Clarion Books.

Park, L. S. (2003). *A single shard*. New York: Yearling.

Parker, N. W. (1996). *Locks, crocs, and skeeters: The story of the Panama Canal*. New York: Greenwillow Books.

Parks, R. (with Haskins, J.). (1999). *Rosa Parks: My story*. New York: Puffin Books.

Paton, A. (1948). *Cry, the beloved country*. New York: Scribner.

Paulsen, G. (2004). *The quilt*. New York: Lamb Books.

Paz, O. (1991). *The monkey grammarian*. New York: Arcade.

Peare, C. O. (1990). *The Helen Keller story*. New York: Bantam Books. (Original work published 1959)

Penn, A. (Director). (1962). *The miracle worker* [Motion picture]. United States: Playfilm Productions.

Perkins, S. (2005). *The not-so-star-spangled life of Sunita Sen*. New York: Little, Brown.

Perl, L. (1996). *Four perfect pebbles: A Holocaust story*. New York: Greenwillow Books.

Perrin, M. (2000). *Magnificent molas: The art of the Kuna Indian* (D. Dusinberre, Trans.). Paris, France: Flammarian.

Peters, J. A. (2003). *Keeping you a secret*. New York: Little, Brown.

Peters, J. A. (2004). *Luna*. New York: Little, Brown.

Philbrick, R. (2002). *The last book in the universe*. New York: Blue Sky Press/Scholastic.

Phillips, S. (2008). *Burn*. New York: Little, Brown.

Phung, V. T. (2002). *Dumb luck* (N. Nguyet Cam, Trans.). Ann Arbor: University of Michigan Press. (Original work published 1936)

Placide, J. (2002). *Fresh girl*. New York: Lamb Books.

Plum-Ucci, C.. (2002). *What happened to Lani Garver*. Orlando, FL: Harcourt.

Polacco, P. (1996). *Rechenka's eggs*. New York: Putnam.

Potok, C. (1987). *The chosen*. New York: Fawcett.

Pramoj, K. (1999). *Four reigns* (Tulachandra, Trans.). Chiang Mai, Thailand: Silkworm Books.

Presilla, M. E. (1996). *Mola: Cuna life stories and art*. New York: Holt.

Pressler, M. (2007). *Let sleeping dogs lie* (E. J. Macki, Trans.). Asheville, NC: Front Street Books.

Radzienda, T. (2002). *A promise for Siam*. Bangkok, Thailand: Pentameter Press.

Ramanujan, A. K. (1986). *Second sight: New poetry in India*. New York: Oxford University Press.

Rees, C. (2003). *Pirates!* New York: Bloomsbury.

Reynolds, M. (2001). *Love rules*. Buena Park, CA: Morning Glory Press.

Ringelblum, E. (1958). *Notes from the Warsaw Ghetto* (J. Sloan, Trans.). New York: Schocken Books.

Rizal, Jose. (2006). *Noli me tangere* [Touch me not] (H. Augenbraum, Trans.). New York: Penguin. (Original work published 1887)

Rodman, M. A. (2004). *Yankee girl*. New York: Farrar, Straus & Giroux.

Rodriguez. B. (2000). *Sarah's sleepover*. New York: Viking.

Rodriguez, R. (1983). *Hunger of memory: The education of Richard Rodriguez*. New York: Bantam Books.

Rojas, F. de. (1958). *The Celestina: A fifteenth-century Spanish novel in dialogue* (L. Byrd Simpson, Trans.). Los Angeles: University of California Press.

Roley, B. A. (2001). *American son*. New York: Norton.

Romulo, L. E., & de Leon, J. (2000). *Filipino children's favorite stories*. Berkeley, CA: Periplus.

Rosenblatt, L. (1938). *Literature as exploration*. New York: Modern Language Association.

Roskind, R., & Roskind, J. (2002). *The gathering of the healers*. Blowing Rock, NC: One Love Press.

Ross, D. (1995). *Returning to A*. San Francisco: City Lights.

Roth, M. (2006). *Never mind the Goldbergs*. New York: Push.

Roumain, J. (1995). *When the tom-tom beats: Selected prose and poetry*. Washington, DC: Azul.

Roumain, J. (1978). *Masters of the dew* (L. Hughes & M. Cook, Trans.). Portsmouth, NH: Heinemann. (Original work published 1944)

Rowe, P. (2007). *Silent time*. St. John's, Newfoundland, Canada: Killick Press/ Creative Book.

Russo, M. (2005). *Always remember me: How one family survived World War II.* New York: Atheneum Books.

Ryan, P. M. (2002). *Esperanza rising.* New York: Blue Sky Press/Scholastic.

Ryan, P. M. (2004). *Becoming Naomi Leon.* New York: Scholastic.

Rylant, C. (1989). *But I'll be back again: An album.* New York: Orchard Books.

Saldaña, R. (2002). *The jumping tree: A novel.* New York: Laurel-Leaf.

Salinger, J. D. (1991). *The catcher in the rye.* New York: Little, Brown. (Original work published 1951)

Salisbury, G. (2006). *House of the red fish.* New York: Wendy Lamb Books.

Salisbury, G. (1995). *Under the blood red sun.* New York: Yearling.

Sanchez, A. (2003). *Rainbow boys.* New York: Simon Pulse.

Sanchez, A. (2007). *The God box.* New York: Simon & Schuster.

Santacroce, J. P. (1998). *Nine thousand miles to adventure: The story of an American boy in the Philippines.* San Antonio, TX: Four Oaks.

Santiago, E. (1999). *Almost a woman.* New York: Vintage Books.

Santiago, E. (2006). *When I was Puerto Rican.* Cambridge, MA: Da Capo Press.

Satrapi, M. (2004). *Persepolis: The story of a childhood.* New York: Pantheon.

Satrapi, M. (2005). *Persepolis 2: The story of a return.* New York: Pantheon.

Saxon-Ford, S. (1999). *The Czech Americans: The immigrant experience.* Philadelphia: Chelsea House.

Say, A. (1993). *Grandfather's journey.* New York: Houghton Mifflin.

Schmidt, G. D. (2004). *Lizzie Bright and the Buckminster boy.* New York: Clarion Books.

Scott, V. M. (2000). *Finding Abby.* Hillsboro, OR: Butte.

Sebestyen, O. (1997). *Words by heart.* New York: Yearling.

Sender, R. M. (1990). *The cage.* New York: Bantam Books.

Sender, R. M. (2000). *To life.* New York: Simon Pulse.

Sevela, E. (1989). *We were not like other people* (A. Bouis, Trans.). New York: Harper & Row.

Sherlock, P. M. (1983). *Anancy the spider man* (M. Brown, Illus.). Oxford, England: Macmillan Caribbean.

Shepard, A. (1995). *The gifts of Wali Dad: A tale of India and Pakistan.* (D. San Souci, Illus.). New York Atheneum.

Shepard, A. (1997). *The sea king's daughter: A Russian legend.* (G. Spirin, Illus.). New York Atheneum.

Shikibu, M. (2002). *The tale of Genji* (R. Tyler, Trans.). New York: Penguin.

Shin, H. K. (2001). *Remembering Korea, 1950: A boy soldier's story.* Reno: University of Nevada Press.

Shusterman, N. (2006). *The schwa was here.* New York: Puffin Books.

Siegal, A. (2003a). *Grace in the wilderness: After the liberation 1945–1948*. New York: Farrar, Straus & Giroux.

Siegal, A. (2003b). *Upon the head of the goat: A childhood in Hungary 1939–1944*. New York: Farrar, Straus & Giroux.

Sienkiewicz, H. (2000). *On the field of glory* (M. Lipinski, Trans.). New York: Hippocrene Books. (Originasl work published 1906)

Silverman, R. L. (1997). *A Bosnian family*. Minneapolis, MN: Lerner.

Simic, C. (1992). *The horse has six legs: An anthology of Serbian poetry*. St. Paul, MN: Graywolf.

Simmons, M. (2003). *Pool boy*. New York: Roaring Brook Press.

Singer, M. (2004). *Face relations: Eleven stories about seeing beyond color*. New York: Simon & Schuster.

Sis, P. (2001). *The three golden keys*. New York: Farrar, Straus & Giroux.

Sis, P. (2002). *Madlenka's dog*. New York: Foster Books.

Slaughter, C. (1994). *The dirty war*. New York: Walker.

Sleator, W. (2008). *Test*. New York: Amulet Books.

Smith, R. (1999). *Jaguar*. New York: Hyperion Books.

Smith, W. J. (2000). *The Cherokee lottery: A sequence of poems*. Willimantic, CT: Curbstone Press.

Softic, E. (1995). *Sarajevo days, Sarajevo nights*. St. Paul, MN: Hungry Mind Press.

Solzhenitsyn, A. (1971). *Stories and prose poems*. New York: Farrar, Straus & Giroux.

Solzhenitsyn, A. (1978). *A day in the life of Ivan Denisovich*. New York: Signet.

Soto, G. (1986). *Small faces*. Houston, TX: Arte Publico Press.

Soto, G. (1992). *Living up the street*. New York: Laurel-Leaf.

Soto, G. (1998). *Big bushy mustache*. New York: Knopf.

Soto, G. (2003). *Pacific crossing*. New York: Harcourt.

Soto, G. (2005). *Help wanted: Stories*. New York: Harcourt.

So-un, K. (2004). *Korean children's favorite stories* (J. Kyoung-Sim, Trans.). Tokyo, Japan: Tuttle.

Spiegelman, A. (1986). *Maus I: A survivor's tale; my father bleeds history*. New York: Pantheon.

Spiegelman, A. (1992). *Maus II: A survivor's tale; and here my troubles began*. New York: Pantheon.

Spinelli, J. (1997). *Crash*. New York: Yearling

Spinelli, J. (2002). *Stargirl*. New York: Knopf.

Spinelli, J. (2003a). *Loser*. New York: HarperTrophy.

Spinelli, J. (2003b). *Milkweed*. New York: Laurel-Leaf.

Stahler, D., Jr. (2004). *Truesight*. New York: HarperCollins.

Staples, S. F. (1995). *Haveli*. New York: Laurel-Leaf.

Staples, S. F. (2003). *Shabanu: Daughter of the wind*. New York: Laurel-Leaf.

Staples, S. F. (2005). *Under the persimmon tree*. New York: Farrar, Straus & Giroux.

Staples, S. F. (2008). *The House of Djinn*. New York: Farrar, Straus & Giroux.

Stewart, C. (2001). *Driving over lemons: An optimist in Andalucia*. New York: Vintage Books.

Stine, C. (2005). *Refugees*. New York: Delacorte Press.

Stine, R. L. (1997). *Into the dark*. New York: Simon Pulse.

Stoker, B. (2004). *Dracula*. New York: Candlewick Press. (Original work published 1897)

Stolz, M. (1988). *Zekmet the stone carver: A tale of ancient Egypt* (D. Nourse Latimore, Illus.). New York: Harcourt.

Strand, M. (Trans.). (2002). *Looking for poetry: Poems by Carlos Drummond de Andrade and Rafael Alberti and songs from the Quechua*. New York: Knopf.

Strasser, T. (2005). *The wave*. New York: Laurel-Leaf. (Original work published 1981)

Students of Fundacion Creando Cambio. (2005). *Stories of life and death / Historias de vida y muerte*. Excelsior, MN: SangFroid Press.

Sullivan, C. (Ed.) (1997). *Ireland in poetry*. New York: Abrams.

Sun-Won, H. (1997). *The descendants of Cain* (Suh-Ji-Moon & J. Pickering, Trans.). New York: UNESCO.

Swift, J. (1999). *Gulliver's travels*. New York: Signet.

Szymborska, W. (1995). *View with a grain of sand: Selected poems*. New York: Harcourt Brace.

Taylor, J. W. (2004). *Gentle hand to victory: The life of Annie Sullivan (Helen Keller's teacher)*. Philadelphia: Xlibris.

Taylor, M. (1997). *Roll of thunder, hear my cry*. New York: Puffin.

Taylor, T. (2002). *The cay*. New York: Yearling.

Telemaque, E. W. (2000). *It's crazy to stay Chinese in Minnesota*. Nashville, TN: Nelson.

Temple, F. (1995). *Tonight, by sea*. New York: HarperTrophy.

Thomas, P. (1997). *Down these mean streets*. New York: Vintage Books.

Toll, N. S. (1993). *Behind the secret window: A memoir of a hidden childhood during World War Two*. New York: Puffin Books.

Tolstoy, L. (1997). *A calendar of wisdom*. New York: Simon & Schuster.

Tolstoy, L. (1982). *War and peace*. New York: Penguin. (Original work published 1865)

Triana, G. (2005). *Cubanita*. New York: Rayo/HarperCollins.

Trout, R. (2005). *Cayman gold*. Los Angeles: Pelican.

Trueman, T. (2000). *Stuck in neutral*. New York: HarperTempest.

Twagilimana, A. (1997). *Teenage refugees from Rwanda speak out*. New York: Rosen.

Twain, M. (2002). *The adventures of Huckleberry Finn*. New York: Penguin. (Original work published 1885)

Uchida, Y. (1988). *Journey to Topaz* (D. Carrick, Illus.). Berkeley, CA: Creative Arts Book.

Uchida, Y. (1992). *Journey home*. New York: Aladdin Books.

Vallejo, C. (2007). *The complete poetry: A bilingual edition* (C. Eshleman, Trans.). Berkeley: University of California Press.

Van de Velde, V. (1998). *A coming evil*. Boston: Houghton Mifflin.

Van Huy, N., & Kendall, L. (Eds.). (2003). *Vietnam: Journeys of body, mind, and spirit*. Berkeley: University of California Press.

Van Laan, N. (1998). *So say the little monkeys*. New York: Atheneum Books.

Veciana-Suarez, A. (2002). *Flight to freedom*. New York: Scholastic.

Venkatraman, P. (2008). *Climbing the stairs*. New York: Putnam.

Villegas, B., & Borda, J. G. C. (1998). *Presidential homes of Colombia* (A. A. Reid, Trans.). Bogota, Columbia: Villegas Editores.

Volavkova, H. (Ed.). (1994). *I never saw another butterfly: Children's drawings and poems from Terezin Concentration Camp, 1942–1944* (2nd ed.). New York: Schocken Books.

Walker, P. R. (1991). *Pride of Puerto Rico: The life of Roberto Clemente*. London: Odyssey.

Warren, W., & Tettoni, L. I. (1999). *Thailand: The golden kingdom*. Berkeley, CA: Periplus.

Wheeler, S. (1999). *Travels in a thin country: A journey through Chile*. New York: Modern Library.

Whelan, G. (1993). *Goodbye, Vietnam*. New York: Yearling.

Whelan, G. (2000). *Homeless bird*. New York: HarperCollins.

Whelan, G. (2001). *Angel on the square*. New York: HarperCollins.

Whelan, G. (2003). *The impossible journey*. New York: HarperCollins.

Whelan, G. (2004). *Burying the sun*. New York: HarperCollins.

Whelan, G. (2005). *Chu Ju's house*. New York: HarperTrophy.

Whyman, M. (2005). *Boy kills man*. New York: HarperCollins.

Wiesel, E. (2006). *Night* (S. Rodway, Trans.). New York: Hill and Wang. (Original work published 1972)

Wieseltier, M. (2003). *The flower of anarchy: Selected poems* (S. Kaufman, Trans.). Berkeley: University of California Press.

Wilde, O. (2005). *The importance of being Earnest*. Clayton, DE: Prestwick House. (Original work published 1895)

Wilhelm, D. (2003). *The revealers*. New York: Farrar, Straus & Giroux.

Williams, N. (1998). *A history of the Cayman Islands* (2nd ed.). Grand Cayman: Government of the Cayman Islands.

Williams-Garcia, R. (2002). *Every time a rainbow dies*. New York: Amistad/ HarperCollins.

Winter, J. (2004). *The librarian of Basra: A true story from Iraq*. Orlando, FL: Harcourt.

Wisniewski, D. (1996). *Golem*. New York: Clarion Books.

Wittlinger, E. (2007). *Parrotfish*. New York: Simon & Schuster.

Wolff, V. E. (2001). *True believer*. New York: Atheneum Books.

Wolkstein, D. (1997). *The magic orange tree and other Haitian folktales*. New York: Schocken Books.

Woodson, J. (1995). *From the notebooks of Melanin Sun*. New York: Blue Sky Press/Scholastic.

Woodson, J. (2001). *The other side*. New York: Putnam.

Woodson, J. (2007). *Feathers*. New York: Putnam.

Wray, E., Rosenfield, C., & Bailey, D. (1996). *Ten lives of the Buddha*. New York: Weatherhill.

Wulffson, D. L. (2003). *Soldier X*. New York: Puffin Books.

Yanagisawa, R. (1993). *The invisible room*. Washington, DC: Young Playwrights Program.

Yang, G. L. (2006). *American born Chinese*. New York: First Second.

Yashar, K. (2005). *Memed my hawk* (E. Roditi, Trans.). New York: Pantheon. (Original work published 1955)

Yep, L. (1992). *The star fisher*. New York: Puffin Books.

Yep, L. (2002). *Sea glass*. New York: HarperTrophy.

Yolen, J. (1993). *Briar rose*. New York: Tor Books.

Yolen, J. (2004). *The devil's arithmetic*. New York: Puffin Books.

Youme, L. (2004). *Selavi, that is life: A Haitian story of hope*. El Paso, TX: Cinco Puntos Press.

Young, E. (1989). *Lon Po Po: A Red Riding Hood story from China*. New York: Penguin Putnam.

Young, E. (2004). *The sons of the Dragon King: A Chinese legend*. New York: Atheneum Books.

Zamyatin, Y. (2001). *We*. New York: HarperCollins.

Zeng, H., & Hai Zi. (2006). *An English translation of poems of the contemporary Chinese poet Hai Zi*. New York: Mellen Press.

Zeno-Gandia, M. (1999). *La charca* [The pond]. Princeton, NJ: Markus Wiener.

Zephaniah, B. (2006). *J is for Jamaica*. London: Lincoln.

Zindel, P. (2005a). *The pigman*. New York: HarperTrophy.

Zindel, P. (2005b). *The pigman's legacy*. New York: HarperTeen.

Zuehlke, J. (2005). *Poland in pictures*. Breckenridge, CO: Twenty-first Century Books.

Zusak, M. (2006). *The book thief*. New York: Knopf.

Index

Michelle Dixon is a graduate student in English Education at the University of South Florida in Tampa and a member of Golden Key Honor Society. Michelle is passionate about teaching adolescents and believes that all students can learn with the right methods and a willing and caring teacher.

Bonnie O. Ericson is Chair and Professor of Secondary Education at California State University, Northridge, where she has taught courses in methods of teaching English, content area literacy, and adolescent literature. She wrote the "Resources and Reviews" column for *English Journal* for four years and published *Teaching Reading in High School English Classes* (NCTE). Ericson contributed to Volumes One, Two, Three and Four of *Adolescent Literature as a Complement to the Classics* and wrote on *To Kill a Mockingbird, The Odyssey, Fahrenheit 451,* and *Our Town.*

Joan Fowinkle holds a B.S. in English/Speech Education from the University of South Florida and has taught regular and advanced students in both California and Florida.

Jo Higgins holds a masters degree in English Education from the University of South Florida and was recognized as the 1994 Teacher of the Year Award Winner by the Florida Council of Teachers of English (FCTE). Jo then served FCTE as its 2000-2001 President and received the FCTE Honor Award, the Council's most prestigious award in 2005. She has taught English in Florida and in New Hampshire.

Joan F. Kaywell is Professor of English Education at the University of South Florida where she has won several teaching awards. She is passionate about assisting preservice and practicing teachers in discovering ways to improve literacy. She donates her time extensively to the National Council of Teachers of English (NCTE) and its Florida affiliate (FCTE): She is Past President of NCTE's Assembly on Literature for Adolescents (ALAN) and is currently serving as its Membership Secretary; she is a Past-President of FCTE and is currently serving again as its 2007-2008 President. Dr. Kaywell is published in several journals; regularly reviews young adult novels for *The ALAN Review*, The *Journal of Adult and Adolescent Literacy*, and *Signal*; and has edited two series of textbooks: Four volumes of *Adolescent Literature as a Complement to the Classics* (1993, 1995, 1997, 2000); six volumes of *Using Literature to Help Troubled Teenagers Cope with [Various] Issues* (Family 1999, Societal 1999, Identity 1999, Health 2000, End-of-Life 2000, Abuse 2004; and has written one: *Adolescents At Risk: A Guide to Fiction and Nonfiction for Young Adults, Parents, and Professionals* (1993). Her latest award-winning novel, *Dear Author: Letters of Hope*, is her first trade book (Philomel, 2007) which is intended to get students to choose reading as a healthy escape. Kaywell fervently believes that teachers and authors are often the unsung heroes of children on the brink of self-destruction. By offering books to children to help them momentarily escape the pain of growing up, teachers offer teenagers a constructive way to survive the crisis, find hope, and know that they are not alone.

Patricia P. Kelly is Professor Emerita of Teaching and Learning at Virginia Tech in Blacksburg, Virginia. She is currently working on international projects in the Center for Research & Development in International Education in the School of Education. She has published articles in *English Journal, Research in the Teaching of English*, and *The ALAN Review*, and is co-author of *Questioning: A Path to Critical Thinking* and *Two Decades of The ALAN Review*. Kelly was awarded the 2007 Ted Hipple Service Award at the ALAN Workshop having served as an ALAN President and as co-editor of *The ALAN Review*. Kelly contributed to

Volumes One, Two, and Four of *Adolescent Literature as a Complement to the Classics* and wrote on *A Doll House, The Miracle Worker*, and *The Crucible*.

Kara Larson holds a B.A. in Literature/Gender Studies from New College of Florida. She teaches developmental writing at Hillsborough Community College and is currently completing a graduate degree in English Education at the University of South Florida. She is committed to multicultural and non-sexist quality public education.

Jennifer Loadman is working on a degree in English literature at the University of South Florida and hopes to work in publishing.

Tara Lorentsen teaches English language arts at Crews Lake Middle School in Pasco County, Florida, and has taught regular, gifted, and ESE students. She is a graduate student at the University of South Florida in the English Education program and is a member of NCTE and ALAN. Tara lives with her husband Fred and step-son Elijah in Port Richey, Florida.

April Templeton holds a Masters degree in English Education from the University of South Florida and has taught high school English for 12 years. She is currently pursuing her Ph.D. in English Education from the University of South Florida.

Leandra Sambrine Vera is currently a graduate student at the University of South Florida and a member of the Sun Coast Area Teacher Training (SCATT) program. She currently teaches English to English Language Learners (ELLs) and regular students at King High School in Tampa, Florida. This is her first publication.